Does God Speak to Us? What About Me?

Does God Speak to Us? What About Me?

A HUSBAND, FATHER, AND DEACON
TALKS TO HIS DAUGHTERS
ABOUT FAITH, HOPE, AND LOVE
IN THE CHURCH TODAY

§

John Catalano

ISBN: 1536909866
ISBN 13: 9781536909869

Nihil Obstat: Rev. Kevin J. O'Reilly, S.T.D.
           Censor Librorum

Imprimatur: +Timothy Cardinal Dolan
           Archbishop of New York
           December 5, 2016

The above designations mean that this work has been reviewed and it has been determined by the competent ecclesiastical authority that it contains nothing contrary to
Catholic faith and morals.

All bible references are from the '*New American Bible, Revised Edition*. Charlotte, NC:
Saint Benedict Press, 2010', unless otherwise designated.

Deacon John Catalano,
Ordained at St. Patrick's Cathedral,
June 25, 2016

To My Mother:

Barbara Rose

Who Started Me on My Journey of Faith

Table of Contents

Introduction

§

Do you believe in God? If your answer to that question is anything other than "absolutely not," then this book may be worth reading.

I'm just an average person. I am an average person who has lived a full life and has some things to share. I've had the same experiences as most people in this country. I have been disappointed, frustrated, hurt, and scared. I have had cancer, lost some friendships, lost jobs, took some risks that didn't work, and have had many things in life just not go the way I wanted them to go. I have been thoughtless and unkind to people, and people have at times been unkind to me.

But I've also been richly blessed. I've had a wonderfully successful marriage and three beautiful children. I've had close, loving friendships and great associations with some fabulous people. I've traveled to many beautiful places in the world and lived in a vibrant, supportive community. I've been to the top sporting events, played some great golf courses, and suffered for years with the Mets and Knicks. I grew up in New York, went to college in Ohio, and have lived in and around New York my whole life.

I've grown to love Jesus and His church, and I have developed a rewarding spiritual life. I've worked on and discovered many things about myself and about the world. I've learned about something called an interior life. It's not an insular life—quite the contrary. It is a window into a wider world—a world of peace and love, accompanied by the virtues of faith and hope. It is at once deeply personal and yet also a universally shared experience. I discovered something that seems brand new, and yet it has always existed. I'm still afraid to die, but now I yearn for a promise, a promise of an eternal life—something Jesus once referred to as "paradise." And this eternal kingdom of God is actually with us here, right now, and it will be, forever.

I now realize that my body—and everything that I own and everything that happens to me and every person I know—will pass away, and soon. But my essence and true self—my soul and spirit—is joined with the Holy Spirit of the Creator, and through Jesus I will be joined with this almighty God in eternal life forever.

I'd like to share some things I have learned along the way, but sharing one's faith is not easy. I would love to talk to young people in college, or those starting out in their careers and marriages, and offer something that might be helpful. But even my own children, who were brought up by two Catholic parents, are a hard sell. I have two beautiful daughters: Angela, who is twenty-six, and Christina, who is twenty-four. They're both single, and they're sweet and smart. They both went to Catholic colleges run by the Jesuits: Angela to Georgetown and Christina to the College of the Holy Cross. They got good educations and now have good jobs—Angela in banking and Christina in media—and they are doing well. They travel, have great friends, and they enjoy life. Now that they are out on their own, I notice they and their friends don't have particularly lively prayer lives. Religion is not currently part of their weekly schedule. And when I talk to them about faith, they're not as accepting as before. Like most millennials, they don't go to church.

You may fit this profile. If you are a millennial, you are part of the most affluent and ethnically diverse generation to date. You are a digital native, and you lean left politically and socially. You got a great education but may now be faced with college debt. You're slower to marry and have children. On most surveys, you'll check the box "not very religious."

If you fit the majority profile, you practically live on social media. You text, tweet, friend, and unfriend people. You're comfortable with Instagram, Snapchat, and Pinterest. You like YouTube, Netflix, and Xbox. You'll tire of Facebook soon if it doesn't keep introducing clever new applications. You post complaints—mostly about relationships, school, and general pet peeves. You don't get your information from traditional media outlets, but tend to share articles, quiz results, and top-ten lists from BuzzFeed. You live-tweet during sports and prime-time shows, and you're more likely to be nostalgic than the middle-agers—reminiscing about your own childhood TV shows and movies like *Land Before Time* and *What's Eating Gilbert Grape.*

You know all the appropriate hashtags to use during shows like *Game of Thrones*, the *Bachelorette*, and the Emmys.[1] You don't watch the nightly news, read newspapers, or write formal e-mails. Every day, you know where your friends eat, hang out, or listen to music. If you're like my daughters, some nights you'd rather stay home and watch Netflix with your friends and save your money for an interesting vacation. You can feel the pace of life quickening, but no worries; it's the digital age, and it is what it is.

Like Angela and Christina, you see what is going on all around you. To an increasing extent, your peers and friends live more and more in a virtual world—or a world of entertainment and information that they have designed—avoiding stuff they don't like. There is more isolation, people wrapped up in their own worlds. There is bullying and nastiness, and some people feel alienated, angry, and embittered. Just below the surface of affluence and political correctness, there's nitpicking, jealousy, resentment. Comments posted online are hateful. Mistrust is spreading. There's more violence, now called domestic. Suicide now surpasses highway fatalities as the number-one cause of death in America. And every five weeks, another person goes off and kills teachers, cops, gay people, coworkers, or young kids, and rips another community apart. Then we talk about guns for a few days. Politicians and their elections don't produce satisfactory results, or any results at all; they're to be ridiculed or made fun of on Colbert, John Oliver, or *Saturday Night Live*.

You know you have some decisions or choices to make about what direction your life will take. There is a ton of information out there about everything, and you know there is a career path out there for you. The big challenge is maintaining the level of affluence your parents have provided for you.

Like my daughters, you're respectful of religion but don't have time for it right now. And all religions are pretty much the same anyway, right? It's up to each individual to decide what's right or wrong. You don't need church to help you believe in God.

But as long as you're keeping your options open, I'd like to describe an option, or a way of living, that I have found, and I'd like you to consider it—assuming that you have an open mind and can listen with your own ears, instead of through the filter of the popular culture and social media.

What have you got to lose? We live in a very small sliver of space and time. You will go through your entire life knowing only the two generations that precede you and the two generations that follow you. Most of us haven't met the parents of our grandparents, and we will probably never meet the children of our grandchildren. So we will have to be content with about eighty or ninety years of this life, and fifty years after we're gone, no one on earth will have even heard of us—much less care. If there is a life beyond history, if there is an afterlife, wouldn't it make sense to explore and to try to know more about it? Why not devote a little time and effort to see if it's worth animating or investing in a spiritual dimension to your life? Why not see if there is a way to feel more connected to a higher power... or to develop a surer sense that your life has more meaning than a career and a great place to live?

This book is a dialogue. I spoke directly to my adult Catholic, single daughters, but not all in one conversation. Over a period of many months, they would question and challenge my point of view, and I tried to respond thoughtfully and sincerely. We have a good relationship, and I love them dearly. I want them to know the presence of God. I don't have all the answers, and some of the things I say do not satisfy them.

I'm not a theologian or a scholar. I had a decent career in a good industry: advertising sales in New York. I am a husband, father, and ordained deacon, offering my daughters and their friends a personal point of view about knowing God in today's real world. I've organized the chapters according to my own way of thinking, and you may think of them very differently. When my daughters question me, I don't want to seem defensive, but if I do it's because I hear so much that is negative, cynical, and dismissive from people who haven't taken the time or effort to explore. Given that they went to Catholic colleges, I'm amazed that my own children are surprised by some things I say.

I'm from another generation altogether: the baby boomers. Perhaps you are a baby boomer as well, and can relate to this book as a parent of a millennial, or as someone who became disenfranchised with the church somewhere along the way. We all went to school in the late 1950s, the '60s, and early '70s. My, how times change. Many of us now only go to church on Easter Sunday, and sometimes at Christmas. Some of us only go to church when there is a funeral or a wedding. Many of us are barely connected to the church but still identify ourselves as Catholic. I have an update for my friends: This book explains what it's like inside the church today and what it's like to be a practicing Catholic. It's about how God speaks to us.

Our experiences are similar. We all went to Catholic school and were taught by the nuns. We memorized our catechism, went to confession, and received Holy Communion. We learned songs and heard stories about the saints. We went to mass on First Fridays during Lent, and some of us learned the mass in Latin. But during high school and college, the world tipped over. The Civil Rights Movement, the war in Vietnam, the assassinations, the demonstrations, the music, and the drugs all seemed to accelerate everything into a manic state. By the time Watergate unfolded, and the corruption scandals in the FBI and CIA came out in the mid-seventies, any kind of trust or faith in institutions was severely damaged. Many kids we knew had already gagged on institutional religion and were glad to be free from any overhanging authority—no more commandments, precepts, obligations...no more saying I'm sorry. And no more church on Sunday, for God's sake. We didn't march off. We just faded away. Disco and cocaine had arrived, and everybody danced right into the AIDS era. The Catholic church for many became a faded memory, an old decaying institution, rigid and unchanging, better-suited for our parents. For some, it was a relief just to get away. For others, the church was to be reviled, blamed, and rejected. Some people who left held a grudge.

But you and I survived. We have our health, we have our kids, and we have Facebook. We just want to enjoy some music, have dinner with good friends, take a couple of vacations, and hug each other. It hasn't been easy. Our parents have been getting sick and dying, and our kids have to navigate challenges that are different than those we faced. We're proud and thrilled when our children succeed, and we blame ourselves and suffer when they hurt. But, hey, we're still here.

And that old Catholic church is still here, and has more than survived. As I explain my faith in God to Angela and Christina, see if you would handle their questions in the same way, if you were born before the millennial generation. I want to give you a peek inside the modern, twenty-first century Catholic church. Much of what you'll read you have already heard, but some stuff will definitely surprise you because there is so much misinformation and so many misconceptions about the church. Everything I share is based on real-life, first-hand experience. This book poses a question and then provides at least one answer.

Yes, to Angela and to Christina and to all my disengaged Catholic friends, I believe that God speaks to people today—profoundly, vaguely, intermittently, loudly, clearly, softly, impatiently, suddenly, often. God speaks to us when we are asleep, when we are awake, when we are in a trance, or when we are just walking down the street. God speaks to us through other people and through events. Sometimes God uses words. Many people are witnesses to this. Being in dialogue and relationship with God can somehow help everything make sense and have meaning. Many people will tell you, in a variety of ways, that they have a personal relationship with God.

So what about you?

Endnote

1. Jack Loechner, "General Social Media Behaviours," *Media Post*, Research Brief, June 30, 2014, http://www.mediapost.com/publications/article/228996/generational-social-media-behaviors.html.

CHAPTER 1

"Spoken through the Prophets"

§

ALL RIGHT, LADIES, IF WE'RE asking *Does God Speak to Us?* we have to start with these questions: When did human beings first become conscious of God? How did people first encounter God?

You know from attending Mass that at one point we recite our Creed. We stand up and, together, we say what we believe. It's the profession of faith, the Nicene Creed (from the first ecumenical council, in Nicaea, in AD 325).

I believe in one God, the Father almighty...
I believe in one Lord Jesus Christ...
I believe in the Holy Spirit, the Lord, the giver of life...

...who has spoken through the prophets.

Most of us don't give every word our full attention. But we're saying that the God we believe in, the one God, has spoken to us. We believe that He has spoken to us, first, through prophets.

Now who are these prophets, and what did they say?

Angela: *Dad, really? Are you taking us back to the beginning of time?*

Stay with me here because everything we discuss later depends on this. Prophetic messages began to come from the Jewish prophets of Israel well over two thousand years ago. The messages from the prophets were mostly focused on the contemporary scene at the time: the abuse of power by judges, the treatment of the poor and disadvantaged, and public morality in general. They warned the ruling class that if society did not practice justice and righteousness, it would not survive.

In ancient Israel a prophet was understood to be an intermediary between God and the community. He was thought to have heard from God through a variety of ways, mostly through dreams and visions. Prophets were believed to have been called by God to become a messenger. In Israel and throughout Asia Minor, these prophets were employed in temples and royal courts.

The prophets conveyed messages from God through public pronouncements, speeches, sermons, and writings. They didn't just condemn or judge. They pointed to a better future. They tried to encourage people to live better lives, and they announced salvation from misery.

You've heard of the prophet Isaiah. He said this:

"The spirit of the Lord God is upon me, because the Lord has anointed me; He has sent me to bring good news to the afflicted, to bind up the brokenhearted, to proclaim liberty to the captives, release to the prisoners, to announce a year of favor from the Lord and a day of vindication by our God..." (Is 61:1–2).

Was there a reason to hope? Throughout the ancient world there were countless calamitous wars, and injustice reigned. The Babylonians had destroyed the city of Jerusalem. The Hebrews had been taken into bondage, enslaved, and forced into hard labor by the Egyptians. And yet the prophets were pointing to a promise, to a time of peace and freedom. Isaiah said that another time was coming, a new world: "Then the wolf shall be a guest of the lamb, and the leopard shall lie down with the young goat. The calf and the young lion shall browse together, with a little child to guide them. The baby shall play by the viper's den, and the child lay his hand on the adder's lair" (Is 11:6, 8).

Technically, the writings of the Jewish prophets in the Old Testament are contained in a section called the Prophetic Books—including Ezekiel, Daniel, Micah, Zachariah, and Malachi. Prophets like Jeremiah, Hosea, and Amos observed the evil and bad living they saw all around them—including idolatry—and they wanted to shake the people from their blindness. They told people to change and pointed to times of abundance. Prophetic literature came in the form of exhortations, threats, announcements of punishment, and promises of deliverance. Their primary concern was communicating the interests of the Jewish God. For example, a prophet's announcement of impending doom because of idolatry would begin with the words "thus says the LORD" (Is 44:24). A divine exhortation and promise from God would begin "hear the Word of the LORD, O people of Israel" (Hos 4:1).

God was speaking through the prophets and calling people to look for the light. Through the prophet Amos, God said, "Seek good and not evil, that you may live. Then truly will the LORD, your God, be with you…" (Am 5:14).

God was here!

"The LORD, your God, is in your midst, a mighty savior, He will rejoice over you with gladness, and renew you in His love, He will exult over you with loud singing, as on a day of festival" (Zep 3:17).

Christina: *But were people listening to this? Did the people of that time believe that* God *existed?*

Well, some did. Most would later come to God kicking and screaming. But here's the thing. It wasn't just that God existed or that God was here. This God of creation was manifesting an act of love. God had looked down at a people oppressed. God saw their plight, and he heard them cry out to him. They were his people, and they were in bondage, enslaved. God wanted to help them, to make a covenant with them. God chose a people to bring from darkness into the light. He would be their God, and they would be his people.

Biblical scholars tell us that the promises of this Jewish God find their classic expression in the twelfth chapter of the book of Genesis. God challenges a man named Abram to believe in Him. Abram is chosen to be the patriarch of God's people and receive a land, and through Abram all the nations will somehow be blessed.

"I will make of you a great nation, and I will bless you. I will make your name great, so that you will be a blessing. I will bless those who bless you and curse those who curse you. All the communities of the earth shall find blessing in you" (Gn 12:2–3).

Abram said, "O Lord God, what good will your gifts be if I keep on being childless?" (Gn 15:2). Then the word of the Lord came to Abram. The Lord took him outside and said, "Look up at the sky and count the stars, if you can. Just so, will your descendants be" (Gn 15:5). A bond began between God and Abram. "Abram put his faith in the Lord, who attributed it to him as an act of righteousness" (Gn 15:6).

Then the Bible says this in Genesis 17:3–9:

When Abram prostrated himself, God continued to speak to him: My covenant with you is this: No longer shall you be called Abram; your name shall be Abraham, for I am making you a host of nations; kings shall stem from you. I will maintain my covenant with you and your descendants after you throughout the ages as an everlasting pact, to be your God and the God of your descendants after you. I will give to you and your descendants after you the land in which you are now staying, as a permanent possession; and I will be their God. You must keep my covenant throughout the ages.

He would be their God, and they would be His people. He would provide statutes and commands, which he would enjoin on them as a covenant—a covenant that would last forever.

Angela: *Ok, how do we get to Christianity from there?*

Someone else would be needed to carry the story forward. A child was born of Levites, Hebrews, and then adopted by the daughter of Pharaoh in Egypt. The woman named him Moses, for she said, "I drew him out of the water." You know this story. Moses, a Hebrew raised as an Egyptian, had grown up and saw the oppression and forced labor of the Hebrews. He saw an Egyptian strike a Hebrew, "one of his own kinsmen," and slew the Egyptian himself. Realizing he would be found out, he fled to a distant land called Midian. In Midian he married the daughter of Jethro the priest.

One day, while tending Jethro's flock, "an angel of the Lord appeared to him in fire flaming out of a bush." Moses saw that the bush was not being consumed by the fire, so he drew closer to have a look at this remarkable sight. God said, "Come no nearer!" Then God told Moses to remove his sandals because he was standing on holy ground.

I am the God of your father…the God of Abraham, the God of Isaac, the God of Jacob…I have witnessed the affliction of my people in Egypt and heard their cry of complaint against their slave drivers, so I know well what they are suffering. Therefore, I have come down to rescue them from the hands of the Egyptians and lead them out of that land into a good and spacious land, a land flowing with milk and honey…(Ex 3:6–8).

Moses was being called on to lead God's people. But he said, "Who am I, that I should go to Pharaoh and lead the Israelites out of Egypt?"

God said, "I will be with you…"

But Moses persisted, "If I tell the people 'the God of your Fathers has sent me,' and they ask, 'What is his name?' what do I tell them?"

God replied, "I Am who I Am…This is what you shall say to the Israelites: I AM sent me to you" (Ex 3:11–14).

What was this? Was Moses having a dialogue—a relationship—with God? Yes, and this God was a not a distant presence beyond the stars or an old man with a white beard. This God was colorful and dynamic, very human, and very personal. This was a God to know. Through the prophets and other writers in the Old Testament, we, who read this Jewish Bible, encounter a living God. This is a God who creates: "God looked at everything he had made, and he found it very good" (Gn 1:31). This God makes promises: "I will make of you a great nation, and I will bless you…" (Gn 12:2). And this God delivers: "…Lift up your staff, and, with hand outstretched over the sea, split the sea in two, that the Israelites might pass through it on dry land" (Ex 14:16).

And even when God was angry, he might relent in his anger. Abraham appealed to God, on behalf of the few remaining innocent people in the sinful cities of Sodom and Gomorrah. He said, "'Will you really sweep away the righteous with the wicked?…Should not the judge of all the world act with justice?' The Lord replied, 'If I find fifty innocent people in the city of Sodom, I will spare the whole place for their sake'" (Gn 18:23, 25–26).

It was to be a loving relationship between God and his people—something like a marriage…a bond…a promise…yes, a covenant. And the faithfulness of this chosen people to the covenant would give glory to God forever, and through this sacred bond, God would extend his gift of love to the rest of the world.

Christina: *But Dad, do you believe that God spoke to just one group of people, in this one place?*

Well, humanity's awakening to a higher presence was not confined to just the people of the eastern Mediterranean. You've read of the great ancient dynasties that grew up in China, as far back as 2100 BC. The renowned philosopher Confucius and the poet Qu Yuan were influential in helping people develop their own sense of self, or moral compass. Centuries before, a man named Lao Tzu (Old Sage) left a record of his teaching in a profound spiritual book called *Tao Te Ching* (The Way and Its Power). He pointed to a way of living and being, to "dwell quietly alone with the spiritual and the intelligent."

In northeastern India, also around this time (2500 BC), a man named Siddhartha Gautama began to recognize the manic madness that occupied people's minds. He taught people to try to awaken from their own insanity and dysfunction. He became known as the Buddha (the Enlightened One), and he taught his followers to purify the mind of all defilements. Slowly, people began to follow his teachings.

The eastern Mediterranean of the Old Testament was one of the most heavily populated areas of ancient times. It was a dynamic environment with great conflict, upheaval, and madness. People needed to awaken to a higher power, a greater good. They needed to change, grow, and get outside of themselves, to realize their destiny. And these prophets were attuned, awakened to a call, a voice that pointed to a better way of living.

The Jewish prophets were spurred on with a passion, a fire, even in the face of derision and ridicule. And at times they complained to God about the response they got. The prophet Jeremiah wrote this:

You duped me, O LORD, and I let myself be duped; you were too strong for me, and you triumphed. All the day I am an object of laughter; everyone mocks me...The word of the LORD has brought me derision and reproach all the day. I say to myself, I will not mention him, I will speak in his name no more! But the call or the vocation to proclaim God was too strong, and could not be contained. But then it becomes like fire burning in my heart, imprisoned in my bones; I grow weary holding it in, I cannot endure it (Jer 20:7–9).

For the people of Israel, the desert was a likely place to hear from God. It was a wilderness of solitude, with strange and unusual sounds. In one passage from the prophet Hosea, God is leading his people into the desert with the voice of a loving husband or father: "I will allure her; I will lead her into the desert, and speak to her heart" (Hos 2:16).

For Catholics, Isaiah is a particularly important prophet and probably the best-known prophet. We hear him in the first reading at the Mass throughout Advent, a time of anticipation and preparation. When the king of Judah died in the year 742 BC, Isaiah received his call to the prophetic office in the temple of Jerusalem. In a dream or vision, he was summoned to be the "ambassador of the most high."

Isaiah proclaimed the majesty, holiness, and glory of the Lord God. He was convinced that God was good and that God was holy. By great contrast, he saw the pettiness and sinfulness of all those around him. He was aware of the moral breakdown of the people of Jerusalem, and he tried to get people to reform their lives, to have courage, and to have faith in the sovereign God.

Actually, the book of Isaiah was written not only by the prophet himself, but by him and at least two of his followers over a period of more than one hundred years. It is a huge work—sixty-six chapters in all—filled with beautiful imagery. It is poetic and offers a sense of hope. It is obviously written by people utterly convinced of the reality of a loving god.

Angela: *But isn't the Old Testament also filled with stories of deception, infidelity, and murder?*

Ok, yes. But as we read through the story, what is the one consistent theme? Despite all the failures, lack of faith, and sinfulness of the people in the Old Testament story, God keeps His promise. He made a covenant with His people, and His patience seems to endure forever.

And watch this: the prophetic wisdom passed through the prophets does not only apply to the situation and people of ancient times. It is the wisdom of the ages, spoken by God. God's words spoke to people then, and they speak to us now.

How do we break from our own bondage of sin? "For thus says the Lord GOD, the Holy One of Israel: By waiting and by calm you shall be saved, In quiet and in trust, your strength lies" (Is 30:15). The prophets proclaimed so many truths. We know these things are true because they stir our own hearts, even today.

But back to our story. There was no going back when the Jewish people left Egypt. The prophets were pointing forward and inward: out of Egypt, out of bondage, out of slavery, out or darkness, and into an awareness of God.

Read something else from Isaiah 9:1–3:

The people who lived in darkness, have seen a great light. Upon those who lived in the land of gloom, a light has shone. You have brought them abundant joy and great rejoicing, as they rejoice before you as at the harvest, as men make merry when dividing spoils. For the yoke that burdened them, the pole on their shoulder, and the rod of their taskmaster, you have smashed, as on the day of Midian.

And the God who has spoken through the prophets was not only pointing to freedom from the bondage of slavery and a land flowing with milk and honey. Something even more wonderful was coming.

CHAPTER 2

Jesus

§

How DOES A FATHER TALK to his two adult daughters about Jesus? Let's start this way:

What do you say to a friend who is down and out or to someone who has just lost a loved one? How do you help a person who is often depressed or ill at ease? Do you know what to say to someone who is consumed by anxious thinking, worried about the future, or deeply regretful about the past? Ever speak to a newlywed who is disillusioned with marriage because her husband is already paying her less attention? Do you know people who are addicted to alcohol or drugs or gambling or pornography and who can't seem to shake the cycle of isolation and debt? How about people who are just bitter because life has dealt one bad hand after another, and they're sick and tired of negative outcomes: loss of a job, a failed relationship, or a diagnosis of cancer. Could you help a person who can't sleep or someone who finds it hard to get up in the morning to face another day of bad news? What could you say to any of these people?

"Come to me, all you who labor, and are burdened, and I will give you rest" (Mt 11:28).

What is Jesus, or who is Jesus? How does Jesus exist for us? Many people of faith can answer with confidence, but for people who are seeking truth in their lives, those questions are not easy. Anyone who wants to encounter Jesus will have questions. If Jesus was born two thousand years ago but still exists today, He transcends time. And if He once lived in the Middle East but now lives through people everywhere, then He transcends space. If Jesus transcends time and space, then an encounter with Him is a profound experience—an encounter with God. And this encounter, through Jesus, has been experienced and expressed by different people, in different cultures, for many centuries. To almost one-third of the world's population, Jesus exists and is alive today. But how?

The Light

In the Bible, in the Gospel According to John, Jesus is introduced this way: "A man named John was sent from God. He came for testimony, to testify to the light, so that all might believe through him. He was not the light, but came to testify to the light. The true light, which enlightens everyone, was coming into the world" (Jn 1:6–8).

Light, as a metaphor, can be overused, but it represents something real. Children say, "I'm afraid of the dark; please leave the light on tonight" because light represents safety and security. When we say that a teacher's lecture is enlightening, we mean that it opened our minds and was a source of knowledge and wisdom. When a third party is brought in to "shed some light" on a subject, it means we are looking for new information or broader perspective. A shimmering light represents healing, and light from an eternal flame represents steadfastness and loyalty. From ancient times, the authors of the Bible used light to describe safety, understanding, wisdom, knowledge, healing, and even God Himself.

"The Lord is my light and my salvation; whom should I fear?" (Ps 27:1).

The author of the First Letter of John wrote this: "…God is light, and in Him there is no darkness at all. If we say, 'We have fellowship with Him,' while we continue to walk in darkness, we lie and do not act in truth. But if we walk in the light as He is in the light, then we have fellowship with one another, and the blood of His Son Jesus cleanses us from all our sin" (1 Jn 1:5–7).

When St. Paul recounts the story of his conversion on his way to Damascus, he uses this imagery: "…I saw a light from the sky, brighter than the sun, shining around me and my traveling companions." They all fall to the ground, and he hears a voice: "Saul, Saul, why are you persecuting me?" When Paul asks, "Who are you?" St. Luke writes that this was the answer: "I am Jesus whom you are persecuting" (Acts 26:13–15).

Jesus Himself says, "Whoever walks in the dark does not know where he is going. While you have the light, believe in the light, so that you may become children of the light" (Jn 12:35–36). And when Jesus explains why He will help the blind man regain his sight near the pool at Siloam, He says, "When I am in the world, I am the light of the world" (Jn 9:5).

In the wisdom book of Proverbs, we read, "The light of the just gives joy, but the lamp of the wicked goes out" (Prv 13:9). We get these references to light from Isaiah: "I, the LORD, have called you for justice, I have grasped you by the hand; I formed you as a covenant for the people, a light for the nations, to open the eyes of the blind, to bring out prisoners from confinement, and from the dungeon, those who live in darkness" (Is 42:6–7). "I will make you a light to the nations, that my salvation may reach to the ends of the earth" (Is 49:6). "The people who walked in darkness have seen a great light; upon those who lived in a land of gloom a light has shone" (Is 9:1).

On the very first day in the story of creation, when "the earth was without form or shape, with darkness over the abyss," it says in the book of Genesis, "Then God said: Let there be light, and there was light. God saw that the light was good" (Gn 1:3–4).

And, again, Isaiah says, "Arise! Shine, for your light has come, the glory of the Lord has dawned upon you. Nations shall walk by your light, kings by the radiance of your dawning" (Is 60:1, 3).

Jesus is the light of healing and the light of forgiveness. And this healing, saving light glows from within.

MINISTRY

Christina: *Yes, God is light, but what can you say about the human Jesus?*

When we discuss Jesus as a human being, we must always be mindful of his dual nature. He is both fully divine and fully human. Creation itself is an act of love by God. So is the Incarnation. We believe that God "so loved the world" that he entered into our humanity through the body of a woman in the form of a man. Jesus is God made man.

The person of Jesus, the historical Jesus Christ, is a fact. People met Him, listened to Him, were called by Him, and were healed by Him. Some people came to believe in Him, told others about Him, and then wrote about Him. Others resisted Him, challenged Him, arrested Him, and killed Him.

During the ministry of Jesus on earth, literally thousands of people heard Him and saw Him. Remember that he fed four thousand people one day and five thousand people another, not counting women and children. When he entered Jerusalem for the final time, more and more people encountered Him. And after the events around His trial and execution, His story became even more widespread.

The first witnesses were the people He chose: His apostles. Other disciples were quickly added, and word about this dynamic, new preacher spread. After His death, a dedicated group of followers formed, and they kept His story alive. People testified that He appeared to them—that they actually saw Him. And these witnesses, led by the apostles, fanned out and told other people the stories about Jesus. Peter went to Antioch and then to Rome. John went to Ephesus. James gathered a following in Jerusalem. Philip traveled to Ethiopia, and Thomas was believed to have traveled to India. Jude went to what is now Syria, and Mark went to Alexandria.

St. Paul went around the Mediterranean, from Greece to Rome, three times. Although he had not met Jesus during His ministry, he had a life-changing encounter, and he told everyone about it. He had been blinded by a light, but he also heard a voice. He told everyone in every city he visited about his sudden and definite conversion—from a persecutor of Christians to a slavery for himself of this Christ. There are thirteen letters in the New Testament attributed to Paul, and from these we learn much about his personality and faith experience. He wrote, "...The Son of God...loved me and gave Himself for me" (Gal 2:20) and this: "I have been crucified with Christ; it is no longer I who live, but Christ who lives in me..." (Gal 2:19–20).

The number of believers continued to spread. Small communities formed in various places. Jesus had said, "I am the way," and some of His followers became known as the People of the Way. "...It was in Antioch that the followers of Jesus were first called Christians" (Acts 11:26). So the church was formed and growing. We know this because of Paul's letters that were sent to places like Corinth, Thessalonica, and Philippi. He was exhorting these communities—this church—to pull together, to help each other, and to behave correctly. He was teaching about a new way of living, about a way of believing and following in the footsteps of this Christ Jesus. He was giving advice on how to live—to husbands, wives, children, even slaves. He gave instruction to presbyters and to bishops. So, even before the gospels were written—before the New Testament—the church that Jesus established on the rock of St. Peter was flourishing. But it wasn't easy to be a Christian.

Over in Rome a small community of followers had formed, and they worshiped and prayed together. In AD 64 a fire broke out and spread quickly, destroying more than half the city. Stories tell of the Emperor Nero, who reportedly wrote an epic poem while the city burned. He was unbalanced, crazy, and he blamed the Christians for the fire. He had them arrested and killed. Anyone who was a follower of Jesus was under constant threat, and it was tempting to lose hope. It was in this context of isolation and hopelessness that the Gospel of Mark was written.

Mark, or John Mark, was an associate of Paul and Barnabas. He had traveled with them and then separated for an unknown reason. His gospel was believed by many to have been the first one written, and it focused on what true discipleship meant—and what was required—even in the face of brutal persecution. Just a few miles away from this unstable emperor, whose subjects thought of him as a god, Mark boldly began his writing this way: "The beginning of the gospel of Jesus Christ, the Son of God" (Mk 1:1).

Christina: *When you speak of Rome and Peter, when does the Pope come in?*

The Pope is known as the Bishop of Rome, among other names. St. Peter was martyred in Rome and is believed to be buried beneath the basilica that bears his name. His successors were the bishops of Rome, Linus, Anacletus, as well as others, and eventually, over time, church authority was gathered at Rome. The Bishop of Rome became known as the First Among Equals. Since Jesus handed Peter the "keys to the kingdom," the successors of St. Peter were also known as the Vicar of Peter and later, the Vicar of Christ. In Italy the Pope was referred to as Il Papa, the Father.

WITNESS

Angela: *How do we encounter Jesus, if He himself wrote nothing?*

We have His witnesses. As the apostles began to age, it occurred to more and more people that it was important to make some kind of record of everything they had heard and seen.

This first generation was passing along their eyewitness accounts, and at one point a man named Luke—a Syrian, a non-Jew from Antioch, possibly a physician by trade—wrote this:

> Since many have undertaken to compile a narrative of the events that have been fulfilled among us, just as those who were eyewitnesses from the beginning and ministers of the word have handed them down to us, I too have decided, after investigating everything accurately anew, to write it down in an orderly sequence for you...so that you may realize the certainty of the teachings you have received (Lk 1:1–4).

Luke addressed this to someone named Theophilus ("lover of God"), a prominent non-Palestinian, and he was writing to an audience that was largely made up of Gentile Christians. At the same time, Matthew, who was either an apostle or close associate, wrote his gospel, and this one was written for Jews, with many references to the Hebrew Bible.

Some years after this, we have more written accounts, such as the First Letter of John. We believe that the author of this epistle is the same person who wrote the fourth gospel. The "disciple whom Jesus loved" was either this apostle or a very dedicated follower. First John is a beautiful testimony to the belief that awareness and knowledge of God are inseparable from love of one another. "Beloved, let us love one another, because love is of God; everyone who loves is begotten by God and knows God" (1 Jn 4:7).

The beginning of 1 John, chapter 1, states that the writer and his friends are true witnesses: "…what we have heard, what we have seen with our own eyes, what we have looked upon, and touched with our hands…" (1 Jn 1:1). Had the writer heard Jesus preach? Seen Jesus with his own eyes? Yes. Was he saying he had looked upon Jesus Christ, the man, and touched Him with his own hands? Yes. "…What we have seen and heard, we proclaim now to you, so that you too may have fellowship with us; for our fellowship is with the Father and with His Son, Jesus Christ. We are writing this so that our joy may be complete" (1 Jn 1:3, 4).

So, by the end of the first century, in addition to the oral tradition—the story being passed along by word of mouth—we have the writings of Paul and Mark and Matthew and Luke and John. The good news of Jesus Christ was being circulated and proclaimed. We can say with assurance that some people met Jesus and knew him and passed along what they knew to others. And those people wrote many things down about him so that all could experience the joy that they had experienced through being with Him. Evangelization was under way.

CALL TO CONVERSION

Some people responded to Jesus readily. As Jesus moved about during his ministry on earth, He called people to follow Him. As He was walking by the Sea of Galilee, He came upon Peter and His brother Andrew, and He said, "Come after Me, and I will make you fishers of men" (Mt 4:19). Then He saw James and his brother John, and He called them, "and immediately they left their boat and their father and followed him" (Mt 4:22). Later Matthew, also called Levi—a tax collector no less—immediately left his post and followed Jesus. Why were some people eager and ready to follow this Jesus right away?

First, they had a referral. John the Baptist had been out preaching, exhorting people to clean up their lives, and preparing them for the savior that all the prophets of old had promised. This prophesied savior was on the minds of people. St. Luke wrote, "Now the people were filled with expectation, and were all asking in their hearts whether John might be the Messiah" (Lk 3:15). John said he was not the Messiah. "I am baptizing you with water...but the one who is coming after me is mightier that I" (Mt 3: 11). All through history, some believers have answered the call of Jesus readily. Once they heard about Him and were taught His message, they accepted Him with gratitude and followed Him with joy.

Consider for instance, St. Paul; his conversion was a sudden and dramatic moment in his life. He had been threatening Jesus's disciples, and he went to the high priest in Jerusalem, asking for letters to take to the synagogues in Damascus. He was determined that if he should find any men or women who followed Jesus, he would have permission to bring them back to Jerusalem in chains. But on the way to Damascus, Paul was stopped in his tracks and called by Jesus. His complete conversion would take some time, but at that moment he was changed, and he would never be the same again.

Does this sudden transformation, or rebirth, ever happen to average Christians? Well, we've heard of people finding Jesus when they hit rock bottom. When all seems lost, the light shines, and we hear someone has "found Jesus." Or expressed another way, "I once was lost, but now I'm found."

Angela: *Well, if you are brought up in a Christian environment and taught about Jesus at a young age, there really is no dramatic conversion.*

We believe that we enter into Christ at baptism. But many people have the experience of conversion in response to an event. In all cases, true conversion is a process.

HEALING

Angela: *Do you think people believe that Jesus heals in this day and age? I mean, young people who are not sick don't see an urgent need for a relationship with Jesus.*

Healing is such a fundamental aspect of life in Christ. As He began His ministry, Jesus would travel around and heal those He encountered. These were acts of compassion and love but also a way to get people's attention. When He entered a synagogue one day, He met a man with a withered hand. Jesus said to him, "Stretch out your hand," and He healed him (Mk 3:1–5). Another time, the people brought Jesus a paralytic lying on a stretcher. When Jesus said, "Rise, pick up your stretcher and go home," the man went (Mt 9:1–8). A leper approached Him, and said, "Lord, if you wish, you can make me clean." Jesus touched him, and said, "I will do it. Be made clean" (Mt 8:2–4). When Jesus entered Peter's house and saw his mother-in-law lying in bed with a fever, "He touched her hand, the fever left her, and she rose and waited on him" (Mt 8:15).

Believing that Jesus could do these acts was important. Sometimes Jesus asked people if they believed that he could heal them before doing so. At other times people proclaimed their belief without being asked. When the Roman centurion approached Jesus about his servant, who was lying at home suffering with a paralysis, Jesus said right away, "I will come and cure him." But the centurion answered Him with words that would be repeated by people of faith forever. He said, "Lord, I am not worthy to have you enter under my roof; only say the word and my servant will be healed." (See Matthew 8:5–13.)

In this same town of Capernaum, Jesus entered the synagogue on the Sabbath and began to teach. There was a man there who was possessed, and screamed at Jesus, "'What have you to do with us, Jesus of Nazareth? Have you come to destroy us? I know who you are—the Holy One of God!' Jesus rebuked him and said, 'Quiet! Come out of him!' The unclean spirit convulsed him, and with a loud cry came out of him" (Mk 1:24–26). People were astounded by what they witnessed. "What is this? He commands even the unclean spirits and they obey him," (Mk 1:27). "We have never seen anything like this" (Mk 2:12).

Jesus kept telling those who witnessed these acts not to tell anyone. "He warned them sternly not to make him known" (Mk 3:12). And when He raised the daughter of Jairus—who was a synagogue official—"He gave strict orders that no one should know this" (Mk 5:43). Why would He not want people to know of these things? Wasn't Jesus calling people to be become fishers of men? The scholars tell us that He didn't want the people to be distracted by the healings. He didn't want them to think of Him as just a faith healer or a miracle worker. As wonderful as these things were, they were only signs. They pointed to something greater. The meaning of His ministry and His purpose on earth was still yet to be revealed.

Still, people came. "When it was evening, they brought Him many who were possessed by demons, and He drove out the spirits by a word, and cured all of the sick, to fulfill what had been said by Isaiah the prophet, 'He took away our infirmities and bore our diseases'" (Mt 8:16–17). And at every turn those who opposed Him plotted and planned how to stop Him. There were those who were threatened by Him and did not believe, and those people wanted to do away with Him.

When He returned to Nazareth, where He had grown up, He went into the synagogue there on the Sabbath, according to the Jewish custom. He opened the scroll and read a passage from the prophet Isaiah: "The Spirit of the Lord is upon me, because he has anointed me to bring glad tidings to the poor. He has sent me to proclaim liberty to the captives and recovery of sight to the blind, to let the oppressed go free, and to proclaim a year acceptable to the Lord." St. Luke then writes that Jesus rolled up the scroll, handed it back to the attendant, and sat down. And then He said something provocative. "Today this scripture passage is fulfilled in your hearing." (See Luke 4:16–21.)

What? He was telling people in his own hometown, those who knew his mother and his father—the carpenter Joseph—that He Himself was the fulfillment of the Old Testament prophecy? He was saying that the hopes and expectations of God's people would now be taken on by His ministry on earth? The people who heard this proclaimed in the synagogue could not handle it. "They rose up, drove him out of the town, and led him to the brow of the hill on which their town had been built, to hurl him down headlong. But he passed through the midst of them and went away" (Lk 4:29–30).

Angela: *It seems the ministry could have ended right there!*

Yes, but the crowds still grew bigger, and the word continued to spread. I love the account of Jesus going off to the mountain to pray all night. In the morning He selected His twelve apostles. And as they were coming down the mountain, a huge throng of people awaited. Jesus was about to deliver His sermon on the plain. St. Luke writes, "And everyone in the crowd sought to touch Him, because a power came forth from Him, and cured them all" (Lk 6:19). It was a power of grace and healing. And with the signs and the power came a message. This message had to be repeated and told in many different ways. His disciples constantly misunderstood. He was teaching them to serve and to love, and it was a hard, counterintuitive message.

I also like the story of the young, rich man (Mt 19:16–30) who approaches Jesus one day and asks, "Good teacher, what must I do to have eternal life?" Now that's a really good question from an industrious young man. He was probably good at managing money and people, and his father probably placed increased responsibility on his shoulders. He is aware that although some of his father's friends and relatives have plenty of wealth, they still die. And so he figures he had better investigate what some people have been talking about—this life that exists after death, this eternal life with God. Who better to ask than this exciting new preacher? Jesus answers directly: "You know what to do; follow the commandments."

At this point, the rich man should have been really smart and said something like, "Thank you, teacher, that's great advice. I'm pretty good on about seven or eight of those commandments, but I should probably keep working on a couple—like three and four in particular. Thanks, and I'll get back to you on my progress."

Instead, he says, "I do that already." That was a mistake. So now Jesus says, in effect, "Oh, you do? Hey, that's great—always happy to meet people who understand and follow all ten of God's commandments. You are definitely ready for the next step. Now go and sell everything you own, give the money to the poor, and follow me." (I'm sorry, I thought I heard you say, *sell everything you own*, and *follow me*. Follow you where?)

The young man went away sad (and maybe thought, "I was just looking for some good advice or direction; is He crazy?"). And then St. Matthew writes, "And Jesus loved him." Jesus will always ask for more, but He will never ask for more than we can give. He meets us where we live and loves us as we are, but He calls us to follow him to the cross and into eternal life.

Jesus told His followers to stop judging. He told them to forgive others who had harmed them, and they themselves would then be forgiven. It was Peter who one day approached Him and asked, "'Lord, if my brother sins against me, how often must I forgive him? As many as seven times?' Jesus answered, 'I say to you, not seven times but seventy-seven times'" (Mt 18:21–22). He was teaching them that they could only expect forgiveness from God to the extent they themselves could forgive others. Being joined to the God of love required a loving heart. And to develop and achieve a heart filled with love required discipline and prayer. So when we pray to God in the Lord's Prayer, we say, "Forgive us our trespasses, as we forgive those who trespass against us."

He taught, He preached, He admonished, He rebuked, and He loved. Jesus had a message of peace, a message of self-surrender. He came to complete the joy of His Father. To teach us, He gave us images of Himself. He Himself was living water, the good shepherd, the true vine…and something else.

The Bread

One evening, Jesus's disciples approached Him and said, "'This is a deserted place and it is already late, let's dismiss the people so they can go to the villages to get food.' Jesus said, '…Give them some food yourselves.' They said, 'We only have two fish and five loaves of bread'" (Mt 14:15–17). What happened next is a very important part of the Jesus story and of the entire Christian movement. It is the story of a miracle, and it is the only miracle that is recounted in all four gospel accounts. Jesus asked for the food and ordered the crowd to sit down. "Taking the five loaves and the two fish, and looking up to heaven, He said the blessing, broke the loaves, and gave them to His disciples, who in turn gave them to the crowds. They all ate and were satisfied, and they picked up the fragments left over—twelve wicker baskets full" (Mt 14:19–20). This is the miracle of the feeding of the five thousand; it's worth reflecting on for a moment:

Everyone was gathered to hear the message of Jesus. His heart was moved with pity for them, and He cured all their sick. Now they needed to be fed, and there was not nearly enough food. He did not dismiss them or abandon them. He was there for them;

they were His people, the ones He came to love and save. The people were all gathered around, sitting and waiting. Jesus looked up to heaven and said a blessing. So, this was a moment made holy by the presence of God. Jesus broke the bread and gave it to His disciples. (Jesus would do this again at His last supper on earth. That's when He took the bread, said the blessing, broke it, and gave it to them, saying, "This is my body, which will be given for you; do this in memory of me" (Lk 22:19).) The disciples, in turn, gave the food to the crowds. This is our example of ministry. They all ate, and they were all satisfied.

God was present, Jesus was present, and the people were present. They were all in communion together, and all were satisfied. And not only that, but there were twelve wicker baskets of fragments left over. In this we see that when we receive Jesus, we receive an abundance, more than we may ever need. We are satisfied now, having been fed by Him. And this miracle hearkens back to the Old Testament; it reminds us that God provided for His people at the time of the Exodus by feeding them manna in the desert, the flakes like hoarfrost that came each morning. That manna could not be stored and saved; it would go bad. But there was enough to satisfy everyone for each day—one day at a time. God provided the bread for them then, as He does for us now.

Back to our story, after they had eaten, Jesus said, "...It was not Moses who gave the bread from heaven; my Father gives you the true bread from heaven. For the bread of God is that which comes down from heaven, and gives life to the world." His followers said, "Hey, give us this bread always!" So Jesus said, "I am the bread of life; whoever comes to Me will never hunger, and whoever believes in Me will never thirst" (Jn 6:32–35).

Jesus would include this concept in His prayer, the Lord's Prayer. He teaches us to reverently and constantly ask our Father in heaven to "give us this day, our daily bread." Followers of Jesus say the "Our Father" every day of their lives.

Angela: *Thus, the consistent emphasis of "presence" in the Church?*

Oh yes. St. Luke writes that precious passage about two travelers who are walking from Jerusalem after all the events of the crucifixion had taken place. They are heading to a town called Emmaus. At one point another traveler joins them and walks along with them. They tell him what happened. As they approach the village, they ask him to stay with them. Luke writes, "And it happened that, while he was with them at table, he took bread, said the blessing, broke it, and gave it to them. With that their eyes were opened and they recognized him, but he vanished from their sight" (Lk 24:30–31).

They recognized Him when He took bread, said the blessing, broke it, and gave it to them. And from those days until this day, we recognize Jesus in the bread when we receive Him in the Eucharist at the mass. Through transubstantiation, the bread and wine that we receive is no longer bread and wine, but the sacramental sign of the Real Presence of Jesus Christ in the Eucharist. Over and over and over again, we recognize the presence of Jesus in the bread, and we receive Him. Again and again, week after week, season after season, year after year, and down through the centuries, we do this in memory of Him because He told us to. We take Him into ourselves, and He takes us into Himself, and we become one with Him and with the Father and with each other. It is Holy Communion with God. Are we obsessed with this? Yes, we are.

RELATIONSHIP

To be a Christian, you have to have a relationship with Christ. To be a follower of Christ, you have to know whom you are following.

I'm not telling you that. I'm just saying that to believe in Jesus, you yourself have to define that belief.

After His disciples had been in various locations preaching and seeing people, Jesus asked them, "Who do the people say that I am?" They said Elijah or John the Baptist. Then Jesus asked them directly, "But who do you say that I am?" (See Matthew 16:13–16.) Peter answered first, but it is a question for each one of us. Who is Jesus to you? No one can answer this question for you.

DOUBTS AND DENIAL

Christina: *Dad, now that you are a deacon, do you ever have doubts?*

Absolutely, we all have doubts. Is God hearing my prayers? Faith is elusive at times. When Jesus had been raised, St. John wrote that He appeared to His disciples, and they said to Thomas, who was not there that day, "We have seen the Lord!" But as we know, Thomas—who had been with Jesus for the entire ministry and had seen everything unfold as He predicted, for goodness sake—said, "Unless I see the mark of the nails in his hands and put my finger into the nail marks and put my hand into his side, I will not believe." But after Thomas had the chance to experience the presence of the Lord once again the following week, he said, "My Lord and my God!" Jesus said, "Have you come to believe because you have seen me? Blessed are those who have not seen and have believed" (Jn 20:25–29).

The call is not only to believe but to love. At the Sea of Tiberius, Jesus would again appear to His followers after His death. While the apostles were fishing, they saw Jesus on the shore. He called to them, "Come, have breakfast." After they shared some fish and bread, Jesus said to Peter, "Simon, son of John, do you love me more than these?" Peter said, "Yes, Lord." Jesus replied, "Feed my lambs." Then Jesus asked a second time, "Simon, son of John, do you love me?" Peter said, "Yes, you know that I love you." Jesus said, "Tend my sheep." A third time Jesus said, "Simon, son of John, do you love me?" Peter was now distressed and said, "Lord, you know everything; you know that I love you." And Jesus replied, "Feed my sheep." Peter's three confessions were meant to counteract his three earlier denials during Jesus's arrest. And it is believed that this is when Jesus gave Peter the authority to become bishop, the shepherd and ruler of the flock of Jesus, the Church. The passage ends with Jesus saying simply, "Follow me" (Jn 21:15–19).

Following Jesus

How did those who saw and heard Jesus react? I already mentioned that they reacted in various ways, but Jesus said it best in a parable about a sower planting seed on his fields. In the parable, the seed is the word of God, and it falls on a flat path, rocky ground, among thorns, and then on rich soil. The people who are like the path are the ones who have heard, but they do not believe. The people who are like rocky ground receive the word with joy at first but then lose interest and fade away. The people who are like thorns hear and accept the word, but as they go along in life, the riches, pleasures, and anxieties of life distract them and get in the way, and their faith fails to produce mature fruit. "But as for the seed that fell on rich soil, they are the ones who, when they have heard the word, embrace it with a generous and good heart, and bear fruit through perseverance" (Lk 8:15).

Oh, Jesus used many wonderful parables. To teach about the greatest commandment—"You shall love the Lord, your God, with all your heart, with all your being, with all your strength, and with all your mind, and your neighbor as yourself" (Lk 10:27)—He told the parable of the good Samaritan, the foreigner who went out of his way to help someone in need.

Jesus offers us something: life with God. But He wants us to change. And Paul helps us with this: "I urge you therefore, brothers, by the mercies of God, to offer your bodies as a living sacrifice, holy and pleasing to God, your spiritual worship. Do not conform yourselves to this age but be transformed by the renewal of your mind, that you may discern what is the will of God, what is good and pleasing and perfect" (Rom 12:1–2).

To teach us about discovery, loss, forgiveness, reconciliation, and awareness of God's presence, He told the parable of the lost son. After the father in the story has forgiven his son for abandoning him after he gave the younger son his share of the inheritance, he embraces his son and celebrates his return. He turns to the older son, who has a doubtful and unforgiving heart, and says, "My son, you are here with me always; everything I have is yours. But now we must celebrate and rejoice, because your brother was dead and has come to life again; he was lost and has been found" (Lk 15:31–32).

Jesus taught those who had ears how to pray. He told them that when they lifted their hearts up to God, they shouldn't show off and make a big deal about it, like the hypocrites who prayed in public places; they had already been paid. "But when you pray, go to your inner room, close the door, and pray to your Father in secret. And your Father who sees in secret will repay you" (Mt 6:6). Jesus taught that talking to God is personal and intimate.

And to encourage them (and us) Jesus said, "...Ask and you will receive; seek and you will find; knock and the door will be opened to you. For everyone who asks, receives; and the one who seeks, finds; and to the one who knocks, the door will be opened." Jesus says that our Father in heaven is glad to "...give the holy Spirit to those who ask him..." (Lk 11:9–13).

Jesus then said that whenever two or more were gathered in His name, He would be present with them. We can, and should, express ourselves to God, together as a community. Again, He gave us a voice ("Our Father, who is in heaven…"). The Lord's Prayer is a shared prayer, for all to pray together, and that's why we recite it when we gather at worship services.

Born Again

Angela: *Dad, some of my friends refer to themselves as "born-again Christians."*

Although Catholics do not use the expression "born again," there is no doubt about the reality and necessity of spiritual rebirth. When Nicodemus, a Pharisee and ruler of the Jews, comes to Jesus, he says, "Rabbi, we know you are a teacher who has come from God, for no one can do these signs that you are doing unless God is with him." Jesus responds, "…No one can see the kingdom of God without being born *from above*" (Jn 3:2–3, emphasis mine). The Greek word *another* means both "again" and "from above," and Nicodemus thinks Jesus means "again."

"How can a person once grown old be born again? Surely he cannot reenter his mother's womb and be born again, can he?" Jesus gets aggravated with this, and in effect he says to Nicodemus, "You guys drive me crazy; here you are, a leader and teacher in Israel, and you still don't get this? Your body, which is born of flesh, is flesh, and your body will die. But your spirit, which is your connection to God, is different. Your spirit has to be refreshed, enlivened, and, yes, reborn. You must become conscious of God, be present with God, born 'from above' so that you can become part of God forever, eternally." He says, "…No one can enter the kingdom of God without being born of water and Spirit" (Jn 3:4–5). Catholics are born of water and spirit at baptism.

Receiving

Catholics do not think in terms of accepting Jesus as their personal Lord and Savior, although that is certainly part of it. For Catholics, it is about receiving Jesus in the Word and in the bread.

Remember how your teachers prepared you for your first Holy Communion? They tried to give you a sense of wonder. They told you to prepare a place in your hearts for Jesus to dwell. They told you to examine your conscience and think about the times when you may have been unkind to a sibling or friend or thoughtless toward other people. After you brought to mind your sins, they reassured you that Jesus forgave everyone—whoever asked for forgiveness—and He sometimes said to those people "now go in peace, and sin no more." After confession they told you that your hearts were now ready to receive Jesus in the bread and wine. We call Communion at the Mass a holy sacrifice because we are re-enacting the sacrifice Jesus made, by giving Himself up for us on the cross, the instrument of salvation. We receive Jesus in the bread at Mass because He told us to.

I like to keep first Holy Communion in mind as often as possible at Mass because it helps keep the ritual fresh and original for me. When I am alert and conscious, I often really experience the presence of God in my life at that moment—even with, or because of, all the other people present.

It also helps to keep first Communion in mind for another reason. At one point, the disciples stopped to have a conversation with Jesus. The ministry was thriving. They were watching people being healed, in tears, their lives changed. They were helping Jesus every day, and they were beginning to feel good about themselves and their role in the ministry. Maybe there would be some special recognition or some payoff in this kingdom Jesus spoke of. So they asked him, "Who is the greatest in the kingdom of heaven?" He called a child over and placed the child before them, and said, "...Unless you turn and become like children, you will not enter the kingdom of heaven" (Mt 18:1–3).

Wait, don't I have to prepare, learn, and teach? Don't I have to live a lifetime free of sin and prove myself by living in all righteousness? Well, yes, but Jesus says something else here: "I want you to lose the cynicism. Quit being so judgmental. Stop always comparing yourself to everyone and measuring yourself favorably against others. I want you to go back to the way you were when you were little. See these kids? They're almost completely dependent on their parents. They depend on their parents for everything: for their clothes, their meals, everything! That's how I want you to relate to God. I want you to place all of your trust in God, completely! It's not about 'who is the greatest.' Once you trust and place yourself fully in the hands of God, eternal life is yours!"

As we go deeper in our relationship with Jesus, more of the stories become intelligible. St. Matthew wrote, "And He was *transfigured* before them; His face shown like the sun and His clothes became white as light" (Mt 17:2, emphasis mine). What does the word "transfigured" mean for us? Remember that Isaiah had said, "The people who lived in darkness, have seen a great light" (Is 9:1). Now on Mt. Tabor, the face of Jesus shone as bright as the sun. We are taught that the divinity of Jesus is expressed in this light. Whenever God is near, a light shines—the light of Christ within us. A voice from the cloud said, "This is my beloved Son, with whom I am well pleased; listen to Him." The divine Jesus appeared, now transfigured, surrounded by the prophecy of Elijah, and the law of Moses, and our witnesses. Peter, James, and John "fell on their faces and were filled with awe" (Mt 17:6). Peter gathered himself and said for all of us, "Rabbi, it is good that we are here!" (Mk 9:5).

PRESENCE

Christina: *Dad, can't we encounter Jesus on our own, without going to church?*

That's a tricky question. Catholics believe that we encounter Jesus through the Eucharist and through the Word, and those things come together at the Mass. We can talk about going to church later. But we know that people do encounter Jesus in everyday circumstances.

But first, did you ever notice people in a quiet church, sitting in front of the tabernacle, the Blessed Sacrament? They were placing themselves in the presence of God, often trying to clear their mind of any and all thoughts. Just being present. Yes, I believe something similar to this can also be done in private. If you and your friends are currently not going to church, try something simple. Try some contemplation in the privacy of your own bedroom, and see if you can go a little deeper. Let's borrow a now-popular meditation technique that our Eastern friends have taught us.

Ok, turn off, or get away from all distractions. No TV, radio, iPad, or cell phone. Be as quiet as possible. Set aside thirty minutes when you can be alone, undisturbed, and silent. Light a candle if that helps. Sit in a chair in a comfortable position, with your back straight, and your hands relaxed in your lap. Start to breathe in slowly, and exhale slowly. Let all thoughts drift away—yes, all five or six of them. Let them drift away, one by one, and allow your mind to be clear of any thinking. Begin to concentrate on your diaphragm and on your breathing. Breathing slowly in and exhaling, your heartbeat will begin to slow. Allow yourself to be completely relaxed and to begin breathing naturally. You can extend this as far as you are able: no thoughts, just the awareness of calm, quiet, and peacefulness. You can sense a stillness, an uninterrupted calm—no rush, no worry, no anything.

You are awake, and you are conscious. What are you aware of? It's not really even a "what," or an "it," at all. What is inside of you, or what are you connected to? What are you conscious of? Can it be…Christ? A peace that is eternal? You are aware of a stillness inside of you that you cannot describe and don't need to. The peace of the risen Christ is an inner peace and a quiet, certain joy. It is the indwelling Spirit of God. It cannot be reached for, grasped, or attained. It is already inside of you, and it cannot be taken away. It is your eternal presence with God, and if you are awakened to it, you know without a doubt, that you will live eternally in this presence, in the consciousness of God.

And with this God consciousness, this Christ within you, there is an impulse. From within you there is a desire, a calling…to love. With the awareness of an indwelling Holy Spirit, you begin to see the world differently, and you are now uninclined to judge, criticize, doubt, and fear. The inner peace that surpasses understanding is now part of your life—no, it is your life—and you will never be the same person again. Oh, why can't we hold on to this connection, this presence? Why does it seem so elusive?

The world and its allure calls to us. We want to get ahead; we want to acquire, own, possess, and consume. We have to compete and win. We have to strive and succeed. And yet, at the end of our lives, we have to surrender everything. We have to let go of our money, our houses, and all of our stuff. Even our very bodies are burned or buried.

Here's something to ponder. What should you do if you are passing a homeless person on the street one day, and you feel the slightest urge to give something? Do it. Or what if, during the Christmas holiday season, you think of a family member who you have been estranged from, and you sense the desire, however reluctant, to call that person? Just do it! Couldn't that be the indwelling Spirit urging you to love, against your own will or judgment? Isn't that God within you—Jesus—calling you to love? Why not respond readily?

Jesus is calling us. But He is calling us from within. He wants us to receive Him, and He wants to dwell in us. And since He is one with the Father, He joins us to the Father, and then we are joined with God, forever. At the Last Supper, Jesus prayed to the Father in heaven for His apostles and for us:

> I pray not only for them, but also for those who will believe in Me through their word, so that they may all be one, as You, Father, are in Me and I in You, that they also may be in Us, that the world may believe that You sent Me. And I have given them the glory you gave Me, so that they may be one, as We are one, I in them and You in Me, that they may be brought to perfection as one, that the world may know that You sent Me, and that You loved them even as you loved Me" (Jn 17:20–23).

Angela: *But when Jesus asks us to be perfect, isn't that asking too much?*

St. Matthew recounts a part of his sermon that Jesus may certainly have said more than once. He is preaching earnestly. He is fired up, and he wants to stir into flame the hearts and minds of the people. He wants to get their attention and get them to change their ways. You can see the veins bulging in his neck. "If your eye causes you to sin, pluck it out! If your hand causes you to sin, cut it off" (Mt 18:8–9)! It's extreme, but a preacher is entitled to use a variety of techniques, hyperbole if necessary.

Jesus says, "So be perfect as your Father in heaven is perfect" (Mt 5:48). Your question is a good one. How is it possible to be perfect when we are so aware of our chronic weaknesses and shortcomings? What this passage says to me is "listen, God is perfect. You come from God. You are a part of God. Therefore, come into your perfection, fulfill your divine destiny. God made you good and holy. Be perfect and live with God in goodness and holiness—yes, with God, forever."

To come into our perfection, we need a heart that loves. Jesus speaks to every human heart. And every heart hungers; yet, this hunger can only be satisfied by God. In the Old Testament, God says to the people through the prophet Ezekiel, "Cast away from you all the crimes you have committed, and make for yourselves a new heart and a new spirit" (Ez 18:31). And there's this: "A clean heart create for me, God; renew within me a steadfast spirit" (Ps 51:12). We don't have to be afraid to look deeply within ourselves; what we find is goodness itself stirring. We long for a loving heart, one that loves with a perfect love—the sacred heart of Jesus Christ.

"Peace be with you; it is I. Do not be afraid." He said these words then, and He says them to us now. We hear His voice, and we know. God wants to be with each one of us. "Listen, I stand at the door and knock. If you hear my voice and open the door, I will come in and dine with you, and you with Me" (Rev 3:20).

Spreading the Good News

The story of Jesus Christ has spread around the world. On Pentecost Sunday, the flame of the Holy Spirit was ignited, and the apostles were fired up. We know that down through the centuries, people were willing to die for Jesus. People would be asked to denounce their faith or deny Christ, and they would be asked to die in the name of Jesus. St. Stephen was the first martyr, and others who died for their faith included the early Roman Christians, St. Iraneaus, St. Agnes, Thomas Moore, Charles Lwanga, and so many others. They were willing to die because they believed there was no other life for them, only life in Christ.

Many great missionaries and teachers have spread the gospel. St. Patrick, Thomas Aquinas, St. Francis of Assisi, St. Ignatius of Loyola, St. Benedict; all were helping new Christians to nurture and increase their faith through every generation.

Christina: *But haven't many awful things been done in the name of Jesus?*

Yes, some people misunderstood, and misused the name of Jesus. Some events in history cause people to question Christianity. The Crusades in the eleventh and twelfth centuries were taken up by the popes to recapture the Holy Lands from the Turks, who had destroyed the churches in and around Jerusalem. The Crusades were fueled by religious fervor, and much blood was spilled. They failed militarily, and although they served to hold the leadership of the Church together for a time, they certainly did not serve the cause of true evangelization.

And what about the discovery of the New World in the fifteenth and sixteenth centuries? Wasn't part of the goal to have missionaries bring the gospel to new lands? In addition to new discoveries, a new world of oppression, injustice, and misery had begun. Your point is valid. Can we see what resulted and say that the work of Christopher Columbus was truly done in the name of Jesus?

There have always been disputes over religious beliefs. Heretics were rooted out, condemned, punished, and killed all the way back to the time of Constantine in the fourth century. But not all Christians were misguided in their belief. Not every believer thought this practice was right. John Chrysostom, who became a saint after his death in AD 407 once wrote, "To kill a heretic is to introduce upon the earth an inexpiable crime."[1]

Can we not point to every century and see evidence that the Gospel message has been misunderstood, abused, and wrongly carried forth by those who still lived in their own darkness? What was the dispute in Northern Ireland about? And why are there so many versions of Christianity today? When Jesus built his church on earth, is this what He intended? No wonder people are still wary of a gospel of love, when it has been so consistently misrepresented.

Angela: *So why didn't Jesus just come and assume more earthly power? Why didn't he come as a king? Wouldn't he have gathered more people? Wouldn't he have had more control and be better able to inhibit injustice?*

That's a tempting thought. St. Matthew wrote the following account:

> Then the devil took Him up to a very high mountain, and showed Him all the kingdoms of the world in their magnificence, and he said to Him, "All these I shall give to you, if you will prostrate yourself and worship me." At this, Jesus said to him, "Get away, Satan! It is written: 'The Lord, your God, shall you worship and him alone shall you serve.'" Then the devil left Him and, behold, angels came and ministered to Him (Mt 4:8–11).

Jesus did not come as king and ruler. When Pilate asked Him, "Are you the King of the Jews?" He answered, "My kingdom does not belong to this world" (Jn 18:33, 36). God's kingdom is not a worldly place that we travel to after death. It is eternal life with God. What is it like? How can we imagine it? While hanging on the cross that Good Friday, one of the criminals condemned to die turned and said, "Jesus, remember me when you come into your kingdom." Jesus replied, "Amen, I say to you, today you will be with Me in Paradise" (Lk 23:42–43).

It was not God's will to send His only son into the world to rule it for a time and then pass away. What did Jesus accomplish? What impact has he made? Consider all the wars and all the conflicts that have occurred, and still occur, and all the blood spilled in the name of righteousness. Everyone who has ever tried to establish a perfect world on earth has failed. We still have wars and poverty. Pope Benedict XVI posed and answered this question in his personal reflection on Christ, *Jesus of Nazareth*:

> What did Jesus actually bring, if not world peace, universal prosperity, and a better world? What has He brought? The answer is very simple: God. He has brought God. He has brought the God who formerly unveiled His countenance gradually, first to Abraham, then to Moses and the prophets, and then in the wisdom literature...It is this God, the god of Abraham, Isaac, and Jacob, the true God, whom He has brought to the nations of the earth.
>
> He has brought God, and now we know His face; now we can call upon Him. Now we know the path that we human beings have to take in this world. Jesus has brought God and with God the truth about our origin and destiny, faith, hope, and love. It is only because of the hardness of our heart that we think this is too little.
>
> Yes, God's power works quietly in this world, but it is the true and lasting power. Again and again, God's cause seems to be in its death throes. Yet over and over again it proves to be the thing that truly endures and saves. The earthly kingdoms that Satan was able to put before the Lord at that time have all

passed away. Their glory has proven to be a mere semblance. But the glory of Christ, the humble, self-sacrificing glory of His love, has not passed away, nor will it ever do so." [2]

Endnotes

1   John O. P. Vidmar, *The Catholic Church through the Ages: A History—Second Edition*. (Mahwah, NJ: Paulist Press, 2014), 148.

2   Joseph Ratzinger, Pope Benedict XVI. *Jesus of Nazareth* (New York: Doubleday 2007), 44.

CHAPTER 3

The Bible

§

ANGELA: *DAD, WHY DID YOU buy us new Bibles for Christmas this year?*

§

Well, now that you are living out on your own, I would love for you to read the Bible regularly. All Christians should. It's got some great stuff in it. Remember this?

"The LORD is my shepherd; there is nothing I lack. In green pastures He makes me lie down; to still waters He leads me; He restores my soul" (Ps 23: 1–3).

That's the beginning of the famous Psalm 23. Just two lines and you get a sense of reassurance and hope. The Psalms have been sung, read, and prayed by many people, for many centuries, and some read the Psalms every day of their lives.

The Psalms were poems meant to be sung, and many of them are attributed to King David, the ruddy youth who hurled the smooth stones into Goliath the giant's head. David was the man after God's own heart, who became the great warrior king of Israel. Many Psalms give praise to God and thanks for victories over David's enemies. Other Psalms were written at various times through Jewish history, and were composed precisely for religious worship. Some are laments, and some are Psalms of thanksgiving. They give us models to follow, and can inspire us to voice our own feelings and aspirations. When you read the Psalms, you come across allusions to such things as Meriba and Massah, the Jordan, or "a priest like Melchizedek of old," so understanding Jewish history helps to appreciate the Psalms. But when you just read them for yourself, even without a lot of historical understanding, you can still encounter and experience the same sentiments the psalmist expressed, and discover for yourself what they mean. The Psalms are a source of comfort and inspiration. The Liturgy of the Hours is based on the Psalms, and all 150 Psalms are found in the Bible.

Now did you know all that, or is this news to you? You both went to Catholic universities; how much exposure to the Bible did you get while you were in college?

Christina: *For several theology and philosophy courses, the Bible was one of the reference books required. I personally did not specifically study the Bible in college.*

Angela: *There were courses offered purely based on the Bible, but they were mostly taken by theology majors. I majored in math and music.*

So on a scale of one to ten, with ten being the highest level of scholarship, how would you grade your level of fluency and knowledge of the Bible?

Christina: *I'd say a five—no, probably a four.*

Angela: *Probably a four, trending toward a three.*

I'll bet you both know more than you realize, but you're like most Catholics; you don't feel confident in your own knowledge about the Bible. Let's start with the basics, and we can go from there.

The Greek word *biblia* means "books." The Bible is a collection of writings that took centuries to write. The Bible has some of the greatest stories ever told, but it's not a history book. It includes the works of many different people who wrote in different languages to different audiences. It has been translated into every language and is distributed around the world.

It is the revealed word of God, as expressed through the authors. The Bible is about history, language, culture, anthropology, art, prayer, and poetry. It is about truth, promises, wisdom, warnings, and fulfillment. It's about war and peace, triumph and failure, victory and defeat. It is about suffering and waiting, hope and joy, and love.

It's the story of a people and their God, and it is the story of Jesus Christ.

We can read the words of Noah, Abraham, Moses, and Isaiah… and the words of John the Baptist, and the words of Mary, the mother of God. And the most important words we find in the Bible are the words Jesus spoke.

The Holy Bible, as we know we know it today, is comprised of two major parts: the Old Testament (OT) and the New Testament (NT). In the Catholic Bible, the Old Testament includes forty-six books. The most important event in the OT was the Exodus. Under the leadership of Moses, the Hebrew slaves left Egypt and journeyed through the desert to a place called Canaan, the Promised Land. To this day, the Jewish people celebrate this event at Passover. Most of the OT (not all) relates back to this event in some way. And for Christians, the OT points forward to the coming of Christ and the establishment of a new covenant. It is in the OT that we get the commandments of God.

The New Testament tells about Jesus Christ and the life of His first followers. The most important event in the New Testament is the death of Jesus on the cross and His resurrection from the dead. There are twenty-seven books in the New Testament, and everything else in the New Testament relates to this event. The life, death, and resurrection of Jesus Christ—and the impact on His followers—are good news for the entire world. And this good news, the Gospel message, is recounted in the first four books of the NT, written under the names of Matthew, Mark, Luke, and John.

Taken together, here's what the Bible says: God is the creator of all things. "God looked at everything He had made, and found it very good (Gn 1:31). And "...God so loved the world that he gave his only Son, so that everyone who believes in him might not perish but might have eternal life" (Jn 3:16).

Angela: *Ok, that's a good summary. But how do you actually read the Bible, one book at a time?*

First, you have to be motivated to read the Bible. There's something in it for everyone. We are all seeking something, so the Bible can be thought of as a gift to the seekers. Since we encounter Christ in the Bible, we read it if we want to develop a life of discipleship to Jesus. We study it so we can follow Jesus with a more lively faith. And as it enriches us and changes us, we can begin to share more worthily in our new life with Christ. It's not easy at first. The Bible is like a vast ocean, and you can swim in it endlessly and actually drown. So, you don't just dive right in.

We need help in getting a good starting point, which enhances our understanding of the Bible. Two references touch on the need for instruction: In the Acts of the Apostles—the second part of St. Luke's great masterpiece—there's a short story involving Philip. He is traveling on a road from Jerusalem, and he encounters an Ethiopian eunuch returning home riding in a chariot, reading the Hebrew scriptures, the book of the prophet Isaiah. Moved by the Spirit, Philip says, "Do you understand what you are reading"? And the Ethiopian replies, "How can I, unless someone instructs me?" The passage he was reading had to do with a "sheep being led to the slaughter," and so he asks Philip, "I beg you, about whom is the prophet saying this? About himself, or about someone else?" St. Luke writes, "Then Philip opened his mouth and, beginning with this scripture passage, *he proclaimed Jesus to him*" (Acts 8:27–35, emphasis mine). So this Ethiopian seeker was given a new and deeper way of understanding the Bible.

The second reference is found in Luke. Two men were walking together on the road to Emmaus when they encountered a stranger. They were bewildered by all "the things that have taken place" in Jerusalem in those days. When the stranger asked what sort of things, they answered, "The things that happened to Jesus of Nazareth, who was a prophet mighty in deed and word before God and all the people." They said that this Jesus had been arrested and crucified, and they were hoping He was the one to redeem Israel. They were amazed that some women had been to His tomb and did not see His body, but rather "a vision of angels" who announced that Jesus was alive. The stranger (whom they had not yet recognized as Jesus) then said, "Oh, how foolish you are! How slow of heart to believe all that the prophets spoke! Was it not necessary that the Messiah should suffer these things and enter into His glory?" St. Luke wrote, "Then beginning with Moses and all the prophets, He *interpreted to them what referred to Him* in all the scriptures" (Lk 24:17–27, emphasis mine). Jesus took them through the Old Testament and provided new meaning to the familiar scriptures. What a conversation that must have been!

So the seeker who opens the Bible has to approach with an open mind and a heart that is willing to be moved. The meaning of the scriptures can seem hidden at first. God's revealed word is something that has to be explored and discovered. Each time the Bible is proclaimed to us, it is possible to hear new things. And each time we read the Bible, we can discover things we never seemed to hear before.

Christina: *So, how did you get so into the Bible, Dad?*

When I was in my late thirties, I was experiencing some serious spiritual urgings. Mom and I had been married for a couple of years. Angela was about two, and we were awaiting our second child (you, Christina). I was in a whirlwind of mixed emotions. I was thrilled that we were having another child. The marriage was off to a good start, and Angela was happy and thriving. I had just left a more secure position in ad sales at an established company, to join a start-up in a new industry. It was a risk. I was restless and unsettled. The pregnancy was making me nervous and excited, but it represented more responsibility. I thought I was loving Jesus, but my spiritual life was in disarray. I was not connecting at church, and my prayer life was not focused. I was worrying too much, eating too much, and drinking too much. I knew God had blessed me, but I didn't know how to express gratitude to God. I didn't know what to ask for or how to ask. I was jumpy and anxious. Something was nudging me, urging me.

So, one cold March Saturday morning, I took my Walkman, my *New York Post*, a bottle of water, and a beer with me and drove to the beach. I also threw in a Bible, figuring I'd take a look at it after my run. It was the *New American Bible*, which had been a wedding present. It was a beautiful book, in a box wrapped with paper, but I had only admired it from the outside. After I stretched and ran my four miles, I sat in the car, sipping my water and beer.

I opened the Bible to the New Testament—to the Gospel According to Matthew—and when I got to chapter 7, I read, "Ask and it will be given to you; seek and you will find; knock and the door will be opened to you. For everyone who asks, receives; and the one who seeks, finds; and to the one who knocks, the door will be opened" (Mt 7: 7–8).

I was arrested…deeply moved…and amazed. Something released in me. I felt that for the first time, Jesus was actually speaking to me. I heard His Word.

Angela and Christina: *Dad, what, are you saying Jesus spoke to you?*

Well, yes. What I heard were the words, "Believe in me!" That's all. Three words. And it was quiet after that.

I felt calm…reassured. I read the rest of the Gospel that day, as if reading all of it for the very first time. And then I rolled right into Mark.

And so I read and read. I decided to read through the entire New Testament, from the Gospel According to Matthew to the Book of Revelation. Over the next few months, off I went: Matthew, Mark, Luke, and John, Acts, Paul's letters, the Epistles, Hebrews, and Revelation, and back again. For about a year and a half, I read every word in the New Testament, three times! I read quickly and loved everything I read: Matthew 28, John 6, Acts 2, and Romans 5. I read, checked off each book I read, and kept going. Did I understand what I was reading? Well, lots of stuff seemed familiar, but how could I understand without instruction? What did I need to know?

Now, during this time, I came upon a book. On Palm Sunday in 1994, I opened the book-review section of the *New York Times*. There was a photo of the book being reviewed, and the cover had a depiction of the crucifixion on it. The title in the headline was "The Death of the Messiah." Since I had been reading the New Testament just about every day, I thought this was exactly what I was looking for. I thought it might be a book along the lines of the more recent *Killing Jesus* by Bill O'Reilly. (A good book in its own right, I recommend it.) But this was something very different. The author was someone I had not heard of: a certain Raymond Brown, a Roman

Catholic priest, a teacher at Union Seminary in New York, a protestant seminary. Father Brown was one of the young biblical scholars who grew up in the '50s, encouraged and spurred on by Vatican II. The book was two volumes, an analysis of the Passion narratives in the four Gospels.

The Passion accounts, everything written from immediately after the Last Supper up to the burial of Jesus, were arranged in sequence. So act 1, scene 1, would be the account of the entry into the Garden of Gethsemane near the Mount of Olives, the agony in the garden. Father Brown would line up each evangelist's account of that scene for comparison and contrast. He would focus on only what was actually written about a given scene, and he would analyze the point of view of the evangelist and note the similarities and differences in the four accounts, with all the varieties of criticism at his disposal. And in this way, Raymond Brown interpreted for me all that referred to Jesus Christ in the scriptures.

Oh, I was amazed. First, this work was a bear to read. It was a textbook, and half of each page had footnotes, page after page of footnotes. In discussing even the minutest point in scripture, he would explain what ten, twelve, or fifteen other scholars had written about it: German, French, and English scholars, professors, clergy, and theologians. He would tell the reader everything that had been written about a given point and then sort through it. I couldn't believe the level of scholarship that had been built up around the Bible, again coming from my limited perspective as a Catholic. But now I was hooked, and I was going to hold on tight.

Angela: *So wait, you did this on your own? You didn't enroll in a Bible course?*

Yes, all on my own; it was weird! I couldn't get enough, and I spent all my spare time reading it. Looking back, I would explain it this way: I had an encounter with Jesus, and I needed to understand it. I needed to read and learn about this Jesus, who was calling me to believe in Him.

Here's what I learned from Raymond Brown about the New Testament. First of all, the Gospels are not literal records of the ministry of Jesus. Decades intervened between Jesus's death and the writing of the gospels. Jesus was a Galilean Jew of the first third of the first century who spoke Aramaic. His words were being translated into Greek, a language He did not normally speak. Greek was the broader language of the time, and the authors used it so that midcentury urban Jews and Gentiles could understand the story. This translating and spreading of the story to different groups and points of view contributed to multiple versions and accounts of the words and actions of Jesus's ministry.

Second, most scholars in the last 150 years have come to recognize that the evangelists themselves may not have been actual eyewitnesses of Jesus's ministry. But they were intimate associates and dedicated followers of the apostles, the first followers of Jesus. This is important in understanding the differences among the Gospels. Mark and Luke were clearly not apostles and did not meet Jesus. Matthew was traditionally thought of as the tax collector, the apostle of Jesus, but recent scholarship has challenged this.

From Father Brown I learned plenty of details. There are ninety-six chapters in the four Gospels, and at least 25 percent of the material deals with the Passion of Jesus. I learned that the first three Gospels are called synoptic because they can be viewed side by side (syn-optically). All three have very much in common, but they also have dramatic differences. Mark has 661 verses, Matthew has 1,068, and Luke has 1,149. Eighty percent of Mark's material is reproduced in Matthew's Gospel. So scholars conclude now that the writer of St. Matthew's Gospel was not the apostle; why would a witness to the ministry draw so heavily from material written by a nonwitness?

Luke used 65 percent of Mark's gospel. Matthew and Luke used much of Mark's gospel but also used other sources. Common material that is found in Matthew and Luke, but not in Mark, is thought to come from a hypothetical source known as *Q* (from the German word *quelle*, meaning "source").

Christina: *Dad, hold on. Matthew was not the tax collector, and his was not the first Gospel written. He copied from Mark? Are you sure?*

The biblical scholars have analyzed this nine ways from Sunday. Father Brown provides very convincing evidence. But there's more. The original material of Matthew and Luke is, oh, so rich and rewarding. To begin with, Matthew provides a genealogy. He reassures his Jewish audience that Jesus Christ is from the house of David, the son of Abraham, and he traces the ancestry from Abraham, Isaac, and Jacob, down through David and Solomon, and down through Joseph "the husband of Mary. Of her was born Jesus, who is called the Messiah." (See Mt 1:1–16.) Luke also provides a genealogy, but he traces Jesus's heritage back up through history. He begins with Jesus's earthly father, Joseph, and goes up all the way through Jacob, Isaac, and Abraham, up through Noah, and on up to "Seth, the son of Adam, the son of God." (See Lk 3:23–38.) There's no genealogy in Mark or John.

When we remember that the Bible is not history nor biography, we understand more. Take the birth narratives. In Matthew, Joseph's betrothed is found with child through the Holy Spirit. Since he had had no relations with her and was unwilling to expose her to shame, he intended to divorce her quietly. But "the angel of the Lord appeared to him in a dream" and told him not to be afraid to take Mary into his home. "She will bear a son and you are to name him Jesus, because he will save His people from their sins" (Mt 1:18–21). God's promise of deliverance in the Old Testament is seen by Matthew as fulfilled in the birth of this Messiah. And Matthew gives us magi, who first meet Herod and then followed a star, which led them to the Christ child. When they saw the child with Mary, "They prostrated themselves and did Him homage. Then they opened their treasures and offered Him gifts of gold, frankincense, and myrrh" (Mt 2:9–11). The magi would return to the East and carry the message of this newborn king beyond the Jewish nation.

The birth account in Luke is different. First, we get the announcement from the angel Gabriel. "Do not be afraid, Mary, for you have found favor with God. Behold, you will conceive in your womb and bear a son, and you shall name him Jesus" (Lk 1:27–31). Mary is stunned but responds, "Behold, I am the handmaid of the Lord. May it be done to me according to your word" (Lk 1:27:38).

When Mary visited Elizabeth, the wife of Zechariah, Elizabeth says, "Most blessed are you among women, and blessed is the fruit of your womb." Mary responds to Elizabeth with what we now know as the Magnificat, the Canticle of Mary: "My soul proclaims the greatness of the Lord; my spirit rejoices in God my savior. For He has looked upon His handmaid's lowliness; behold, from now on will all ages call me blessed." (See Lk 1: 46–55.)

Luke gives us the Christ child wrapped in swaddling clothes, laid in a manger—and another prayer, the Gloria, from a "multitude of the heavenly host…praising God and saying: 'Glory to God in the highest, and on earth peace to those on whom His favor rests'" (Lk 2:13–14). In Luke we meet the shepherds, who are keeping night watch over their flock, and are visited by an angel of the Lord. They are struck with fear, but when the good news is proclaimed to them, they decide to go find Mary and Joseph and the infant lying in the manger. Then Luke says, "When they saw this, they made known the message that had been told them about this child. All who heard it were amazed by what had been told them by the shepherds" (Lk 2:15–18).

St. Luke is someone special. Only in St. Luke do we get the birth of John the Baptist, the presentation of Jesus in the Temple (where we meet Simeon, the old man, and Anna), and the young Jesus's disappearance in Jerusalem. There are six miracles and eighteen parables in St. Luke. This book is the only place we learn of the prodigal son (where we learn about true forgiveness) and the healing of the ten lepers (all were healed, but only one returned to give thanks). We also read about the woman who washed Jesus's feet with her tears. We meet the good thief ("Jesus, remember me when you come in to your kingdom) and walk the road to Emmaus. Luke is the most prolific of the New Testament writers. His Gospel and the Acts of the Apostles contain 37,800 words, yet we know very little about him personally. By contrast the thirteen letters that are attributed to St. Paul use some 32,350 words, and from these we learn a lot about Paul's motivation, personality, and relationships.

The fourth Gospel, John, is different from the other three in style and substance. There is no genealogy or account of Jesus's birth. It is beautifully written, with wonderful signs and imagery. It is a highly theological work and is the favorite of many priests, Bible teachers, and students. The author is believed to be a person who regards himself in the tradition of "the disciple whom Jesus loved." It was probably written in Ephesus, a place where there may have been a school of writing disciples devoted to the apostle John. This helps explain the differences found in the Gospel According to John, the three Epistles of John, and the Book of Revelation—all thought at one time to be written by John the Apostle, the brother of James, the son of Zebedee. Some of that material probably came from these devoted associates and followers of John. But when they say, "what we have seen," they are surely proclaiming the eyewitness testimony that they received firsthand from the apostle.

Angela: *Dad, this is a bit confusing. Each Gospel account is different. Is one more accurate than the others? If they differ, which one are we supposed to believe? Do they fit together?*

The evangelists all had the same goal: to proclaim that Jesus was the Son of God, who came into the world, suffered, died, and rose from the dead so that all mankind would be saved from sin. That's the good news! They each came to the story from a different angle. They each wrote to a different audience and from a different point of view. You can see these differences more clearly when you line them up and contrast them, a la Raymond Brown. Let's try it:

Take an example from the Passion: one scene in biblical history, a dramatic one. Let's look at the very moment in history when Jesus was hanging on the cross. What did Jesus say on the cross, right before He died? We read/hear Him saying different things. There were no reporters or cameras there that day, but there were eyewitnesses. We rely on the evangelists to reveal what happened:

> In Matthew (also in Mark, but let's use Matthew here) Jesus says, "My God, My God, why have your forsaken me?" (Mt 27:46).
>
> In Luke, Jesus says, "Father, forgive them, they know not what they do" (Lk 23:34).
>
> And in John, Jesus proclaims from the cross, "It is finished" (Jn 19:30).

Why would there be these differences, and how should we understand them? Can they all be true? Did Jesus actually say them? And can the differences be made to fit together? Let's look at each account.

Matthew is writing to a Jewish audience, and to help connect his audience to this new Messiah, he draws words, images, and examples from the Old Testament in every one of his twenty-eight chapters. To convey the crucifixion, Matthew draws from the Psalms and places words from Psalm 22 on Jesus's lips. "My God, my God, why have you abandoned me?" (Ps 22:2)

Psalm 22 starts off as a lament, depicting the despairing attitude of a people held in the bondage of slavery for centuries. The Psalm itself continues in that vein: "My God, I call by day, but you do not answer, by night, but I have no relief" (Ps 22:3). As you continue reading the Psalm, a call for help goes up: "Do not stay far from me, for trouble is near, and there is no one to help" (Ps 22:12) and "save me from the lion's mouth, my poor life from the horns of wild bulls" (Ps 22:22). But now comes a sense of determination and hope: "Then I will proclaim Your name to my brethren; in the assembly I will praise You: 'You who fear the LORD, give praise!'" (Ps 22:24).

This hope leads to realization and acknowledgment. For God "did not turn away from me, but heard me when I cried out…my vows I will fulfill before those who fear Him" (Ps 22:25–26). Then we read "all the families of nations will bow low before Him. All who sleep in the earth…will kneel in homage (Ps 22:28, 30). And finally, "the generation to come will be told of the Lord, that they may proclaim to a people yet unborn the deliverance You have brought" (Ps 22:32).

So, Psalm 22 is not only a cry of despair but also an acceptance of God's will—a proclamation of praise and trust and a joyful acknowledgment of fulfillment! You have to read the whole Psalm. The Jewish audience that Matthew was writing to would have known and understood this Psalm. And with the help of Bible scholars, now we do as well.

St. Luke took a different approach. "Father, forgive them, they know not what they do" (Lk 23:34). Again, Luke was a non-Palestinian, non-Jew, writing to an audience of largely Gentile Christians. He wrote this Gospel and Acts, and the scholars tell us that he knew the Greek versions of the Old Testament traditions and was literate in Hellenistic Greek writings. He may have been a physician, and knowing that helps us when we read all of his references to healing and curing.

For Luke there was no need for the readers of the Gospel to assign blame. Luke lays out the history of the early church and the origins of the path to salvation. The Jesus who died on the cross, and those who followed Him and believed in Him, did not blame the Romans, or the Jewish leaders of the time, for their part in the story of salvation. Luke goes out of his way to establish this. He has Pilate declare three times that Jesus is not guilty, and he places the Roman centurion at the foot of the cross to declare that truly, this man was the Son of God. We are all responsible for the death of Jesus on the cross because of our sinfulness. For believers, this act was carried out so that our sins would be forgiven. So in St. Luke, Jesus cries out to God for forgiveness for all those who participate in this crucifixion.

In John we read "it is finished" (Jn 19:30). By the time the Gospel of John was written, a second generation of believers was growing in or around Ephesus. They are referred to as the Johannine community. They were somewhat unique in their dedication to a deep understanding of the Son of God.

When John looked back at the Passion and death, he had the benefit of a longer view than the writers of the three synoptic gospels. Thoughts of the brutality of the crucifixion had given way to a deeper meaning of Jesus's death on the cross. In recounting the events at Calvary, John provides a longer—can we say more hopeful—view. When Jesus saw His mother and the disciple whom He loved, He said to His mother, "Woman, behold your son." Then he said to the disciple, "Behold your mother." We can understand this to mean that Jesus was placing responsibility for mother church in the hands of the apostles. When his side was lanced, blood and water flowed out—the life-giving water of baptism and the blood of the new covenant.

The will of God had been completed. John had written "for God so loved the world that He sent His only Son, not to condemn the world, but that the world might be saved through Him." And now, on Calvary, the signs—the Last Supper discourses and the suffering in Jerusalem—are now complete, according to the Father. "It is finished" proclaims not the shortcomings of His followers but the fulfillment of God's plan for salvation on earth.

Christina: *But doesn't every Jesus movie combine all these accounts?*

Angela: *And every Nativity scene always includes shepherds and magi!*

Yes, since the very beginning there has been a pull or desire to try and harmonize the four accounts in the New Testament. If you're going to make a movie and you think of the Gospels as history, it makes sense to put the accounts together to fill out a more complete version of the story. But that is not how to read the Bible. Putting the stories together distorts them.

You accept each account for what it is and accept each one at face value. Did Jesus say all these things? Yes. Are they all true? Yes!

Christina: *All different and all true?*

Yes, as I said earlier, each evangelist was coming from a different place and was telling the story in his own way. The stories were passed along by different people, and the details were recalled differently some thirty to ninety years after Jesus died. The languages were different. We just have to conclude that it was God's will that these words come to us this way. The goal was the same: through the Gospel, according to their perspective, we might come to believe in Jesus. And it is by faith that we can say, without reservation or doubt, that the Holy Bible is the revealed word of God.

One more thing: if all we had was the Gospel According to Mark (just sixteen chapters, the shortest account), we would have everything we need. We would still have Jesus, revealed. But that's not all we have.

I love the Bible; it's like two others things I love, jazz and baseball. It is enduring, but it always seems fresh. No matter how long you're away from it, it always seems familiar. Baseball is similar: it's all about context. Every time there's a big play, you think you've never seen one quite like it before, and at the same time, it reminds you of another game from long ago. Even when I watch games today by myself, I instinctively connect to games I saw with my father when I was a kid. It seems that every home run recalls another home run from another time. In the Bible, every parable seems to remind you of a dependable lesson learned long ago and simultaneously provides insights that you've never realized before.

When you listen to jazz live, something similar happens. You may recognize the tune, but it is played differently than the last time you heard it. You feel comfortable because you love the form, and the excitement comes from the fact that everyone is improvising. When you study the Bible in a group, everyone is bringing his or her own take. Jazz has a restlessness to it, with an urge to keep regenerating. You know you're heading someplace, and it's a fun ride. The Bible is like that; it's taking you someplace good, to enjoy. It's been around forever but always seems to provide fresh inspiration. It lives and breathes because you yourself bring life and breadth to it.

Angela: *Dad, you know you're completely crazy, right?*

Yeah, but do you still love me anyway?

Christina: *Yes, Dad, we do.*

THE CATECHISM

Well, I didn't always love the Bible. As a Catholic student in the late '50s and early '60s, I was not taught how to read the Bible. I had my Baltimore Catechism for school and my missal for Mass. I knew all my Bible stories; we all did.

Like you, I knew the story of the prodigal son and the good Samaritan. I learned about the wedding at Cana, the twelve apostles, and the Last Supper. We knew about the healings and about Lazarus being raised from the dead. We learned the Ten Commandments and the Beatitudes. We knew the Christmas story and acted it out in plays. We knew about Palm Sunday, Holy Thursday, and Good Friday. And we learned to love Jesus because He suffered for us and gave Himself up and died on the cross. We celebrated Easter Sunday because Jesus rose from the dead and will come again and is with us always.

Christina: *But you couldn't locate these things in the Bible?*

No, at that point what Protestants said about Catholics was right; Catholics just didn't know their Bible.

From the late eighteen hundreds right into the 1960s, the Baltimore Catechism was the standard text used by Catholic schools in the United States to teach Catholic children their religion. This was a carefully arranged document that the bishops in the United States had discussed and worked on for much of the nineteenth century. A large Catholic population had grown in and around Baltimore, and this is where the bishops met in a series of councils. At the Third Council of Baltimore in 1884, a revised text was voted on and approved, and this textbook of Christian doctrine, the Baltimore Catechism, was released and published.

It was a series of well over one thousand questions and answers, covering the Creed, the commandments, Sacraments, and prayer. After a number of revisions, the Baltimore Catechism evolved and was reissued, containing 421 questions and answers in thirty-seven chapters. This little book gave millions of American Catholics unity to the teaching and understanding of the faith. It is the document that baby-boomer Catholics grew up on. We didn't just read it. We memorized it. Here is a sample:

"Who made you?" God made me.

"Who is God?" God is the Creator of heaven and earth and of all things.

"Why did God make you?" God made me to know Him, to love Him, and to serve Him in this world and to be happy with Him forever in heaven.

There were questions about every aspect of faith—about the Creed, the Trinity, sin and redemption, and salvation.

"What do you mean by the Incarnation?" By the Incarnation I mean that the Son of God was made man.

"How was the Son of God made man?" The Son of God was conceived and made man by the power of the Holy Ghost, in the womb of the Blessed Virgin Mary.

Angela: *The nuns made you memorize the entire Catechism?*

All the important questions and answers, yes. That's how we learned our faith. Our Catholic faith was based on oral tradition and on the Bible.

And the nuns didn't make us memorize it because it was a neat idea or because they were mean. In the sixth chapter of Deuteronomy, Moses was giving the people of Israel God's commandments. He said, "…You shall love the LORD, your God, with your whole heart, and with your whole being, and with your whole strength," and then he gave further instructions. "Take to heart these words which I command you today. *Keep repeating them to your children.* Recite them when you are at home and when you are away…let them be as a pendant on your forehead. Write them on the doorposts of your houses and on your gates" (Dt 6:4–9, emphasis mine). Believing in God and loving God was a commandment of faith, and it needed to be taught, understood, and remembered! The good sisters took this very seriously.

Christina: *But, Dad,* were *the nuns mean?*

I suppose many of the stories about hitting, slapping, and yelling were true, but you have to be somewhat compassionate. They themselves were influenced/victimized by their training, and maybe they carried some over-the-top disciplinary methods into the classrooms. But they were good teachers. I've talked to a few of those who used to strike fear in me, and meeting them as older, retired sisters, I find them to be kindly, loving people of faith.

Angela: *Ok, so your learned your faith through the teaching of the Catechism. Was the Bible itself simply not taught by the church?*

No, the church is the source of insight into the meaning of the scriptures. The Catholic church has always had brilliant teachers and preachers of the Bible. From Irenaeus to Polycarp to Augustine to Aquinas, and to hundreds of others, great scholars of the church provided interpretation and insight into the sacred scriptures. The words "ignorance of scripture is ignorance of Christ" are attributed to St. Jerome, one of the four original doctors of the Western church (along with St. Gregory the Great, St. Ambrose, and St. Augustine). Many insightful sermons on the Bible have been written by these and other great doctors, and they are still read today regularly in the Divine Office.

St. Jerome is revered and worth mentioning. Here's what Pope Benedict XVI said about him:

Jerome's literary studies and vast erudition enabled him to revise and translate many biblical texts, an invaluable undertaking for Western culture and for the Latin church. On the basis of the original Greek and Hebrew texts, he revised the four gospels in Latin, then the Psalter, and a large part of the Old Testament. Taking into account the original Hebrew and Greek texts of the Septuagint, the classical Greek version of the Old Testament, as well as earlier Latin versions, Jerome was able to produce the "Vulgate," which continues to be the "official" Latin text of the Roman Catholic Church.[1]

Angela: *But these great scholars did not encourage people to read the Bible.*

The church fathers did not believe that the people could discern the meaning of the Bible on their own. They thought they would get lost. So the church used a variety of means to pass along the "deposit of faith" to the people down through the centuries. By the middle of the fifteen hundreds, the church had been providing instruction on the faith in some variation of the formal teaching we now know as the Catechism. But the Bible itself was not being taught to the average believer.

Christina: *Many of the Protestants I know are very proud of their scripture knowledge, and they can quote you chapter and verse.*

They have a strong tradition of scholarship. The printing press and the Protestant Reformation are part of the story. By the early fifteen hundreds, Martin Luther, John Calvin, and others were rejecting what they regarded as the nonbiblical expressions found in the Roman church. They instigated and inspired a rededication to the Bible as the only place in which a true explanation of faith could be found (*sola scriptura*). The Reformers said there was no need for the Pope, the Magisterium, or any authoritative interference between God and man. Luther translated the Bible into German, and Bible study and instruction began to grow. Church historians tell us that from roughly the sixteenth to the nineteenth centuries, the Protestant Reformers were the drivers of biblical scholarship. That finally began to change again as the twentieth century approached.

SCHOLARSHIP

Angela: *What happened? Vatican II?*

Even before Vatican II, big changes in Catholic scholarship and Bible study were underway. In September of 1943, Pope Pius XII issued his encyclical on "The Most Opportune Way to Promote

Biblical Studies," *Divino Afflante Spiritu* (literally, "Inspired by the Divine Spirit"). The Pope was confirming a new openness to studying the Bible. He was saying, in effect, let's not be afraid. Let's follow the path to discovery and insight and see where it leads. Pius was encouraging Catholic scholars to continue to unpack the riches of the Bible and to not be deterred by unresolved inconsistencies or by what might be found. He exhorted bishops and priests to make great use of scripture in their preaching and teaching. And he instructed seminaries to train all future priests in the means of exegesis (critical interpretation) so that they would be instilled with a love of the Divine Word.

This wasn't completely new thinking. Fifty years earlier, in 1893, Pope Leo XIII had issued his own encyclical: *Providentissimus Deus* ("The God of All Providence"), which itself had represented a cautious opening to historical criticism of the Bible. "Historical criticism" meant learning about what was going on in the world the author was writing in—the languages, beliefs, and customs of the time—in other words the historical context of the writing. Pius was now pushing the movement forward. New, young scholars were emerging and being trained at Catholic institutions such as the Catholic University of America and the Pontifical Biblical Institute.

The 1950s was the right time for renewed scholarship. In 1945 a large number of primary Gnostic Gospels were found in Egypt, texts once thought to have been lost during the early Christian struggle to define orthodoxy. These were the Gospel of Thomas, the Gospel of Philip, the Secret Book of James, the Gospel of Mary, and the Gospel of Truth. Then between 1947 and 1956, the Dead Sea Scrolls were found—a collection of some eight hundred documents in tens of thousands of fragments.

This discovery aroused greatly renewed interest in the Bible. The Dead Sea Scrolls gave us manuscripts of the OT some one thousand years older than any we had previously—and remarkably, they agreed with what we had for the most part. The Scrolls date from around 250 BC to AD 68 and were written in Hebrew, Aramaic, and Greek; this material helped our understanding of the history of Judaism, the development of the Hebrew Bible, and the beginnings of Christianity. They showed Christianity to be rooted in Judaism and have been called the evolutionary link between the two.

Vatican II would pull all of this together for the church. It was the professed aim of the Second Vatican Council to place the Bible and the liturgy squarely in the mainstream of the spiritual lives of all members of the church, to a greater degree than had been the case for centuries. The "Constitution on the Sacred Liturgy" asserted that if Catholic church worshipers were to derive maximum profit from the liturgy, they needed to know the scriptures. It said, "The sacred scripture is of the greatest importance in the celebration of the liturgy," and it urged a "sweet and living love for sacred scripture."[2]

So, by 1970 the Catholic Church was armed with a newly revised Bible (*The New American Bible*) and a completely revamped liturgy. The Sunday and weekday lectionaries were redesigned to expose churchgoers to the greatest amount of scripture possible. The Gospels now rotate in three-year sequences, and the use of the Old Testament, the Epistles, and the Psalms include more chapters and verses, providing a much richer menu of Bible readings at the Mass, during the week, and on Sundays. The church believes that the Bible becomes more fully alive when it is joined with the liturgy. The words of the Bible are the words that God uses to speak to His people, and they are the words that people use to address their God.

Catholics today are much more knowledgeable about the Bible than their ancestors. Granted, fewer people go to church regularly, but those who do now participate in a world rich in Holy Scripture.

That's why you two, as regular churchgoers in high school and college, find so much more of the Bible at least vaguely familiar; you've heard it read at Mass. Bible-study groups are now found in most parishes. Books about the Bible are more popular, preaching at Mass is greatly enhanced, and it can be said that the Bible has been restored to the center of Catholic life.

Christina: *Dad, you are truly exhausting. Ok, Old Testament, New Testament—how did the Bible, as we know it today, come together?*

Let's start with the Old Testament. Scholars tell us that the first five books (Genesis, Exodus, Leviticus, Numbers, and Deuteronomy) were written about 1250 BC. This was the Torah, the scripture of the Israelites. Some scholars acknowledge Mosaic authorship, but many believe there was later editing; some think that different sources for the Torah stem from the tenth century BC and after, with final editing coming in the exilic period, or shortly thereafter, in the sixth to fifth century BC. As Jewish identity was solidified, and as God revealed more and more of His plan, Jews wrote down more and more books that explained these developments. So, Joshua, Judges, the books of Kings, and the books of Chronicles were recorded, as well as the prophetic books of Ezra and Nehemiah. In addition to these, other books, opinions, and commentaries were written and circulated, and there was apparently no clear line that defined for all what we now call the Old Testament.

By around 200 BC, the successor to Alexander the Great—Ptolemy Philadelphus, the new pharaoh of Egypt—provided some inadvertent help. Ptolemy wanted his great library of Alexandria to have at least one copy of every book in the world, all arranged in order. He commissioned seventy Jewish scholars to come up with a standard canon of Jewish scripture and a standard version of each book in that canon. The seventy men on this committee came up with forty-six books, and this volume was called the Septuagint, from the Latin word for seventy: *septuaginta*.

Jews universally used the Septuagint right up to the time of Christ. Jesus knew this scripture and quoted from it, although He and the apostles used Hebrew or Aramaic translations, since the original Septuagint was in Greek. Although it may not include everything, the Septuagint is the official canon of the Old Testament in the Roman Catholic Church. It's in your Bible.

The New Testament was written and canonized pretty firmly within about three hundred years. As I said earlier, the oral tradition and the writings of Paul, Mark, and Luke began to circulate. Matthew, Peter, James, Jude, and John added accounts of Christ's teachings, and they too were being read in the assembly of the Eucharist. Over time, the bishops began to set a standard for which books were to be read at assembly, based on their credibility and consistency with one another. Essentially, they were saying, "These are the writings that contain the essential deposit of our faith." The other writings, those left out, were not consistent with one another and therefore, were less credible.

In his Easter letter from Alexandria in AD 367, St. Athanasius published the definitive list of twenty-seven New Testament books, saying, "Let no one add to them or take anything away from them."[3] This new canon became more widely accepted among all the bishops and was adopted in 382 by Pope St. Damasus I. It was confirmed by every subsequent council that took up the question of scripture, and in 419, at the Second Council of Carthage, Pope Boniface confirmed the canon and promulgated it officially. The New Testament as we know it today took less than one hundred years to write, but over three hundred years to come together!

Angela: *When I saw the movie* The Da Vinci Code *a few years ago, it said that there was a hidden conspiracy in the church to keep certain information about Jesus out of the Bible. Was that true?*

That movie stirred renewed interest in material that was left out of the New Testament. There were articles online detailing a hidden conspiracy at church councils. They supposedly closed the doors and decided to keep stuff out of the Bible about the life of Jesus that would be scandalous. (He was married, Mary Magdalene was a prostitute, whatever.) Or maybe the expunged material was destroyed because church secrets would be revealed or would open up the door for women as priests or some other teaching that would promote heresy.

Here's what I would say to all the conspiracy theorists: go read it. Read everything for yourself. It's no longer hidden. Read all the notes from all the councils. Read the Gospel of Pseudo-Matthew, which has information about Christ's childhood and about the widower Joseph. Read the Gospel of the Birth of Mary, which introduces to us Joachim and Anne, her parents. The Gospel of Nicodemus has an account of the thieves crucified with Christ "whose names are Dismas and Gestas." Read also the Gospel of Thomas (the apostle who carried the Gospel to India), which has many wonderful sayings of Jesus.

The Didache is also well worth reading. It is a brief treatise from the early second century, also known as the Teaching of the Twelve Apostles, and it deals with Christian ethics, the sacraments, and church rules. I would also say to read the Gospel of Mary Magdalene, which has been in circulation now for over sixty years. Although this material does not have the same theological authority as the approved canon, it's still out there. If this material, or anything else you discover, draws you into a closer relationship with Jesus Christ, all the better. But if it only serves to invalidate for you the Bible as we know it today, what good does that do for you, or anyone else?

Christina: *Aren't there tons of books written about the Bible?*

Yes, and many of them are great; I can recommend some. But some are unusual. Thomas Jefferson was impressed with the teachings and sayings of Jesus, so he set about to edit the gospels. We've read that in his later years of respite in Monticello, he took to cutting and pasting together with a razor and glue those sections that would best summarize Jesus's philosophy. *The Life and Morals of Jesus of Nazareth* is notable because it extracts and excludes all of Jesus's miracles or any mentions of the supernatural or the divine or references to the Resurrection. This must have been more appealing to Jefferson's scientific mind, but it can hardly be considered a valuable tool for those seeking spiritual truths.

Charles Dickens also took on scripture in his writings, called *The Life of Our Lord*, which when published included the subtitle "Written for his children during the years 1846–1849." It has a gentle, fatherly tone and is a simple retelling of the life of Jesus, but again, no miracles, sin, or repentance. It's aimed more at portraying Jesus as a comforter of the downtrodden (Dickens's major focus). Jesus exists to make people feel better and help them to greater prosperity. Nice, but not the whole story.

There are also other versions of the Bible that attempt to be of help. There's a *Good News Bible*, *The Poverty and Justice Bible*, and the *Freedom Bible*. There are youth Bibles, children's Bibles, men's Bibles, and a *Bible for Today's Family*. Then there are books that illuminate certain aspects of the Bible: *Messages from God* looks at stories from the Bible and provides interpretation, and *Women of the Bible* introduces some seventy legendary biblical figures and shows how they can teach us lessons for today's living. You can also just buy the New Testament by itself, or one that includes the Psalms and Proverbs.

Christina: *So how many translations are there? Which is the best Bible to have?*

There are many legitimate translations of the Bible. Everyone has heard of the King James Version (KJV) of the Bible. Scholars of the church of England wrote this translation in the seventeenth century. It took a learned team of men almost seven years to complete, and their goal was not to come up with a whole new translation of the Bible, but to make the existing good one better. Revised several times, English-speaking peoples have deeply revered it because of the accuracy of the translation and its majesty of style. The King James had great influence on the English language, with its many unique expressions and idioms: "the powers that be" for example.

It is the Bible that has been most often quoted. Take this passage: "For by grace are ye saved through faith; and that not of yourselves: it is the gift of God: Not of works, lest any man should boast" (Eph 2:8–9). If you grew up with this version, it is difficult to let go. After all, this is the style in which you heard God's word revealed. But newer translations make it clearer to us now that Paul, the Jew from Tarsus, did not use words like "ye," "lest," or "thou." Jesus himself surely did not speak the King's English, so for modern American ears, a more recent translation is often preferred.

The Bible has been translated for centuries, and there are now over fifty versions in English alone. We have the NIV (New International Version), the NASB (New American Standard Bible), the NLT (New Living Translation), and the NRSV (New Revised Standard Version). I recommend the *New American Bible* (NABR), the modern Catholic version most Roman Catholics use today. It is read at Mass each day, has good footnotes and introductions to chapters, and has been around since 1970, with revisions in 1986 and 2010.

You know that I have been in a weekly Bible-study class for over sixteen years, with Christians of various denominations, and we all use different Bibles. I can tell you that in all those years, with thousands of chapters in the New and Old Testament that we have read together, only once did we ever encounter a passage where the various translations yielded a different or opposite meaning, and it was on an obscure and noncritical theological point. We constantly say to each other, "What does your Bible say?" So, we are always comparing various texts. I don't believe the different versions of our Bibles should separate us as Christians.

Angela: *All right, so we each have our own New American Bible. Where do we start?*

Start with the Gospel According to Mark. It was probably written first, and it is the shortest—just sixteen chapters. It darts from one dramatic moment to the next. Before you begin, say a prayer: "Lord God, open my mind to this holy scripture, so that I might come to know you better." Remember, Mark is writing to a community of Christians that understand suffering. The Romans were terrorizing them. Their freedom was taken away, their beliefs compromised, and their very lives were threatened. It was tempting to lose hope. Mark's Gospel tells how Jesus faced the same temptations and the same feelings of isolation and hopelessness the people were experiencing. The Gospel of Mark teaches that Jesus stayed faithful to His beliefs even when it led to suffering and death on the cross. And true discipleship means following that model—staying true to one's beliefs in the face of suffering. "Take up your cross, and follow me."

Christina: *Dad, I've heard you use the expression "praying the scriptures." What does that mean?*

Once you've learned a bit about the Bible, you can navigate yourself, and you can begin to do something called *lectio divina*, literally, divine reading. Traditionally, there are four separate steps or movements to *lectio divina*—read, meditate, pray, and contemplate—but there are mild variations of this practice, and they're all fine.

The most important thing is that divine reading should be approached as an enjoyable way of praying. It is a privileged, time-honored way of sitting with God. You can look at it as spending time listening to God, who speaks to us in the words of the Bible.

Again, always open with a gentle prayer: "Dear Father, open my mind to your word; Lord Jesus, come into my heart; Holy Spirit of God, fill me with light." Sit for a moment, allowing yourself to relax. Then, with faith and trust, open your Bible and begin reading your selected passage. (Suggestions to start are Luke 15, John 13, Philippians 4, and Proverbs 3.)

Read slowly, peacefully, joyfully, and prayerfully. Read through the entire text, and then read through it again, aloud. Ask yourself some questions. What does the text say? What was my first impression? What was my favorite part? Was there a phrase I'd like to memorize or keep near? Where do I fit in the story? What does the passage mean to me? What is God saying to me? Was there anything that disturbed me or that I did not understand? And finally, what do I now say to God? How will I respond to God's word?

The origin of this practice has been credited to St. Benedict in the sixth century, and it was formalized into four steps by the Carthusians in the twelfth century. At Vatican II, Dei Verbum recommended *lectio divina* to the general public, and many lay people today embrace this practice in parishes throughout the world. Anyone can do it. It is a prayerful attempt to be formed and molded by the revealed word of God. *Lectio divina* transforms us and strengthens us.

Angela: *How often should we read the Bible?*

Regularly. Every day. When you want to encounter Jesus, read the Bible. And Christina, you mentioned books about the Bible; some provide great insight. I'll mention two: *Introducing the New Testament*, by Mark Allan Powell, is a very friendly guide for anyone who wants to really get acquainted with the Gospels and the Pauline Literature. It is not as onerous as Raymond Brown's works, and it's accompanied by an amazing collection of Christian illustrations and artwork.

Another book is about the story of David. Once you get through the first five books of the Old Testament—the Pentateuch—there are then eleven works known as the historical books. You have Joshua, Judges, and Ruth, and then you come to the first and second books of Samuel. This section of the Bible tells how Israel made the transition from a period when judges ruled into a relatively brief time when a monarchy was established. Great biblical characters are introduced: Samuel himself, the seer and kingmaker; Saul the great king and his son Jonathan, who befriended David; and David, the root of Jesse, the ruddy youth with beautiful eyes anointed by Samuel to succeed Saul. He would become the great king of Israel but would fall from grace. He took Bathsheba for himself and had her husband killed and then would suffer his own great loss. He would write music and poetry to God but would be chased from his own throne.

All of this is recounted and explained brilliantly in a book by Robert Alter. Its full title is *The David Story—A Translation and Commentary of 1 and 2 Samuel*, and it may help you understand and appreciate the richness and value of the Old Testament. I highly recommend it. To find other books that may interest you, just Google "books about the Bible." You'll be amazed.

Forgive me, but one more suggestion: Everyone should read the Book of Job at least once in their adult life. It makes you think. Why does an innocent person suffer? How do we understand our own hardships and suffering?

The unknown writer of this Old Testament classic confronts these questions initially through a conversation—a conversation between God and the devil. One day, the Lord says to Satan, "Have you noticed my servant Job? There is no one on earth like him, blameless and upright, fearing God and avoiding evil" (Jb 1:8).

Satan is not impressed. "Sure," he says, "with his big, prosperous family and all his livestock and property—sure, Job is upright and blameless. What if you took everything away from him and then caused him to suffer? I bet then he would curse you to your face!"

"Ok," God says, "Do what you want with him, and let's see. Just don't kill him."

Then it all begins to fall apart for poor Job. He goes through a series of catastrophes, even boils on his skin from head to toe. His own wife even says to him, "Why don't you just curse God and die, already; get this over with." And his friends begin to doubt him, question him, and challenge him. Job remains patient. "We accept good things from God; should we not accept evil?" (Jb 2:10).

I won't tell you the end, but if you can make it through all forty-two sometimes tedious, repetitive chapters, you'll be rewarded. And you will have shared something with Bible-readers from all time.

Christina: *Thanks for all this information about the Bible, Dad. By the way, what happened to the Catechism?*

It's still with us, but different. In 1962 John XXIII articulated a vision for the Fathers of the Second Vatican Council. He charged them to guard and present more effectively the deposit of Christian doctrine in order to make it more accessible to the Christian faithful and all people of goodwill. In 1985 a synod of bishops in Rome convened to celebrate the twentieth anniversary of the conclusion of the Second Vatican Council. A proposal to develop a universal catechism for the Catholic Church was made and accepted. The outcome was the *Catechism of the Catholic Church*, published in 1992, and revised with some modifications in 1997. It is arranged in four parts: The Profession of Faith, The Celebration of the Christian Mystery, Life in Christ, and Christian Prayer. It no longer offers a series of questions and answers but is now the place to find out the church's position on articles of faith and doctrine. It is Bible-based, including thousands of words from scripture, with specific references for each citation. When you come visit, you'll see my copy of the Catechism, right on the shelf next to the Holy Bible.

Endnotes

1. "Benedict XVI—General Audience—Saint Peter's Square," Benedict XVI, Libreria Editrice Vaticana, November 7, 2007, https://w2.vatican.va/content/benedict-xvi/en/audiences/2007/documents/hf_ben-xvi_aud_20071107.html.
2. Pope Paul VI, *Constitution on the Sacred Liturgy* 1963, SC 24, dfhttp://www.documentacatholicaomnia.eu/03d/1963-12-04,_Concilium_Vaticanum_II,_Constitutio_'Sacrosantum_Conciluim,'_EN.p.
3. Athanasius of Alexandria, 3th Festal Letter of Athanasius 367 CE The Development of the Canon of the New Testament, http://www.ntcanon.org/Athanasius.shtml.

CHAPTER 4
The Church

§

ANGELA: *DAD, YOU'VE EXPLAINED THE story of the prophets clearly, and some of your insights about Jesus and the Bible really make sense to me, but when you start talking to us about the church, I'm afraid you're swimming upstream.*

Christina: *Yes, Dad, with all due respect, don't you agree that the church today is out of touch? It's too conservative with its stance on abortion and birth control.*

Angela: *There's been too much scandal with the priests and the bishops.*

Christina: *It's male dominated, with no place for women. And it's intolerant of the gay lifestyle.*

Angela: *Also, Dad, there are way too many rules and regulations. Penance? Most of the practicing Catholics I know are older, hard core, and not fun. (Sorry, except for you, of course.)*

Christina: *Those are the criticisms; but I will say this Pope seems friendly, open, and nonjudgmental. Maybe things will change.*

Well, I agree that the church in America today goes against the grain of normal life in our society. You'd have to describe it as countercultural. But there is a lot of misinformation out there about the church. Many Catholics today don't understand their faith and cannot articulate its principles. Many non-Catholics don't understand how the church is set up and what's really going on inside the church.

You guys are both still in your twenties; do you regard yourselves as open-minded? You took basic courses in philosophy or theology in college. Do you still think about the meaning of life and the existence of God? If you're still with me, there are three things I want you to know about the church today, before we discuss anything else: prayer, work, and the parish.

Prayer

Angela: *Dad, obviously we know the church prays.*

Ok, but I think many people, including nonchurch-attending Catholics, are not aware of how the church prays. Let's start with daily prayer.

The Hours

At this very moment, somewhere in the world, people are praying what is known as the Liturgy of the Hours. They are doing the Divine Office, a pattern of prayer based on the Psalms. The word "office" comes from the Latin *officium*, meaning "service" or "something done for someone." The divine office is service given to God in prayer.

As a deacon I am required to pray some portion of the Office. Every bishop, priest, deacon, nun, and brother uses a breviary, the book that contains all the prayers, hymns, readings, and instructions for the Hours. The breviary actually comes in four volumes and breaks the year down into seasons (Advent, Lent, Ordinary Time 1 and 2) but it is also published in a one-book volume.

The Liturgy of the Hours is not the Mass; it is separate from the Mass, but it is part of the public liturgy of the church. It has been prayed since the beginning of the church. Jesus himself learned to pray, according to Jewish custom. He followed the Jewish practice of daily prayer, praying morning prayer at sunrise, afternoon prayer during the sacrifice in the temple of Jerusalem (3:00 p.m.), and evening prayer at nightfall. These hours of prayer were the daily habit of every devout Jew.

Down through the centuries, with help from the Benedictines, the Cistercians, and others, the monks kept the prayer of the Hours alive in the church. And the practice spread everywhere, in order to lead people to a life with God. Here's a quote from a prologue of the Book of Hours used in France around the year 1500: "In these present Hours is briefly proclaimed the Old as well as the New Testament; and with a view to the salvation of every soul, in the calendar is noted the form and manner of living in this world, during the little time God grants us, to grow in goodness and in virtue."

Remember when I went on retreat to the monastery with the monks? Those monks follow the Hours for Vigils and Lauds in the morning, Sext and None during the day, and Vespers and Compline in the evening. Prayer at 9:00 a.m., noon, and 3:00 p.m. mark the third, sixth, and ninth hours of the day. The monks work with their hands in a variety of ways, take their meals in silence, and are dedicated to a life of prayer.

Christina: *But why all this praying all day long?*

St. Paul tells us, "Rejoice always. Pray without ceasing. In all circumstances give thanks, for this is the will of God for you in Christ Jesus" (1 Thes 5:16–18). And Jesus taught us to pray in silence to God, who hears us in silence. And He taught us His own prayer, the Lord's Prayer, a shared public prayer in which we ask for our "daily bread." The Our Father is very much a part of the Liturgy of the Hours and Daily Mass.

So, the church prays.

And with the encouragement of Vatican II, lay people now also pray the Office. Many people who work at the center of parish life—the Eucharistic ministers, the lectors, CCD teachers, members of the choir—now join the clergy in daily prayer, most often just for Morning and Evening Prayer, which each take about twenty minutes. Yes, it takes time and some discipline. But people who enter into a daily prayer life find it to be a sustaining and enriching way to live each day.

Angela: *How does it work?*

The Office is designed to be prayed in groups and features a call-and-response flavor to it. The Psalms for Morning and Evening Prayer are selected and arranged to best fit and aid a Christian form of worship. Morning Prayer begins with what is called an invitatory, an invitation to pray. It is supposed to focus our minds on God before anything else we are to do that day. The invitatory begins daily dialogue with God, and it continues through the whole Office. Then there is a hymn, a psalm, a short scripture reading, a response, a Gospel canticle, the intercessions, the Lord's Prayer, a concluding prayer, and a blessing. Good so far?

Antiphons are inserted throughout the Office. They are recited responses to the readings and hymns and serve as bridges to the next part of the prayer. A hymn is included because hymns have always been a special part of prayerful worship. In Paul's letter to the Colossians (3:16) it says, "Let the word of Christ dwell in you richly, as in all wisdom you teach and admonish one another, singing psalms, hymns, and spiritual songs with gratitude in your hearts to God."

The Office can be done together or alone, every morning and every evening. It is meant to be sung but can be recited. There is an additional section called the Office of Readings, a special treat for Bible fans and church-history buffs. It is an amazing assembly of selections from the Bible, read in sequence (from the Book of Revelation or Exodus, for example), accompanied by sermons and reflections by some of the greatest scholars and doctors of the church (St. Gregory, St. Augustine, Vatican Council writings, and others.).

And there is a Divine Office App, which not only provides you with everything in proper order and sequence (so you don't have to fuss with all the colored ribbons that come with the breviary) but also includes the singing of the Psalms by some of the greatest choirs in the world. I'd recommend the app just for the music alone!

Christina: *But Dad, praying all day? Please!*

Not a good idea? Ok, I'm not saying that you should even attempt this, at first. For most people this is just not their cup of tea. But if you are a member of the church, whether you like it or not, you are either praying or you are being prayed for. It is a praying church.

The Days

Just as the hours of the day are designated for appropriate prayers, the days of the year are also designated for specific devotion and prayer. Every day of the liturgical year is a celebration of a specific person or a specific event. We celebrate these at Mass.

In every time zone, in just about every country in the world, Mass is being said. The same Mass—with the same readings, same Psalm, same celebration, and the same Holy Sacrifice—said every hour of every day in this world. We'll talk more about the Mass later, but what I want you to know now is that Mass is always being said and has a theme, a dedicated purpose, and meaning.

Everyone knows what day we celebrate on December 25, but do you know what we celebrate on December 26? As we bask in the glow of the newborn baby Jesus, the church pauses to recall the life and death of the first Christian martyr, St. Stephen, who gave up his life for Christ. December 27? John the Evangelist. December 28? The church dedicates a day of remembrance for the Holy Innocents— those children, up to two years of age, whom Herod had killed to ensure that no new messiah would be born in the midst of his own kingdom. In fact, the church celebrates the birth of Jesus for an oc- tave, the eight days following Christmas Day.

Pick a date: July 3? The Feast of St. Thomas, the blessed apostle who doubted. You know of the Franciscan Friars, the Benedictine Monks, and the Jesuit priests of the Society of Jesus, of course. These are orders of people who for centuries have dedicated their lives to Christ, with the inspiration of the saintly founders of those orders. The church sets aside dates in memory of St. Francis of Assisi (October 4), St. Benedict (March 21), and St. Ignatius of Loyola (July 31).

The church has always remembered the quiet lives of beautiful saints like St. Agnes (January 21), a young girl martyred in the third century; and St. Cecilia (November 22), the patroness of church mu- sic, who died at the beginning of the fourth century. Many women, role models for us all, are honored by their own day each year: St. Scholastica (February 10), a nun, the twin sister of St. Benedict; St. Therese of Lisieux (October 3), the Saint of the Little Flower, who died at the age of twenty-four. She is thought of as one of the most inspirational saints of modern times and is now a doctor of the church. And there's St. Monica (August 27), the mother of St. Augustine, and the great St. Catherine of Sienna (April 29), another doctor of the church, who served the sick and dying but was also a counselor to popes and bishops.

There are eleven days of the year that celebrate some aspect of the Blessed Virgin Mary, including the big ones: The Annunciation (March 25), the Feast of the Assumption (August 15), and the Feast of the Immaculate Conception (December 8). Most people know that the Feast of St. Patrick of Ireland is celebrated on March 17, and many people embrace the Feast of St. Joseph on March 19. On November 1 we celebrate the Solemnity of All Saints (formerly All Hallows—for Halloween), so we can recall with reverence the great witnesses to Christ who now reside in heaven. November 2 is the Feast of All Souls' Day, when we pray for all those who have gone before us, the faithful departed, and especially our own friends and members of our own families. Most liturgical celebrations of individual saints during the year are known formally as memorials, but those classified as feasts are reserved for important events in Christian history and for saints of particular significance, such as the twelve apostles.

Angela: *So each one of the 365 days celebrates an event or a saint?*

Not every single day, but when there is no universal celebration on a given day, the local diocese can designate an appropriate saint for honor.

Another thing, in every Catholic Church you walk into, you see the Stations of the Cross—fourteen of them displayed around the church. The Stations are done throughout Lent and on Good Friday, helping us enter into the Passion and death of our Lord, Jesus. I know you've seen the Pope on Good Friday, conducting a Stations of the Cross service inside and around the Colosseum in Rome. It's televised in Italy and can now be seen by all on EWTN.

Christina: *Was it like this when you were a kid? Has it always been like this?*

It has evolved over time, but yes, there has always been a liturgical calendar. The entire church year revolves around the life of Christ and is celebrated by seasons. The liturgical year begins with preparation, as we anticipate the coming of Jesus in the season of Advent. We celebrate the birth of Jesus at Christmas, and then we ponder the mystery and wonder of the Incarnation (He entered humanity through the body of a woman in the form of a man!) during the weeks after Christmas. We begin the Lenten season on Ash Wednesday, and we prepare to celebrate the Resurrection by fasting, abstaining, and doing good works. We celebrate the Resurrection on Easter Sunday, and we rejoice for fifty days throughout the Easter season right up to the Feast of the Pentecost. The remainder of the year is referred to as Ordinary Time (not plain, or usual, but "in the order of"—from "ordinal" meaning number) where we consider and celebrate all the other extraordinary events in the life of Jesus and His followers.

Angela: *So from the church's point of view, every day is a holy day in a sense.*

Yes, in a real sense. Small, devoted congregations of believers gather every morning for prayer and communion at daily Mass all over this country and around the world. Every day. It's the same Mass in every location. You can join in by picking up a copy of the *Magnificat*. It has all the readings and timely reflections for each day's celebration at the daily Mass.

Christina: *I'm a little embarrassed to ask, but do they still pray the Rosary in church?*

Oh yes, with great devotion. I'll bet you still know how to say the Rosary. You remember that the rosary beads are comprised of five decades (groups of ten), with a separate cord or chain leading out to the crucifix with five more beads in between. You start with the crucifix in one hand, blessing yourself and reciting the Apostles Creed. Then, with the first bead, say the Lord's Prayer. With the next three beads, you say three Hail Marys, asking God for an increase in faith, hope, and love. Then you say the Glory Be (the Doxology), and with that fifth bead, you can dedicate the Rosary to some person or special intention, and then you are on to the five full decades. Each decade is concentrated on one of four sacred mysteries (the Joyful,

Luminous, Sorrowful, and Glorious), which draw attention to various aspects of Mary's life. For example, the first Joyful Mystery is the Annunciation; the second, the Visitation; and so forth. To observers it seems monotonous, but there's a lot going on. The person praying may be offering it for a person or cause. They may also be reflecting on the miracle of Mary's life. And they are also doing something like a mantra, repeating the same words over and over, leading potentially to enlightenment. "Holy Mary, Mother of God, pray for us sinners, now, and at the hour of our death." Over and over. The Holy Rosary lives.

Angela: *You have to admit, Dad, you don't really hear or read much about daily Mass and prayer.*

Well, it's not news. And people don't spend a lot of time talking about prayer; they just do it. They do it because Jesus told us to do it. Prayer is talking to God. And many people do it joyfully, with reverence and devotion.

Have you ever said to someone something like, "Hey, I'll be praying for your mother during her surgery today?" Whenever we tell someone that we are praying for them, they appreciate it. No one ever says, "No thanks, I'm good for now." And if you tell them that your whole family is praying for their mother, or that all the people in your prayer group are praying for her, they feel even better. The more spiritual energy that's organized, concentrated, and directed at a particular cause, the greater the force of petition, we believe, is generated. It can't hurt.

And think about people who cannot themselves pray. You've been in nursing homes. People are unwell, medicated, and living with others who are unwell. Some are semiconscious or in and out of consciousness. Some sit together; some sit alone. Some cannot hold up their heads and nod off. Can they pray? Some have families that may visit, but others are quite alone—alone and unable to clean themselves, dress themselves, or feed themselves. Who prays for them? We do. The church is praying unceasingly with, and for, all those people. We are building up and becoming the body of Jesus Christ. St. Paul wrote, "...God has so constructed the body as to give greater honor to a part that is without, so that there may be no division in the body, but that the parts may have the same concern for one another. If one part suffers, all the parts suffer with it; if one part is honored, all the parts share in its joy" (1 Cor 12:24–26). So we pray.

Angela: *Do you think it works?*

Do you know what the nuns used to ask us to pray for in the late 1950s? An end to communism! We didn't even know what communism was, for goodness sake, but we prayed anyway. We prayed to God and prayed to Mary, our intercessor. And look what happened. So the church is at prayer—every hour and every day—in thanks and praise to God and in petition for healing, for grace, and for the salvation of the whole world.

Christina: *But just saying prayers and going to church is not enough, is it?*

Boy, you just reminded me of Thomas Merton, the twentieth century American mystic. He wrote, "Real Christian living is stunted and frustrated if it remains content with the externals of worship, saying prayers, and going to church. The real purpose of prayer is the deepening of personal realization in love...the awareness of God."[1]

WORK

So let's move to the second thing I want you to know about the Catholic Church, which is the stuff that grows out of prayer: the work.

The work of the church is vast. I mentioned some religious orders earlier. There are 296 religious orders around the world—congregations of priests, nuns, and brothers. These orders are dedicated to making the world a better place. Some are specialists in education, like your professors in college, the Jesuits. Others are dedicated to missionary work, like the Missionary Sisters of the Sacred Heart of Jesus or Mother Theresa's order, the Sisters of Charity, now with over forty-five hundred nuns in 133 countries. Still others take a vow of poverty and are dedicated to helping the poor, like the Franciscans, who draw their inspiration from St. Francis of Assisi, the namesake of the current Pope. These religious orders maintain their own finances, and they draw support from donors throughout the world. They are practicing Catholics who follow the gospel proscription to serve. They live their faith and fulfill the call of the Gospel: "Amen, I say to you, whatever you did for one of the least brothers of Mine, you did for Me" (Mt 25:40).

The church is blessed by generous and energetic organizations like the Knights of Malta, the Knights of Columbus, and the Order of the Holy Sepulcher, who provide sustained moral and economic strength to those who do the work of the church. The Society of St. Vincent de Paul is one of the largest charitable organizations in the world. It is an international Catholic lay organization of almost eight hundred thousand men and women who volunteer to provide person-to-person service to the needy and suffering in 149 countries! Much money is needed, and many wealthy Catholics and non-Catholics are asked to donate funds or sponsor worthy events or programs, and many respond. Legatus is an organization of four thousand Catholic business leaders who are committed to live and spread the Catholic faith in their business and personal lives. They call their movement "Ambassadors for Christ in the Marketplace." The list goes on.

Let me tell you about one particular organization that amazes me: Catholic Relief Services (CRS).

At the height of World War II in 1943, the Catholic bishops in the United States established Catholic Relief Services to help resettle war refugees in Europe. As Europe stabilized under the Marshall Plan in the 1950s, CRS began to expand into other regions of need and established operations and opened offices in Africa, Asia, and Latin America. The focus was, and is, two-fold: first, to provide immediate relief in emergency situations and then to seek ways to help people in the developing world break the cycle of poverty—through community-based, sustainable development initiatives. The programs are designed so that the local population is the central participant in its own development, and the local community can sustain the project.

Remember the hurricane that devastated Haiti recently? CRS was there right away, and long after news coverage ended—CRS was still there, establishing clean water projects, health education, and agriculture initiatives…helping families and communities rebuild their lives. CRS is committed to the poor and vulnerable overseas. They are in over thirty countries in Africa, and the first thing they do when they arrive in a local village is make sure the people have access to clean water, the life-force of a community.

CRS deploys professionals with expertise in social safety nets, agriculture, education, HIV and AIDs, microfinance, and peace building. They do God's work, and you don't hear much about them. Because of their growing success at providing relief to the most vulnerable, and because the needs continue to grow, their ambitions to help are growing. You will be hearing more and more because they will need greater publicity to help achieve their funding goals.

Their stated goal is now to call on over 10 million Catholics in the United States to provide the funds to serve 150 million poor and vulnerable people around the world by 2018! More than a third—some 37 percent—of the money goes specifically to emergency relief. All their programs are built to benefit the poor overseas. The next time you read about an international crisis affecting human beings, look carefully to see if CRS is mentioned. Go to their website and find out more, and if you are so moved, tell your friends about CRS, and make a contribution.

What CRS does overseas, Catholic Charities USA (CCUSA) does within the United States. Catholic Charities was founded in 1910 on the campus of Catholic University in Washington DC, and for over one hundred years, the organization has guided and supported a vast network of local Catholic charities nationwide in a common mission to "serve, advocate, and convene." Catholic Charities provides a full range of human services to help the hungry, the homeless, the abandoned, at-risk children, and the developmentally disabled.

When Hurricane Katrina hit, more than 110 local Catholic Charities in the Gulf Coast and beyond provided immediate and long-term aid to more than one million hurricane victims. In addition to disaster relief, CCUSA provides health services, housing, and HIV/AIDS services for those in need. Catholic Charities is more familiar to most churchgoing Catholics than other missions because it reaches out to potential donors at the parish level, where a specific Sunday donation is made in the collection plate at least once a year. Catholic Charities is a member of Caritas International, a federation of over 160 Catholic social-service organizations around the world.

Angela: *When did all of this begin? Who started these organizations?*

The church has done charitable work in every century since its beginning. In 1891, Pope Leo XIII issued Rerum Novarum (Latin for "Revolutionary Change"), an encyclical, an open letter to the bishops, which addressed the condition of the working classes during the height of the Industrial Revolution. Its primary concern was the need for some amelioration of "the misery and wretchedness pressing so unjustly on the majority of the working class."[2] Rerum Novarum is considered the foundational text of modern Catholic social teaching. Later encyclicals expounded on this one and developed into the Seven Themes of Catholic Social Teaching. These themes articulated the rationale for charity. Man has been created in the image and likeness of God and as such, is holy. Man comes from God and has needs, which the church must be aware of and tend to. The bishops in the United States and around the world built on existing charities, started new programs, and began to garner resources in a more coordinated way to make more of an impact as the twentieth century unfolded. The bishops now had a playbook.

In St. John Paul II's Centesimus annus, it was asserted, "While the Catholic Church is primarily concerned with the salvation of souls and with one's eternal destiny, it is also genuinely concerned with man's earthly existence and his temporal welfare during his pilgrimage to his eternal home."

Christina: *Dad, are you feeling defensive here?*

A little, and I'll tell you why. So often you hear people say, "Why doesn't the church just sell everything it owns and give the money to the poor?" I can't say that's an unfair question, but you have to be aware of what's actually being done before you can fairly discuss the answer. People who follow Jesus Christ and find their home in the Roman Catholic Church today are using their talent, skill, education, and money to alleviate pain and suffering in the world. I am glad to belong to a church that seeks to fulfill the second of the two greatest commandments: to love thy neighbor as thyself. There are serious problems in the church today, and we'll discuss them, but the church is at work in the world, every day.

The Parish

The third thing I want you to know about the Catholic Church is the parish. Now both of you basically grew up as members of a parish, right up until you went off to college. That's how you learned to be Catholic. The parish is where everything happens. The universal church is manifested in the local parish. The Eucharist, the sacraments, the praying, the teaching, the celebrating, the suffering, the dying, and the burying, are all done in local parishes across this country and around the world.

To be a part of the life of the church, you have to belong to a community. For most, that's the parish. It is easier, over time, to be a follower of Jesus if we pray with other people who are trying to do the same thing. Right from the beginning, as we can read in the Acts of the Apostles, communities of believers gathered together to support each other in a world that was hostile to their beliefs. People gather together, because they need each other and God.

You remember: it's like a big, extended family. But since you receive sacraments together, there is often a level of closeness and trust that can be deeper than in other organizations. We have picnics, dances, bazaars, festivals, and even bingo, to raise money. Since it is like a family, people disagree with each other and get mad at each other. And they complain about things, about everything: The Mass or sermon is too long; the choir is too loud; the songs are not right. Why don't people dress better? Put more money in the plate? And on it goes. There are busybodies in every parish, and there are know-it-alls in every parish. There are some people who volunteer for everything and get involved in every project and others who don't help at all.

By growing up in a parish, you experienced pretty much everything there is to know about the church. When you sat in the pew each week, you heard about charitable work being done halfway around the world, and then you prayed for the family who just lost a loved one down the street. You heard about the people who were suffering in your community, and you prayed for those who were sick every Sunday at Mass. You prayed for the Pope, for the bishops, for government leaders, and for the children receiving their First Communion.

Just like all parishes, the pastor is in charge. But you saw many lay people with a lively and active role in church. There is usually a parish council, made up of men and women. The pastor can use the council as an advisory board, and ask for help in matters of finance and stewardship.

And you saw some wonderful ways to serve in a parish. People who sing in choirs find it to be an uplifting and enjoyable ministry. Your religious-education instructors were mostly lay people, teaching classes of children from first to eighth grade. You saw both men and women serving at the altar as lectors and Eucharistic ministers, some taking the consecrated hosts to hospitals and shut-ins after the Mass on Sundays.

People who make up the core of a parish often develop stronger prayer lives and a deeper commitment to their faith. Some study the Bible and pray the Office. Over time, people develop deep attachments to their parish and identify strongly with it. Even now, when you tell fellow Catholics where you're from, don't they ask what parish?

Despite falling attendance, people still bring their newborns to the local parish for baptism, the sacrament that welcomes a person into the church. In preparation, that family will receive some basic instruction in the meaning of the sacrament and about their responsibility to teach their child to pray and to grow in faith. Within a few short years, the child will be registered for religious-instruction classes and will begin preparation for the Sacrament of Reconciliation and for First Holy Communion.

Every parish has to have some focus on the poor. That's part of Catholic social teaching. It's up to each local parish to identify the needs in their midst and to have a program to meet those needs. That's why you guys helped out at the soup kitchen and helped organize collections of food and clothing for the needy. Remember the midnight runs into the city to help the homeless? That's how Mom and I were able to expose you to the notion of charity and service, by getting you involved at a young age through the parish.

Angela: *Dad, all true, but—other than the annual picnic—we really didn't socialize that much with other people. There was no youth group for example.*

Christina: *And during the summer in our parish, attendance at Mass was really low. It was depressing at times.*

Well, the health of a parish is determined by two criteria: the spiritual and the financial, and both relate to attendance at Mass. The spiritual health of a parish can be looked at in terms of activity, the quality of teaching, and the outreach. Are there adequate services for the bereaved, the divorced, the addicted…and most importantly, the youth? Our parish was small with just one priest, and although we tried a number of times to get programs going for young people, we never got any traction. That's regrettable. I know of many parishes that have really active youth groups, and it's a very important part of parish life.

And if people are not coming to Mass, it can't be said that the spiritual life of a parish is healthy. Then it becomes a burden on those who do come and a struggle to collect enough money to pay the bills. Let's talk about money for a minute:

Catholics are constantly asked for money and expected to support the parish. The plate is passed at least once at every Mass, and a second collection may be passed for a dedicated cause or mission. You hear many grumblings from both sides about the giving, or lack of giving, done each week. On the one hand, Catholics feel overburdened by all the requests for money. Despite that, many people are extremely generous.

But, often, people are not tuned in to their share of responsibility. You'll hear people say that the person in the next pew only gave a dollar or two. Remember tithing, the call to give a tenth, to the church? You've heard that Tom Cruise or John Travolta gave millions to the Church of Scientology because of the requirement to tithe. Evander Holyfield reportedly provided millions to World Changers Church International in Atlanta. Tithing is not a word that Catholics use much, but it is important to consider how much is appropriate to contribute in one's own local parish.

Let's say a family makes $65,000 per year. A tithe would be an annual donation to the church of $6,500. Well, people say, that's crazy. But $650 would be only 1 percent—less than fifteen dollars per week. And if a local parish has to raise $150,000 per year to meet expenses for example, what is a pastor to do if people give less than 1 percent? Thus the need for all the creative fundraising. Many parishes now use online services like ParishPay, allowing people to use their credit card to plan out their giving over the course of a year and still contribute when they are away. But for every parish, like for most families, money is a nagging, enduring problem.

And listen, I get it. To join a parish today is a radical decision. It's going against the grain. As you said, Angela, it's swimming upstream. But it can be a defining moment in your life. It's not just about doing something; it actually serves to define who you are. Joining a parish is entering into a community of believers and expressing your faith in a public way. It is aligning yourself with a family of saints and sinners, joining them on a journey of faith, helping them, and being helped by them. Look ahead. How will you bring up your own children? If you stay away too long, what will you have to share with them?

I wanted to focus on these three aspects of the church first. By looking at prayer inside the church, the missionary and charity work of the church, and then an overview of the parish, we have a good starting point for discussion, a context for considering the church. If the church today in America is too conservative or too hardcore, too rigid, too strict, why would anyone consider joining? If the people seem odd or out of the mainstream, why join them? Getting up for church every Sunday? Following all the rules and regulations? Who needs it?

The church has problems, and it is at the parish level where they are illustrated. We now have more than two generations of Catholics in America who do not know their faith and so cannot pass it along to their children. Numbers vary, but somewhere between 17 and 20 percent of the people who are registered with a parish come to weekly Mass. Parents want their children baptized but don't teach their children the Hail Mary or take their children to Mass. Many drop their children off for religious education but do not set an example of a religious life.

Divorce has caused a separation from the church for some, without a clear path to reconciliation. You mentioned penance earlier? Well, it's still a sacrament, but it has lost its meaning to too many people. And too many people still think in terms of "what counts" in order to fulfill their obligations. Attendance aside, here's the scariest statistic of all: I've read that as many as 50 percent of Catholics surveyed do not believe in the Real Presence of Christ in the Eucharist. That is a crisis of faith.

When you read any article online that deals with the church, you can scroll down and read the comments people make. The first few may be supportive, respectful, and even thoughtful. Then, something negative—an insult—and then a response, and the rest of the conversation devolves into name calling, vitriol, and hatred. This pattern does not happen just sometimes; it happens every time. Am I right?

We don't really talk to each other about subjects on which we disagree. We yell or avoid each other. We only read and watch the news that supports our own point of view. When people discuss religion, they get upset, so there's no follow-through. When you talk to your friends about religion, would you say they are angry? Or dismissive?

Angela: *I mean, they're not disrespectful, but they're not really informed.*

Christina: *I'd say apathetic.*

What I would say to you—and all young Catholics—is, how are you doing? Are you unhappy? Do you have any complaints about your life or about the world? I hear so many Catholics start their conversation about the church with "see, I have a problem with that." Other common phrases are "what do I get out of it?" or "what's in it for me?"

Take some time, and do a personal inventory by asking yourself these questions: How is my own prayer life? Do I have a relationship with God, and am I in dialogue? Do I speak to Jesus, and is He present in my life? Do I begin my day with gratitude? Am I thanking God for all that He created, for my own life? Do I have a sense that everything in my life, including myself, comes from God? Do I make my desires and my petitions known to Him in prayer? Do I pray for other people in my life? Am I aware of God's presence during the day? Do I end my day with humility and gratitude?

What about the work, the charity, that I do? Do I look outside of myself and really see people: their pain, their anxiety, their suffering? Do I call a friend who might be hurting? Do I visit someone when he or she is sick? Am I a peacemaker in my family and in my own circle of friends? Am I doing enough for others—not big things, just the little stuff?

But speaking of bigger things, am I in a community of prayerful believers who do charity? Do I volunteer my time to visit the local hospital or shelter? Do I share my goodness and my gifts with others? Do I do work for other people? And do I pray with, and work with, other people?

It's a good exercise to look in the mirror, really look. It's necessary, really. It's like an examination of conscience. Why talk about church if you haven't taken personal inventory? Some people say, "I do my own thing with God." That's ok, but it's a long journey, and it's not good for man (or woman) to be alone. If you are doing your own thing, how are you doing? When we look at the church, we can say, "Wow, there's a lot of work to be done." When we look at ourselves, we can say the same thing.

The church doesn't give you God. God exists. God gave us Jesus, Who loves us and saves us. The weak people in the world need God's strength. The strong need His tenderness and love. Those who stumble need God's salvation. The lonely need God's presence and friendship. The self-righteous need God's patience and forgiveness. The caretakers need God to love them and lead them. Through the church you can receive Jesus and His sacraments. But in return, what are you willing to give to God?

In a 2014 Pew Research survey from 2014, 31.7 percent of American adults said they were raised Catholic. Of that group, 41 percent no longer identified with Catholicism. That means that almost 13 percent of American adults are former Catholics. [3]A vast exodus.

Yet, the church is still very much alive. The Catholic population in the United States now stands at about 21 percent, and that percentage of the total population has held steady for several decades, according to the Pew survey. That would put the number of people who consider themselves Catholic upward of sixty-nine million. If we say that fifteen to eighteen million Catholics in the United States today go to church on a regular basis and receive the sacraments, that is not insignificant; believing Catholics have not disappeared.

There are about 17,900 local parishes in 195 dioceses. They are served by thirty-eight thousand priests and just over seventeen thousand permanent deacons. As Catholic populations have shifted, bishops have had to shift resources to meet the needs of the diocese. That means merging or closing parishes. Those beautiful old churches in the inner cities no longer attract congregations big enough to sustain themselves. So schools have closed, and parishes are being merged or closed. That process has been particularly painful for older, loyal Catholics. But good stewardship of resources is necessary and is underway.

Christina: *I have a friend in Boston whose parish was merged.*

The parish you two grew up in has now merged. Even though some fabulous buildings have had to close, there are still many beautiful churches. The Holy Name Cathedral in Chicago is home to one of the largest dioceses in the United States. The Archdiocese of Los Angeles is alive and has a beautiful home in the Cathedral of Our Lady of Angels. Nearly fifty thousand people streamed through the doors of the renovated St. Patrick's Cathedral in New York in 2016, just to receive ashes on Ash Wednesday. There is strong leadership in place; there are currently four cardinals who serve as archbishops: Timothy Dolan in New York, Donald Wuerl in Washington DC, Sean Patrick O'Malley in Boston, and Daniel DiNardo in Galveston-Houston. And three new Cardinals have been appointed in the Unites States, in Chicago, Indianapolis, and Newark.

The bishops have a lot on their plate. They have to provide for adult faith formation, young-adult outreach, black and Hispanic ministry, and the care for all the clergy—newly ordained and retired—in the diocese. They have to foster vocations to the priesthood and permanent diaconate. One of their most vexing problems is figuring out a way back into reconciliation and Holy Communion for those divorced Catholics who don't have an annulment and who stay away from the church out of guilt or fear. There's much work to be done.

Angela: *When I visit my friends in North Carolina, there's like, no Catholics down there.*

Yes, the population is dispersed. States with the highest percentages of Catholics are in the Northeast—topped by Connecticut, New Jersey, and Massachusetts with over 40 percent. The lowest percentages are in the South—with states like Tennessee, Alabama, and Mississippi under 4 percent.[4] You will find active, vibrant parishes along the south shore of Long Island and the west coast of Florida.

The liveliest parishes in the United States today are Hispanic, and they're growing. Hispanics currently account for about 40 percent of all US Catholics, and 55 percent of all US Catholics under the age of thirty are Hispanic! This is the population that will fill religious vocations in the near future, and this is why Hispanic ministries have grown in over forty-two hundred parishes nationwide. Growth in the church will be fueled by Hispanic citizens and immigrants.

The Pope

Angela: *Do you think the new Pope has helped? He seems open, friendly, willing to discuss, open to change. Hasn't the "Francis effect" helped to increase attendance at Mass?*

Yes, he's helped, but let me ask you, what would you say is his central theme as Pope, or his overall message?

Christina: *"Who am I to judge?"*

That comment was made on an airplane in response to a reporter's question about the sexual orientation of priests. The press then took it out of context and exploited it for a variety of purposes, but it is interesting how that one quote has resonated, particularly with young people, more than almost anything else he has said. It projected a sincere tone of humility and kindness, without condemnation, and there is obviously a great thirst for that from church leaders.

The Pope speaks every day, and everything he says is made public. His daily homilies are published in a variety of websites. He is seen on live television more than any other Pope. He has a twitter account (@Pontifex), and I believe that his message is clear and consistent.

Here's another quote:

The great danger in today's world, pervaded as it is by consumerism, is the desolation and anguish born of a complacent yet covetous heart, the feverish pursuit of frivolous pleasures, and a blunted conscience. Whenever our interior life becomes caught up in our own interests and concerns, there is no room for others, no place for the poor. God's voice is no longer felt, and the desire to do good fades. This is a very real danger for believers too. Many fall prey to it, and end up resentful, angry, and listless. That is no way to live a dignified and fulfilled life; it is not God's will for us, nor is it the life in the Spirit which has its source in the heart of the risen Christ.

I invite all Christians everywhere at this moment, to a renewed personal encounter with Jesus Christ, or at least an openness to letting Him encounter them. I ask all of you to do this unfailingly each day. No one is excluded from the joy brought by the Lord. Whenever we take a step toward Jesus, we come to realize that He is already there, waiting for us with open arms.[5]

That's from Evangelii Gaudium ("Joy of the Gospel"), the first encyclical of Pope Francis. It is thoughtful and loving and well worth everyone's time to read through prayerfully. "I invite all Christians... to a renewed personal encounter with Jesus, or at least an openness to letting Him encounter them." I take these words to heart. I know I need to continually renew my relationship with Christ and be open to a personal encounter. Isn't this a good message for millennials, for baby boomers, and for all of us? We are invited to a renewed personal encounter with Jesus—who is living water, the bread of life—or at least an openness to Him, the Good Shepherd, who guides His sheep and protects them.

If you ever want to know what the Pope is saying, that's it! I believe all of his words come down to a central, unifying message: come to Christ, or at least let Him come to you! The Pope may speak about the economy or about the environment, but his central message is fairly simple. Everything the Pope says is made public. He has declared a Year of Mercy. His message is clear and consistent: come to Christ!

I'm sure the Jesuits at Georgetown and Holy Cross rejoiced when one of their own, the first Jesuit, became Pope. Pope Francis has been determined to emphasize charity first, before doctrine. People want to love this Pope, and many people both inside and outside the church see that Pope Francis has already done much to re-energize the church and alter its image around the world. I'm glad you both have a favorable opinion of him.

But his papacy has not just been about tone or images. This Pope had serious work to do. The previous fifteen years or more were a period of turmoil and decline for the universal church. Its image was damaged by the pedophilia scandals. And money was a recurrent source of scandal at the Vatican. Stories had circulated for years about malfeasance and mismanagement at the Vatican Bank and within the Curia. There was an arrest of a onetime Vatican accountant for being part of a cash-smuggling scheme. And when the so-called Vatileaks scandal became news, in which Pope Benedict's butler had smuggled letters to the press that warned the Pope of detailed corruption and cronyism in the Vatican, the cardinals were said to be outraged. The affairs of the Vatican were poorly managed, and people noticed. By 2013 it was clear that the next Pope needed to be someone with the leadership skills to bring professional management to the Vatican and its affairs. The Archbishop of Buenos Aires, Cardinal Bergoglio, was one of the observers of the insular, systemic problems within the Vatican. He had even been quoted as referring to the Vatican as a "royal court." Bergoglio was an outsider and emerged as a popular choice.

The new Pope proved right away to be serious about reform. In the summer of 2013, he summoned seven major Catholic financiers from around the world to discuss strategy. According to an article in the September 2014 issue of *Fortune Magazine*, the Pope essentially said that in order for the spiritual message of the church to be credible, the Vatican's finances needed to be credible as well. It was time to open the books to the faithful—no more secrecy and intrigue. The Pope was quoted as saying, "When the administration is fat, it's unhealthy."[6] He wanted a leaner, more efficient administration, which would free up more money for the poor. That was the goal, and that was the message: more money for charity.

The Pope's approach to the problem was revolutionary but sound. Help was needed from outside. He knew that many of the cardinals and bishops in key positions of authority were less than expert at money matters, and so he began replacing them with Catholic lay experts who started setting financial strategy, doing regulatory oversight, and running more of the day-to-day operations of the Vatican. He made changes and brought in professionals.

Again, according to *Fortune*, at the direction of Pope Francis, the Roman Curia has brought in credible outsiders to get the financial house of the church in order. KPMG auditors started implementing reform, using internationally accepted accounting standards, to replace the Vatican's former archaic bookkeeping. Ernst & Young (now EY) was called in to scrutinize the management of the Vatican's stores, utilities, and other municipal services. And Deloitte & Touche was hired to regularly audit the accounts at the Vatican Bank.

Not all the people in charge are lay people. The Pope appointed Cardinal George Pell from Sydney, Australia, to manage the problems. The *Fortune* article stated that Pope Francis has granted Pell power over finances that no official has remotely held before. Pell is responsible for setting and enforcing all budgets and managing all investments. He's been a no-nonsense executive who is brutally frank about the necessity to radically pare costs.

Cardinal Pell's work on the Vatican's financial reforms moved quickly. With Francis's approval he created a three-part structure: a secretariat for the economy with power to impose fiscal discipline and accountability; a council for the economy composed of the most capable cardinals and business professionals to oversee operations; and an independent auditor general to keep everyone honest. In a short time he reported to all cardinals that his team had discovered $1.5 billion in hidden assets and a shortfall of almost $1.0 billion in the Vatican pension fund. Now audited financial statements are to be regularly forthcoming.

The Pope leads by his own example and is not patient in his call for fiscal responsibility in others. He will publicly chastise church leaders who spend money irresponsibly, as was the case with a bishop in Germany, who reportedly spent lavishly to build a new cathedral.

Financially, the Roman Catholic Church is divided into three branches: the Vatican, the religious orders, and the dioceses. In terms of money, the Vatican stands on its own. The Vatican itself is a sovereign, independent nation with its own laws, courts, and security force (Swiss guards). Politically, it could be described as a totalitarian dictatorship. The Pope is in charge, but he doesn't rule the world—just a little over eight hundred citizens with 110 ceremonial guards, on a plot of land one-eighth the size of Manhattan's Central Park.

The Vatican's second, and principal, function is that of the hierarchy of the church. The Pope heads a large bureaucracy, the Curia, officially known as the Holy See. It has a wide range of influence and provides advice and assistance to the church at large. There are nine congregations, each headed by a cardinal, like cabinet departments in the US government. One congregation, for instance, appoints the world's bishops (almost three thousand). Another does the research work needed to name new saints. The combined workforce of the Holy See and the city-state is around forty-eight hundred. The wages are not super high (an average of $46,000 a year for the cardinals and bishops and an average of $28,000 a year for priests and nuns). But they also receive housing, benefits, and pensions. It is in that pension fund where Cardinal Pell's team discovered that huge liability, and the Vatican has to restock its reserves ($30 to $40 million a year) in the years ahead to meet that obligation.

All the Vatican's assets—its bank statements, its investment portfolio of stocks, bonds, and real estate, and its income from Catholic foundations around the world—are open to scrutiny by multiple financial institutions and thus, the public. It wasn't easy to get there. The old guard who ran the Vatican Bank had resisted lifting the veil of secrecy, and by 2009 real problems began. It had existed as an offshore bank, outside of the European Union (EU), for years. The EU had developed stricter policies on money laundering and financing of terrorism. Under Italian law, the Vatican Bank was not required to notify authorities of clients who transferred money into its accounts in Italy, and so it didn't.

By 2012 the Bank of Italy declared that the Vatican Bank (known as the IOR, for Institute of Religious Works, in Italian) was failing to comply with antimoney-laundering laws and forced all banks in Italy to close their IOR accounts. By the time Francis became Pope, the IOR was on the verge of collapse.

The reforms were finally and speedily put in place, and the IOR is functioning again, now as a potential growth franchise. It's like a savings and loan and is very important. From all around the world, wealthy dioceses, religious orders, and Catholic charities collect huge sums of money—frequently in cash—all destined for needs in the developing world. These funds are deposited in the Vatican Bank. The Vatican Bank wires the funds to all corners of the developing world to build churches and schools, run hospitals, and pay priests and nuns. According to *Fortune*, the idea for the IOR is to gain interest on its deposits and invest the money in government bonds. Cardinal Pell is quoted as saying, "The future of the IOR is asset management." It is no longer a hidden or secret bank.[7]

As one of the three branches, the Vatican has no official claim on, or access to, the wealth of the other two branches it oversees—the religious orders and the dioceses. The 296 religious orders maintain separate finances, and frequently, regional units within each order manage and control their own finances.

Each diocese, headed by a bishop or archbishop, is a separate corporation with its own investments and budgets. Yes, the dioceses send tremendous amounts of money to the Vatican Bank each year, but most of it is earmarked for either missionary work or the Pope's charitable giving. The funds sent by the dioceses to support the Vatican's operations are important but account for under 5 percent of the Vatican's total revenues—thus, the need for the Vatican to generate funding from its own assets, from Catholic foundations, and from its museums.

With the approval of Pope Francis, Cardinal Pell is gathering all Vatican investments into a newly created unit called the Vatican Asset Management (VAM). This will be a great help to the church overall. Pell believes that the religious orders and the dioceses, especially in poor countries, sorely need professional money management. With their growing individual assets, they may be more than willing to entrust their accounts to VAM. And the plan is for VAM to excel in ethical investing, aligning the church's values with those of its clients.

Christina: *It sounds like the church has finally come into the modern world financially. Interesting that you got much of this from print media about the economy. I haven't read or seen much about this in mainstream or social media. Do you think these reforms are real and will hold?*

Real, long-lasting reform is difficult. This nagging notion of hidden assets keeps coming up, beyond the $1.5 billion that Cardinal Pell had already uncovered. And there was a story in the *Wall Street Journal* in 2016 that said Pope Francis had steered Cardinal Pell away from a deeper audit of some smaller Vatican departments. I would guess both Cardinal Pell and Pope Francis have encountered plenty of resistance to change. And Cardinal Pell himself had to deal with accusations that he either sexually abused or failed to report sexual abuse in Australia several decades ago, accusations which he has firmly denied.

But this whole story of financial reform in the church is not a secret; it's out there for all who are interested. By all reports the church is committed to international public-sector accounting standards, even if they haven't yet been completely implemented everywhere. The gains that have been made appear to be irreversible. As Cardinal Pell was quoted as saying, "Once you let the light in, it's impossible to return to a situation where you've had large elements of the truth buried."[8] I've read that, every two weeks, Pope Francis meets with Cardinal Pell for progress reports. The Pope is fully engaged, asks the right questions, and is determined to carry out these long-term reforms in the church. It may be that Pope Francis, for all his public approval and charisma, will one day be known as the Pope who placed the church on the path of fiscal as well as moral responsibility.

§

Pull back and think of the whole church from an international perspective. The center of gravity for the church has shifted southward, with more than two-thirds of the world's Catholic population living in Latin America, Asia, and Africa. The number of baptized Catholics worldwide has grown at a faster rate than that of the world's population. According to the Vatican's Central Office for Church Statistics, the number of baptized Catholics reached 1.27 billion, or 17.8 percent of the global population, by the end of 2014.[9]

Despite these impressive figures, the work of the church is burdensome. The faith has to be handed on from one generation to the next, in a world that is violent, hateful, and poverty-stricken. The church always seems to be fighting against persecution and apathy. There are many people who hate the church and all it stands for. Christians are being killed for their faith in Syria, Libya, and elsewhere. If people within the church do not know, follow, or live their faith, how long can it last?

Angela: *Throughout history, hasn't the church always been in crisis?*

At so many points in history, the church should not have survived. How did it make it through the sixth century when the barbarians invaded and sacked Rome? Fortunately, at that time, it wasn't made of buildings and armies, so it couldn't be destroyed. Why didn't the feuding between East and West cause an irreparable split between the Atlantic and Mediterranean cultures? It would have, except that they were to be reunited again under one Pope and would pull together militarily during the Crusades to try to recapture the Holy Lands from the Turks.

Why didn't the church fail because of the weaknesses pointed out by the Protestant reformers Luther, Zwingli, and Calvin: selling of indulgences, abusing power, and ordaining unfit priests? It took The Council of Trent (which lasted eighteen years, 1545–63) to get the church on track, with many reforms lasting right up till the first Vatican Council in 1870.

And what about the popes? Don't we read in history that between AD 955 and 1057 there were twenty-five popes, half of them appointed by the Roman Emperor, the others creations of Roman aristocracy? The Emperor dismissed five of them, and at least two of them were assassinated. Not until 1073 did the papacy regain its footing, under the guidance of Gregory VII. By the end of the thirteenth century, there would be another split, a schism, when there were two popes (and for a brief time, three!). Popes have led armies into war, lived sumptuous lives, and had illegitimate children. How did the church survive that?

Always in church history, it seems, great men and women of faith emerged to provide moral leadership and direction. Thomas Aquinas, Catherine of Sienna, Ignatius of Loyola, Teresa of Avila, and so many more. The problems in the church today do not seem insurmountable when measured against twenty centuries of sinning and sainthood.

Yes, in a real sense, the church is always in crisis. But the church is at prayer, and this carries on in faith. And the church is at work, so people can have hope. And communities of faith still exist where the gospel of love is proclaimed and received. I believe that the church in the first half of the twenty-first century is---- regenerating. It is tightening up in some places—becoming smaller and more efficient with fewer, more dedicated people. And at the same time, it is examining, discussing, reaching out, and adapting to the new realities of its people.

As long as there is a strong foundation—dedication, sincere prayer, selfless service to the poor and needy, and responsible stewardship of church resources at all levels—then the church is equipped to deal with its problems, however difficult.

After all, what is the church? Is it the Pope and the College of Cardinals? Is it the Order of Bishops, the magisterium? Some people think that when we say "church" we mean the hierarchy, the people who run things. That can't be right. Is it just the people themselves: functioning Christians, the so-called people of God? Or maybe it is a combination? How does it carry on through the centuries without coming to an end, like all other worldly regimes?

In a sense it is a mystery and something that can only be known by divine revelation. But it exists and functions in the real world. So it is better described as a mystical reality, a union of God with His people, manifested in the world but only as it is realized or made real by God. Paul speaks of the body of Christ, of which we are all different parts—not an actual body but the mystical body of Christ. The church, we can say then, is the body of Christ on earth.

We fail, we sin, we fall, but the truth is carried on. We carry the truths of the Gospel like earthen vessels, easily broken. When Jesus said to the Galilean fisherman, "You are Peter, and upon this rock I will build my church," He knew, of course, that the rock of Peter was more like clay really—and that Peter would stumble in his humanity. But once breathed on by the Holy Spirit of God, the rock would hold, and so Jesus could say with confidence and proclaim most assuredly that "the gates of hell will not prevail against it." And so the mystery of this reality carries on, through everything.

Endnotes

1. Thomas Merton, *Thomas Merton: Spiritual Master, Essential Writings.* (Mahwah, NJ: Paulist Press 1992), 375.
2. Pope Leo XIII Rerum Novarum ("Of Revolutionary Change") 1891 Section 3.
3. Pew Research Center, Religion and Public Life, Religious Landscape Study, last modified 2016, http://www.pewforum. org/religious-landscape-study/religious-tradition/catholic/.
4. Howard Chua-Eoan and Elizabeth Dias, "Pope Francis, The People's Pope," *Time*, December 11, 2013.
5. Pope Francis I Evangelii Gaudium ("The Joy of the Gospel") 2013 Section 2, 3.
6. Shawn Tully, "This Pope Means Business," *Fortune* 170, no. 3, September 2014, 67–78.
7. Ibid., 78.
8. Francis X. Rocca, "Vatican Finance Chief Runs Into Resistance," *Wall Street Journal*, September 8, 2016.
9. National Catholic Reporter, Junno Erocho Esteves, Catholic News Service 2016, https://www.ncronline.org/news/vati-can/vatican-statistics-report-increase-baptized-catholics-worldwide.

CHAPTER 5

Priests

§

THERE'S NO QUESTION THAT THE public image of the Catholic priest today has been damaged, to say the least. In recent years the priesthood has been used as a joke on late-night TV. Much has been written about the priesthood as an order in decline—unattractive as an occupation and misguided in its pledge to celibacy. If all you know about a priest is what you see and hear in the media, it's not good.

I wonder what young people think about priests. Do you have any sense of how your peers perceive the order of Catholic priests?

Angela: *I would say most of my peers are respectful of all religions, but they don't think much or know that much about priests.*

Christina: *When we were in college, some of them were great teachers and really friendly and engaging. But I think outside of the university setting, its less positive. I think my friends would say some priests are cool, and some are creepy. And my friends who don't go to church don't actually know any priests.*

Yes, I think the not-knowing thing is similar to other professions, like law-enforcement, for example. If you don't know any police officers, you may think they're all racists because of what you see and hear in the news. But if your father or your uncle is a cop, you know that's not true. It's the same with priests. If you don't know any priests, you might think they're all abusers.

Christina: *Or just not nice.*

Well, I maintain that the public reputation of the priesthood has not been rehabilitated in the eyes of the general public. When other enterprises or groups have been tarnished by scandal—airlines, restaurants, or consumer brands - - or any entity that has been portrayed negatively in the news—their defenders used common-sense marketing programs to promote positive images in the media to the public. And over time, the public begins to see those brands in a better light. There are companies today that professionally manage the search engine results for their clients and make them look their absolute best online. They can actually rehabilitate their client's scandalized reputation by using technology that pushes negative information down in a search and promotes more recent positive stories. That hasn't happened for priests. Catholic priests who have done nothing wrong have had to carry on in recent years in a world that does not hold them with much regard at all, other than with disdain.

I'll tell you what I know. Ever since I was a young boy in Catholic grammar school, I've known priests. Since first grade, I have met, been taught by, served, befriended, and observed many priests—for over fifty years! As a Catholic now just past sixty years of age, I have met and have known literally hundreds of priests, and this is what I have observed.

First, some priests are very smart and some less so. Some preach extremely well—others not as well. Some have a great sense of humor and love to laugh, while other priests are very serious. Some priests come from big families, and others have only one or two relatives. Some are fit and in good shape, while others have health problems. Some priests are professors and very comfortable in academic settings. Other priests are more comfortable visiting hospitals, working in a soup kitchen, or with homeless people on the street. Some priests are natural leaders and run great meetings. Other priests hate long meetings and tend to defer to others in authority. Some priests are friendly and gregarious and love to work the room. Other priests tend to be shy and loathe cocktail receptions. Some love to pray their office every day, and some have to struggle to concentrate on all the material. You get the drift; priests are actually people. And no two priests are the same.

But all priests do one thing the same, and they all do it every day of their ordained lives. They bring Jesus to the altar in the bread and wine at Mass.

That task, that privilege, that calling, we believe comes from God, and it was established on earth by Christ himself at the Last Supper. Without the consecration at the Mass, we don't have a Catholic Church—no priests, no church. Their function is essential.

First and foremost, a priest administers the sacraments to the people he serves. Priests perform baptisms, hear confessions, do weddings and funerals, and visit the sick. They also do prayer services at wakes, anoint the dying, and prepare their parishioners for the sacraments. Priests proclaim the Gospel and preach the good news from the pulpit.

Priests have many different kinds of occupations. They are teachers, writers, administrators, counselors, and fundraisers. Many are assigned to work in a parish. Parish priests interface most directly and intimately with the people, and they are on the front lines of daily ministry in the Catholic Church.

The apostles—the first bishops—were the first priests. As the bishops (*episkopoi*) established church communities around the Mediterranean, they needed help, and they appointed presbyters to carry out sacramental and pastoral duties. We know this from St. Paul because he addressed them directly in some of his letters. A bishop receives "the fullness of the sacrament of Holy Orders"

(*Catechism of the Catholic Church* (CCC) 1557) and thus becomes a successor of the apostles, those men who were there for the first Eucharistic celebration at the Last Supper. Bishops become "transmitters of the apostolic line."[1] Once a bishop ordains a priest, that priest becomes a coworker of the bishop and shares in the bishop's ministry. Priests do not operate on their own. A priest's ministry is directed by the bishop and in communion with him to whom he has taken a promise of respect and obedience. Priests cannot ordain other priests. Only the bishops can ordain.

We believe that the priesthood was established when Jesus took the bread, said the blessing, and gave it to the apostles to eat. He said, "This is my body." Then He took the cup, gave thanks to God, and gave it to them to drink. He said, "This is my blood of the covenant." (See Mark 14:24.) And this blood would be shed the following day for many, for all of mankind. God was making a new covenant with His people, in the blood of His only Son. And when Jesus says in the Gospels, "do this in memory of me," He is passing on to His followers the practice that has been followed to this day, through the hands and prayers of the priests.

In the Old Testament, in Genesis, the great patriarch-to-be Abram is returning victorious from battle. In chapter 14 Melchizedek appears, the king of (Jeru)Salem. He blesses Abram and offers a sacrifice of bread and wine, and he becomes the first priest figure in the Hebrew scriptures. He becomes a symbol of permanence. Psalm 104 verse 4 says, "Like Melchizedek you are a priest forever." Aaron—the brother of Moses—and his sons were chosen to be priests. From the twelve tribes of Israel, one tribe—the Levites—was designated the priestly tribe. They were to serve the people liturgically and as leaders of prayer.

For Catholics, Christ is the true high priest. In Hebrews 7:15–17 it says "another priest is raised up after the likeness of Melchizedek, who has become so…by the power of a life that cannot be destroyed. For it is testified: 'You are a priest forever according to the order of Melchizadek.'" This passage goes on to say the following:

It was fitting that we should have such a high priest: holy, innocent, undefiled, separated from sinners, higher than the heavens. He has no need, as did the high priests, to offer sacrifice day after day, first for his own sins and then for those of the people; He did that once for all when He offered Himself. For the law appoints men subject to weakness to be high priests, but the word of the oath, which was taken after the law, appoints a son, who has been made perfect forever (Hebrews 7:26–28).

The Catechism states that "The Christian tradition considers Melchizadek, 'priest of God Most High' as a prefiguration of the priesthood of Christ,…holy, blameless, unstained."[2]

Christina: *For someone to want to be a priest in this day and age, there must be a true calling, I mean a real vocation, right?*

A priest is called to serve. That's what a vocation means: a strong impulse, a divine call, to serve God and His people. If a person does not have that true calling, how could he function effectively? How could anyone even attempt a life of priestly service, without a true vocation? A young man who wants to be a priest has to enter into a process and a period of discernment. After years of training, study, prayer, and formation in the seminary, a person is ready to be ordained.

It is a profound call. In 1990 there was a synod of bishops in Rome on the subject of the priesthood, called by John Paul II. Then-Cardinal Joseph Ratzinger gave the opening address. He said that the "essential foundation of priestly ministry is a deep personal bond to Jesus Christ."[3] Everything hinges on this bond. A priest must be a man who knows Jesus intimately, has encountered Him, and has learned to love Him. Ratzinger said that a person simply cannot function in this ministry without strong spiritual substance.

The main purpose of a priest's life is working for another, and it is *He* who truly matters. Cardinal Ratzinger saw the need to present a clear definition of a true priesthood. He said in effect that "there has been confusion and misunderstanding of the priesthood, and the church has not always defended it or explained it to critics properly, but now we must state clearly its essence—what it is now and what it has always been from the beginning." This was over twenty-five years ago, and the future Pope was saying that the recent wave of men who had left the priesthood, combined with a decline in new priestly vocations in many countries, was forcing the church to look deeply within and ask why. Even acknowledging all outside forces working against the priesthood, Ratzinger said that the ministry had become dubious—tainted with doubt from within.

Angela: *The priesthood was in doubt even in the 1980s?*

Yes, not only doubt, but to some extent—like the church itself—the priesthood has always been in crisis. During the Protestant Reformation, Luther referred to Catholic priests as leaders of a cult of worship. Along came the Council of Trent, which ran from 1545 to 1563. Primarily it reasserted that the body and blood, together with the soul and divinity of Christ, are truly, really, and substantially in the Eucharist. But other matters were pressing, with the priesthood a particular concern. The council referred to the clergy as "the dregs" and stated they needed rehabilitation. The bishops would now be held responsible for properly educating the priests, and so special colleges were set up near the bishops. The recruitment of future priests was to concentrate on poor boys who would then be assigned to care for the poor. And there was even a rule needed to prevent bishops and priests from sending their illegitimate sons into the seminaries.

The council called for problem priests to be dismissed. The spiritual life of the priest was legislated. Priests were to celebrate Mass every day, go to confession every month, and assist at the cathedral on major feasts. The number of Masses a priest could say each day was limited to one. These reforms and others held, and by the sixteen hundreds the state of the clergy was said to have improved noticeably. The Council of Trent was a dramatic housecleaning, and it paved the way for continued reform from within the Catholic church. Reform and regeneration are always needed.

Holy Orders is a sacrament, a "sign instituted by Christ to give grace." In all four Gospels, Jesus appears as the bearer of a power received from God, "for He taught them as one having authority" (Mt 7:29). And in John 7:16 Jesus says, "My teaching is not my own, but from the one who sent me." So Jesus has no authority in and of Himself, but only that which comes from the Father.

Likewise, when Jesus confers authority upon the apostles, He makes their office parallel to His own mission. "He who receives you receives Me," He says to the twelve (Mt 10:40). So now we can understand these words: "Amen, amen, I say to you, a son can do nothing on his own" (Jn 5:19), and then to the apostles, "without me, you can do nothing" (Jn 15:5). Having nothing of their own drew the apostles into communion of mission with Christ. A person cannot become a priest by his own declaration. One can receive what is God's only from the sacrament. A person becomes a priest by entering into the mission that makes him the messenger and instrument of Christ Himself. "Through the sacrament of Holy Orders, priests by the anointing of the Holy Spirit are signed with a special character and so are configured to Christ the priest, in such a way that they are able to act in the person of Christ the head."[4]

To act in the person of Christ, a priest must develop a priestly heart. He should be a man of peace. His ministry is to heal, reconcile, and unify his parish. He is to guide with a loving heart—especially the ill, the poor, and the most vulnerable. A priestly heart is no small thing. I have heard many priests say when they stand before the congregation as Mass is beginning and look out over the people, they feel a love for *their* people. Something of the Good Shepherd comes over them, and they feel love for the flock, no matter what shape they're in. This is the reason for their vocation: to bring Christ to His people. That sacred, holy responsibility comes over many a priest at the beginning of Mass and manifests itself in a love for Christ's people.

In the first letter to the Corinthians, Paul writes, "So let us be considered as servants of Christ, and as administrators of the mysteries of God." How else could a man say, "this is My body" or "your sins are forgiven"? Only by emptying himself can a priest become one with Christ, and thus become His true representative.

Jesus Himself often said that He came to serve and not to be served. In John's Gospel (only in John's), we have the beautiful account of the washing of the disciples' feet (Jn 13:1–20). Jesus said to them after He finished, "Do you realize what I have done for you? I have given you a model to follow..." (Jn 13:12, 15).

A priest also shares something else in common with every other priest. At some point, he was called—called to love, to serve, to guide. That calling is something special, to be cherished and revered. Even if, over the years, a priest succumbs to disappointment or cynicism, his vocation is the driving force in his life, and from all the giving, he receives grace for healing and reconciliation. Have you ever felt a quiet joy when you have been able to help someone—when you have touched someone in a way that improves his or her life—however modestly? Think of what it's like to be a priest who has the opportunity to do this every day. A priest touches lives profoundly by blessing, forgiving, consecrating, and anointing.

Priests have a patron saint, St. John Vianney—often referred to as the Curé of Ars—who was a French parish priest born in the eighteenth century. He had a humble beginning, with parents who modeled a pious lifestyle. He left a rural upbringing and pursued an education, which culminated in ordination at the age of thirty. He opened an orphanage and began to minister to the people of his local parish in the aftermath of the French Revolution. Saint John was known for his tender heart and was eventually appointed cure, the minister of souls, in the small French town of Ars. His reputation grew, and over time, tens of thousands of pilgrims traveled to seek his counsel. "I often think that when we come to adore the Lord, we would receive everything we ask for, if we would ask with living faith and with a pure heart."[5] He was made a saint in 1925, and his memorial is celebrated on August 4.

I have heard many newly ordained priests say they were inspired by something early in their life. They may say that their father and mother, or an uncle, was extremely devout, and this made an impression on them. Or they will say that they loved being in the sacristy as an altar boy before Mass, inspired by the silent beauty of the chalice and the soon-to-be consecrated hosts and wine. Something of God touched their heart, often at a young age.

Angela: *It's such a challenging calling. Like, you have to be perfect to be a good priest.*

Hey, they struggle with their vocations, like everyone. They wonder if they should pursue a career in business or engineering or the theatre, like all of us do. They may wonder if marriage and a family life are for them or if this is truly their vocation. That's why they need a long period of discernment, plenty of training, and lots of prayer.

Christina: *Wouldn't it be better for everyone if priests could be married?*

A man who becomes a priest makes a choice; he chooses to accept a call from God. He chooses a life of celibacy, which opens a door. Celibacy is an invitation and opportunity to love and serve more widely all the people he will encounter through his ministry. Yes, celibacy means remaining unmarried and not having children. It means being chaste. And it provides freedom from a call to married and family life, freedom to know, love, and serve all the many families whom he will encounter as a priest.

Christina: *But a whole, entire life of chastity? It seems unrealistic.*

Well, I know married men who practice chastity. "Where," you say? Take a married couple dealing with cancer or any serious disease. Let's say a wife is sick and requires treatment. She's ill for several weeks and then has a difficult surgery, followed by chemo or radiation. She's home convalescing, and her family is taking care of her. Her husband feeds her, cleans her, gets her medicine, and rubs her feet. The last thing on her mind is sex; she might not even be physically capable of sexual relations for a while. What is a husband to do? Care for her and love her, of course. But what about his needs? Well he places them aside to fulfill a promise he made. What would a typical man say? "I gotta have sex at least twice a week?" Really? I don't believe that.

Angela: *Some married men don't keep their vows either.*

I know not all men keep their vows. But a married man has made a promise. He stood up one day in front of all of his friends and family, in a church before a witness and before God, and said, "I promise to love you and honor you, all the days of my life." And so in sickness, he honors his wife and helps her. He subjugates his own needs for months, maybe years.

That's what a priest does. He chooses to love and serve God. He makes a promise and places the needs of his people above his own. Call me naïve, but I believe that a man can meet a woman, fall in love, make a solemn pledge before God and man, and keep that pledge until the end of his life. I am a witness to this, and I know other men who have done this as well. And I believe that a young man can grow up, respond to a vocational call by God, be trained, make a promise before God and man, and keep his promise to the end of his life. And I know priests who have done this.

Christina: *How can a priest understand what it's like to be married, when he himself has never had a wife?*

First, all priests I know have a mother and a father. Many have brothers, sisters, nephews, and nieces. They have families; they don't just fall from the sky. They've seen good marriages, and they've seen neglect, abuse, and divorce. When a priest has married and counseled hundreds of married couples, don't you think he gains insight from hearing the same things over and over? What are the battlegrounds in a marriage: money, sex, the kids? What are the issues: control, selfishness, honesty, respect? Many priests, just like many therapists and counselors, are more than capable of providing the guidance, care, and direction to couples experiencing trouble in their marriage. With such a unique vantage point and perspective on marriage, some priests are excellent advisors and counselors.

It's not easy to be a priest. Look at it from their point of view. When a parish priest looks out over a congregation today, what does he see? Sometimes he sees his church only half filled. Some of the people are not participating in the Mass, not singing, or responding. Sometimes, a priest will look out and see people dozing off during Mass or just not paying attention. Sometimes he will see the faces of people he has never met. He's trying to rouse these people with a message; he has good news! He can't always tell if he's connecting, despite all of his preparation. No matter what, at least a few people will stop after Mass and say to him, "Great sermon, Father!" And others will duck out the side or back exits and say nothing.

In this day and age, priests constantly encounter people who don't know their faith or the meaning of the sacraments. Take the Sacrament of Reconciliation. People are uncomfortable confessing their sins out loud to another person. Confession has become widely misunderstood. Priests don't forgive sins of their own accord or of their own mind. They are acting in the person of Christ, and they are not in the confessional to pass judgment. When you go to confession, you are calling to mind your sins and weaknesses and expressing them to a representative of Christ, who has been given authority to forgive those sins and assign appropriate penance. One time I went to confession, and my penance was to read the Bible—John 13–17, the so-called Last Supper discourses. They were inspirational and of great benefit.

It is a sacrament, again, a sign instituted by Christ to give grace. Can you imagine the things a priest must hear in confession? The smaller things like I was unkind to my sister, I neglected to call my father, or I gossiped about a friend. And the bigger things like I lied, I cheated, I intentionally missed Mass. Then, there are the more complicated issues: I've been seeing someone outside my marriage. I stole a large sum of money from my partner. I haven't spoken to my daughter in over a year. And maybe they hear things like I had an abortion. Priests listen to just about every act a human being can commit in the confessional. They do not and cannot repeat or share with anyone else what they have heard from a particular person. They are ordained to ask for penance and to sacramentally forgive those sins. If the person is truly sorry, says the act of contrition, and does penance, the priest is empowered by Jesus through His church to forgive those sins ("whose sins you shall forgive, they are forgiven") (Jn 20:23). The priest performs an outward sign of God's mercy and forgiveness. A priest's work forces him to rise above or put aside his own human frailties and administer the sacraments in the way he was called and trained to do.

And by the way, if you two haven't been to confession in a long time and have a desire to do so, I can assure you that you will be pleasantly surprised. It is a process of healing and cleansing—a regular opportunity for spiritual renewal. Christ Himself did not condemn sinners, and His priests have not been anointed to condemn or judge.

Having a priest available to administer the sacraments is not something we can demand or take for granted. In some parts of the world, even today, priests are murdered for celebrating Mass. Sometimes they have to travel in secret to reach Christians who wish to receive the Eucharist. Because of the threat of persecution, some people have to wait months, even years, to receive the sacraments of Holy Communion and Confirmation. In this country, even in the face of a declining number of vocations to the priesthood, we lose sight of priests' importance and their value.

Christina: *Dad, the movie* Spotlight *won the Academy Award and brought tons of attention back onto the pedophilia scandal. Do you think the church has adequately dealt with this problem?*

Ok, let's talk about the scandal. We can look at it now from the benefit of hindsight. From accounts by news organizations in print, radio, and television, and from a number of movies, we have all learned of what we now call the priest scandal or the scandal of pedophile priests. No short summary can encompass everything there is to know or end the discussion, nor should it. Let's try to plainly state, in overview form, what took place.

Let us say that roughly between the years 1950 and 1995, some Roman Catholic priests engaged in the sexual abuse of children.

The ages of the children ranged from as young as three years old up to the late teen years (sixteen or seventeen), with the majority between the ages of eleven and fourteen. The abuse took the forms of inappropriate touching, tickling, kissing, sexual intercourse, and sodomy. Some victims held in their feelings of shame and guilt for years before coming forward and telling their story and contacting authorities. Some priests who engaged in this behavior managed to keep it a secret from church authorities and managed to abuse multiple children over a period of years.

As more and more victims came forward with their stories, legal authorities became involved, and charges were filed against some of these priests. As some bishops became aware of claims being made against these priests, they made decisions not to remove those priests from ministry but to relocate those priests to other areas, still in proximity to children, where, we have read, additional abuse of children may have occurred. And even some bishops, who may have engaged in covering up the behavior of their priests, have been relocated to avoid prosecution.

Criminal prosecutions of the abusers have taken place. Some cases span several decades and were brought forward years after the abuse occurred. Civil lawsuits have been brought against the church's dioceses and parishes. Cases have also been brought against some bishops who initially did not report sex-abuse allegations to legal authorities. Hundreds of millions of dollars have been paid out in reparations to the victims of this abuse.

What about the victims? First, when parents place their children in the hands of any authority (and we're talking here about the church), they trust that the authority will protect their children and guide them. No adult should ever harm a child in any way. The victims of abuse by priests have suffered mightily. Not only did they suffer physical abuse, but it is not hard to imagine that they have also been damaged emotionally and psychologically, having been betrayed by adults—religious authorities no less—and having lived for years with feelings of fear, hurt, and shame. We've read that many have depression, anxiety, and thoughts of suicide.

What about the reaction by the Catholic people in the United States to this scandal? The movie *Spotlight* illustrated the way some people initially responded. No one wanted to believe it. Maybe it would blow over. I have spoken to many Catholics over the years, and the response has run the full gamut of emotions. First, there was shock and then outrage. How could they? It is disgraceful. It is wrong, evil. It is mortal sin. That any man abused his vows and abused innocent, young children causes one's skin to crawl and blood to boil. Angry, people demanded an explanation. What about the money? What about these settlements? Then there was more outrage. Covering up? Moving abusers around without reprimand? Like everyone, Catholics want to see what the Pope called a "leprosy in our house" removed. They want the perpetrators brought to justice. And there is a strong sense, finally, that strong corrective measures have been put in place.

What was the worst crime of all? Turning children from God. Having children lose trust and grow up unable to believe in God. Manipulating, deceiving, and exploiting children for one's own pleasure taught people, through this example, not to trust Jesus. We, ourselves, are not allowed to judge, but Jesus had this to say: "Things that cause sin will inevitably occur, but woe to the person through whom they occur. It would be better for him if a millstone were put around his neck and he be thrown into the sea than for him to cause one of these little ones to sin" (Lk 17:1–2).

Pope Francis first met with victims of abuse in July of 2014. One news account described the meeting this way: Francis first greeted six victims—two people each from Ireland, Britain, and Germany—on a Sunday after they arrived at a Vatican guesthouse. On Monday morning, he led them in a private Mass at a Vatican chapel, where he offered a strongly worded homily condemning an abuse scandal that began decades ago. Francis also met with each victim individually in sessions that, in total, lasted more than three hours.

"Before God and His people, I express my sorrow for the sins and grave crimes of clerical sexual abuse committed against you," Francis said during his homily, according to a text released by the Vatican. "And I humbly ask forgiveness. I beg your forgiveness, too, for the sins of omission on the part of church leaders who did not respond adequately to reports of abuse made by family members, as well as by abuse victims themselves." In his homily, Francis also vowed "not to tolerate harm done to a minor by any individual, whether a cleric or not" and declared that bishops would be held accountable for protecting minors. He said the abuse scandals had had "a toxic effect on faith and hope in God."[6]

One of the victims who met the Pope said she had told Francis that the church needed greater accountability, and she would not feel as though progress had been made until bishops who covered up the abuse had been removed. Other victims have said that the Vatican still has done too little to create a strong, accountable system to prevent abuse and to stop bishops from protecting abusive priests by reassigning them to other dioceses or by neglecting to report accusations to the civil authorities. But things have changed.

Most people have now seen that Pope Francis has communicated his sorrow and remorse in a genuine, sincere, and personal way. And he has appointed Cardinal Sean Patrick O'Malley of Boston to head up the Pontifical Commission for the Protection of Minors to continue the process resolving remaining cases of abuse and cover-up and to bring those priests and bishops to justice who have not yet paid for their crimes.

The Vatican has placed some bishops under house arrest as they await criminal trial. At the direction of Pope Francis, there are now canonical courts investigating charges of sexual abuse and cover-ups by bishops in the United States, Latin America, and Western Europe. And some bishops have now been laicized (removed) from the clerical state and deprived of all rights and duties associated with being a priest. As late as September of 2016, Pope Francis has appointed a college of jurists who will help the Pope decide whether to remove a bishop from office for failing to protect minors and vulnerable adults from sex abuse.

Pope John Paul II acknowledged abuses, met with victims, and asked for forgiveness. But not enough was done during his time to root out perpetrators. Pope Benedict XVI met with numerous groups of abuse victims, and he called for a zero-tolerance policy. He moved aggressively to weed abusers out of the priesthood. In his final two years alone, he removed over four hundred priests. But the stories of unresolved cases involving bishops continued, which is why Pope Francis continues to address the problem. And we know that this is not just a crisis that occurred in the United States; Ireland, Latin America, and Africa—indeed all corners of the earth—have been scarred by this abuse and by this scandal.

Is it behind us? Three popes have asked for forgiveness and dioceses have paid out hundreds of millions of dollars in settlements. Many of the abusers have been punished, laicized, and have died from old age. Bishops are still being tried and punished. As late as 2016, the Archdiocese of New York initiated a program to provide compensation to victim-survivors of sexual abuse by clergy. Cardinal Dolan asked the famed mediator Kenneth Feinberg to oversee the program, which he hopes will serve as a "tangible sign of the Church's outreach and reparation."[7] However slowly, the church has moved to remove this sin from its midst. New bishops and new priests have been ordained and now live in a church with zero toleration for anyone who does not protect minors.

Every hint of impropriety is now reported, and should be, and many people regard the scandal as a stain and a sin that will never end and can never be forgiven. No reparation will ever be enough to satisfy them. The church needs to be ever-vigilant in making sure this sin is avoided, both now and forever. We have the ideals, and we've taken the vows, now we have to do the work.

So, let us paraphrase a question in the Bible: "How many times must I ask my brother for forgiveness? Seven times?" The answer is probably "no, seventy times seven times." Even after fifteen to twenty years of attempting to heal, we must continue to beg for forgiveness as a church, just as we are called to constantly forgive others. In a sense, the scandal has brought the church to its knees, and that's not a bad place to be for a church that seeks to guide its people to eternal life with God.

Angela: *After all of this, why didn't the Catholic people just walk out? If people were so reviled by the scandal, why didn't they just withhold their offerings, stop going to Mass, and just leave?*

Some, maybe many, have left, and that's painful and sad. But we remember that all Catholics are sinners. And we acknowledge this at every Mass when the priest begins with "let us call to mind our sins." And later, when we stand during the consecration to recite the Lord's Prayer, we say to God the Father, "Forgive us our trespasses, as we forgive those who trespass against us." And just before Holy Communion, we all say, "Lord, I am not worthy that you should enter under my roof." We try to acknowledge our weakness before God and then receive His power, strength, and grace. We acknowledge our weakness before Him who makes us strong. We acknowledge our sins so that we can better understand the meaning of the cross; Jesus is the Lamb of God, who takes away our sins—the sins of the whole world—by emptying himself on the cross so that the world might be saved through Him.

The church has been built on a rock, and the gates of hell will not prevail against it—either from without or within. The priest scandal and the cover-up did not and will not destroy the church.

We have to remind ourselves that most priests are good. Statistics around the scandal vary widely, but the highest estimation of the percentage of priests who have engaged in criminal behavior I have read anywhere is 4 percent (*Spotlight* claimed 6 percent in the 1990s in New England). Even if you allow, for the sake of discussion, that another 4 percent may have engaged in scandalous behavior, but were never accused, you still have over 90 percent of all priests who have done nothing wrong. That is hard to believe for some people, and if you find it hard to believe, ask yourself, do you know any priests personally? If you do know a priest personally, and you have observed firsthand what dedicated priestly service looks like, you can get a sense for what it might feel like to be thrown in with a group of sexual predators who succumbed to the worst kind of sinfulness and who abused the sacrament of Holy Orders.

Christina: *Dad, what about women priests—or at least women deacons?*

Cardinal Sean O'Malley of Boston was asked about this in an interview on *60 Minutes* in November of 2014. In effect he said if we each started our own church, it might look different from the one we now have. But the one we now have was established by Christ on earth, and the Magisterium does not make changes based on changes in society. Jesus interacted with women in the gospels (Martha, Mary, the woman at the well, the woman caught in adultery) and did not ordain them. Pope Francis was recently asked by reporters on a plane about the subject, and he said, "Pope St. John Paul II had the last clear word on this, and it stands, this stands."[8] He was referring to the Apostolic Letter issued by the Pope in May of 1994, in which it was stated the "The Church has no authority whatsoever to confer priestly ordination on women." ⁹ So the subject of "women priests" is not open for consideration and is not being discussed.

As for deacons, that might be different. As you know, Pope Francis has been willing to form a commission to discuss and consider it. Let's see what happens. There are many experienced, intelligent women assuming prominent roles in the church and serving as role models for younger women. They now serve as presidents of parish councils, heads of various charities, and advisors to bishops. The Pope himself is advised by a woman. I know brilliant women who would make great preachers.

Since Vatican II, there has been a revival of the permanent diaconate in the Catholic Church. Deacons go all the way back to the early church and are mentioned in the Acts of the Apostles, but the order went into decline in the Middle Ages. As of now married men who are called by God to serve the church can enter into a period of discernment and pursue their vocation at a seminary. After four and one-half years of training, and with the written approval of their wife and their bishop, they can be ordained as ministers of the church, through the sacrament of Holy Orders. Deacons do not and cannot replace priests. The bishop assigns them to serve in a parish, and they serve that pastor and his community in whatever capacity is needed. Deacons come from all different professional backgrounds and bring a variety of skills and expertise. They can be of great help to a priest by offering help in the areas of law, finance, real estate, construction, and human resources. They can also, in the absence of a priest, perform baptisms, weddings, and wake services, allowing the priest to focus on the essential duties of Mass and the sacraments. They cannot consecrate the Eucharist at Mass, hear confessions, or anoint the sick (which includes the forgiveness of sin), but they can do much work to help the parish and the people of God.

In 1985 there were just over seven thousand permanent deacons in the United States, but as of 2016 there are over seventeen thousand. That's a growing population of clerics trained to support and help the thirty-eight thousand priests we currently have in the United States. A typical configuration of clergy in a parish could feature one priest and two deacons or, in a larger parish, two priests and three or four deacons, with a lay administrator in charge of religious education. If the permanent deaconate is filling parishes with people who have strong marriages, real-life work experience, and a true desire to serve God and His people, then it will provide the muscle and hope to sustain the regeneration and growth of the Catholic Church in the United States, as well as helping the priests.

If I'm not mistaken, a lay person can perform most if not all the duties of a deacon. And if the Pope is willing to discuss women as deacons, all we can do now is pray that the Holy Spirit will continue to guide the church in its consideration of this matter.

As for the priesthood today, it's good to ask what can be done to strengthen the ministry, and the quality of the vocation itself, here in the United States.

As I said earlier, an end to celibacy is not a solution. First of all, we already have married priests in the Roman Catholic Church. Members of the Anglican Church who were married as priests and then converted to Catholicism do exist. But do you think that because a man takes a vow of chastity he is inclined to lose his mind and begin sexually abusing young boys? Pedophilia is an aberration, an illness, and is not caused by celibacy. And you don't hear priests themselves calling for the end of celibacy.

Look, marriage is a huge commitment—a vocation itself, a lifetime promise. Merging the two vocations might cause more problems than it solves. I've been married for over twenty-eight years, and I can tell you, it's not as easy as it looks! It's a full-time job. Balancing kids, work, and marital relations requires a commitment and includes compromises. You make many compromises to maintain equilibrium. Outside commitments have to be carefully considered. Can't you just see a married priest, after telling his wife his plans for the evening, "Another wake? That's the fourth one this week! When are you gonna start spending more time with your family?" And which commitment takes precedence: a sick son or daughter at home or an anointing across town?

No, I have two more practical suggestions that would bolster the well-being of the priesthood, and neither one is new. The first has to do with the training and is being done already: after full criminal background checks have been completed, all applicants should be interviewed about their dating history and sexual orientation. Another course or two in the seminary should be included, maybe in the final year. Call it "Human Sexuality—Your Body" or "The Arc of Desire/Puberty to Old Age"—whatever. Bring in experts, discuss these thing openly, ask healthy, celibate priests to share their experiences. Prepare seminarians for what they will hear and see out in the real world. Show them what pornography looks like and discuss sexual addictions. Don't turn away from it; look it in the eye! Remind these young men to be careful about counseling women in private. Teach them that they must always have another adult present when counseling children, and so forth. Help them to recognize temptation and to be vigilant in avoiding occasions of sin, and tell them the consequences of aberrant behavior: you will lose your ministry and be subject to arrest! Make the seminary the solution to the problem. Teach them and help them to lead healthy lives in the community of the people they have been called to serve, and introduce them to example-setting priests who successfully lead celibate lives.

Second, let's avoid isolating parish priests—no more living alone in a rectory. A parish priest can say Mass, go to work, and then have dinner with other priests or clergy. Require a minimum level of social interaction, so priests can bounce things off different people and hear different points of view. With more social interaction, priests can hold each other accountable. "So, Bill, how was your evening?" Make sure they check in with their vicar of clergy at least every couple of weeks, and have them hear from their bishop more regularly. A lot of this is being done already. Let's do it where it's not being done.

Since the number of practicing Catholic families has been in decline for two generations now, the number of vocations to the priesthood has been in decline. Let's remember that vocations come from God. They can arise from anywhere, in any person, even from the depths of misery or despair. Can't God choose who He wants to serve His people? So, it is a necessary and worthy task to continue to pray to God for vocations to the priesthood.

It's easy for a priest to feel discouraged, with everything always seeming like an uphill climb. Once again, Cardinal Ratzinger addressed this at the synod. He said a priest does not need to worry or bother about himself and his own achievements. He must leave the outcome of his work to the Lord, doing his work without anxiety, maintaining a cheerful countenance in spreading the Gospel of Christ. He said, "If priests today [1990] so often feel overworked, tired, and frustrated, the blame lies with a strained pursuit of results."[10] It's good advice for all of us. Do the work, and leave the outcome to God.

In his "Letter of the Holy Father to Priests for Holy Thursday 2002," John Paul II wrote this:

Dear Priests! Know that I am especially close to you as you gather with your bishops this year 2002. At this time, as priests, we are personally and profoundly afflicted by the sins of some of our brothers who have betrayed the grace of ordination. Grave scandal is caused, with the result that a dark shadow of suspicion is cast over all the other fine priests who perform their ministry with honesty and integrity and often with heroic self-sacrifice. As the church shows her concern for the victims, and tries to respond in truth and justice to each of these painful situations, all of us are called to embrace the "The Mystery of the Cross" and to commit ourselves more fully to the search for holiness. We must beg God in His Providence to prompt a whole-hearted reawakening of those ideals of total self-giving to Christ, which are the very foundation of the priestly ministry.[11]

So we still have our Mass, and we still have our priests. Psychologists will tell us that with all the skill and experience we have in the area of psychiatry, with all the ability we have in treating mental illness, anxiety, depression, and low self-esteem, we still do not have the power to place hope in someone's heart. That can only come from within each person and through connection to a higher power. And in a similar way, we cannot place a vocation to serve God into a person's heart.

A vocation must come from God. And if God does place a vocation to serve into a person's heart, our job is to do everything we can to nurture that vocation. A young person with a vocation needs our support. When a person is called by God and accepts the call, he accepts that his journey will require years of spiritual development and formation.

All Catholics have a role to play in bolstering the priesthood and in nurturing the development of more good priests. We should pray for vocations and encourage those who receive them. And when young men are finally ordained to the priesthood and set out to serve God, we should support them, encourage them, help them, and love them—really, love them.

Endnotes

1   *Catechism of the Catholic Church* (Liguori, MO: Liguori Publications, 1994), 1555.

2   Ibid., 1544.

3   Cardinal Josef Ratzinger, *On the Nature of the Priesthood*, Synod of Bishops, October 1, 1990.

4   *Catechism of the Catholic Church*, 1563.

5   Beloved Saint John Marie Vianney Quotes, http://www.how-to-pray-the-rosary-everyday.com/saint-john-marie-vianney-quotes.html.

6   Jim Yardley, "Pope Francis Asks Forgiveness from Victims of Sex Abuse," *The New York Times*, July 7, 2014.

7   John Woods, "Archdiocese Opens Independent Reconciliation, Compensation Program for Abuse Victims," *Catholic New York*, October 13, 2016.

8   Laurie Goodstein, "Pope Francis Says Ban on Female Priests Is Likely to Endure," *The New York Times*, November 1, 2016.

9   Pope St. John Paul II, Ordinatio Sacerdotalis, May 22, 1994, https://w2.vatican.va/content/john-paul-ii/en/apost_letters/1994/documents/hf_jp-ii_apl_19940522_ordinatio-sacerdotalis.html.

10 Cardinal Josef Ratzinger *On the Nature of the Priesthood*, Synod of Bishops, October 1, 1990.

11 *Letter of The Holy Father Pope John Paul II To Priests For Holy Thursday 2002*, Section 11 https://w2.vatican.va/content/john-paul-ii/en/letters/2002/documents/hf_jp-ii_let_20020321_priests-holy-thursday.html.

CHAPTER 6

The Jews

§

SINCE WE'VE BEEN TALKING IN this book about Jewish prophets, Jesus and the Bible, the practice of praying the hours, and the importance of the Old Testament, it makes sense to consider the relationship between Catholics and Jews.

Something great has actually happened: a major shift, a miracle really, a reconciliation of two great peoples. But you might not have heard about it on social media or in the secular press. In fact, it's been widely ignored and widely unappreciated. Here's the headline: a true and loving peace has broken out between Catholics and Jews!

Why would this matter? Well, we are talking about two of the great religions of the world. Whether people are excited about this or not, it certainly pertains to or involves a large percentage—and an important part—of the American population. American Jews still have a distinct Jewish identity in this country. When asked in a recent survey, "How important is being Jewish in your life, if at all?" Forty-four percent of Jewish respondents said "very important," and 35 percent said, "somewhat Important." On the question, "On Yom Kippur do you usually fast at least part of the day?" Fifty-five percent answered affirmatively.[1] We know that Jewishness is both an ethnicity and a religion, and in this chapter I'm referring to Orthodox, Conservative, and Reform Jews as one large group. There are about

6.7 million Jews in America today (2.2 percent of the US population), with over half (55 percent) living in four states: New York, California, Florida, and New Jersey.[2] People still very much identify themselves as Jewish culturally, although how many Jews are knowledgeable about their faith, not just their culture, is unclear. In any case, being Jewish is still important to almost 80 percent of Jews in America today.

There is also still a strong Catholic identity in America. Despite the increase in the number of former Catholics, even nonchurchgoing Catholics still identify themselves by their religion and make their way to church on Ash Wednesday and Easter Sunday. They think of themselves as Catholic.

Over the last fifty years, since Vatican Council II, interreligious outreach has been encouraged, and progress has been made. The bond between Catholics and Jews is unique, long-standing, and complicated. Any functioning Christian today should know something about this relationship to understand the richness of his or her own faith and for a better appreciation for the world in which we now live.

You guys have read and heard all about the horrors of World War II, and about the extermination of six million Jews in the holocaust. Sadly, anti-Semitism is alive and well today. A recent survey by an international organization determined that anti-Semitism around the world is still on the rise. Not anti-Israel sentiment but old-fashioned Jew hating. The survey revealed a lower level of hostility in Britain and the United States, but overall internationally, resentment toward Jews is increasing. The threat of a nuclear Iran, the rise of ISIS, and continued calls for extermination have kept worldwide attention on Israel, its security, and its ability to survive. A fresh example of anti-Semitism was unleashed as recently as 2014 when the Israeli army was sent into Gaza in response to Hamas activity. Anti-Israeli demonstrations broke out all over Western Europe. The news coverage revealed a level of vitriol and hatred that hadn't been seen in fifty years or more. The *New York Post* editorial board wrote this:

> The demonstrators are ostensibly protesting Israel's ground operation in Gaza, but the stink of anti-Semitism hangs over so much of what is happening. In Paris, for example, eight synagogues have been targeted in the past week alone. Other targets included Jewish-owned stores and kosher butcher shops. In Berlin and other German cities last week, mobs draped in Palestinian flags defaced synagogues to cries of "Hamas, Hamas, Jews to the gas." Said the head of the German Jewish community Monday: "Never in our lives did we believe it possible that anti-Semitism of the most primitive kind would [again] be heard on the streets of Germany." Even in Britain, where demonstrations were not as violent, a group of protesters drove through a heavily Jewish neighborhood shouting, "Heil Hitler."[3]

As a teenager on Long Island in the early 1960s, I didn't know much about the Jewish faith. In Catholic school we were aware that the public schools were always closing for the Jewish holidays, but I didn't know the meaning or significance of them. I awoke in 1965.

The baseball World Series was approaching, and I was psyched. The Dodgers had won the pennant for the second time in three years, and the Series was to start against the Twins in Minnesota. The Dodgers team had great pitching and good defense, and I was rooting for them. Actually, your grandfather and his brothers, my uncles, had been insane Brooklyn Dodger fans, but when the team left for LA, all our loyalties shifted to the Mets. The Mets were not good yet, so I continued to follow the Dodgers. I was thirteen, and Sandy Koufax and Maury Wills were my favorite players.

When the starting pitchers were announced for Game 1, something was wrong. Koufax wasn't starting. He had informed the team that he could not start that day because of religious observance. The best pitcher in baseball would not play in the first game of the World Series because it fell on something called Yom Kippur. I couldn't believe it, and it made an impression on me. I thought it must be really important if Sandy wasn't going to pitch on that day.

I learned, of course, that Yom Kippur was the Day of Atonement, the holiest day in the Jewish calendar, and I've read that countless young Jewish baseball fans never forgot the significance of that decision.

That same month, October 1965, was significant for another reason. On October 28, over in Rome, the Second Vatican Council issued one of sixteen major documents that would define the Catholic Church for the next fifty years. This one was called Nostra Aetate (In Our Time). It said that the Catholic Church rejects nothing that is true and holy in non-Christian religions, called for an end to anti-Semitism, and said any discrimination based on race, color, religion, or condition of life is foreign to the mind of Christ. It would mark a new era of understanding between Catholics and Jews.

Why have Jews had such a hard time throughout history? The story of hostility toward the Jewish people has been recorded by historians in every age. The Egyptians held the Jewish people in slavery over two and a half millennia ago. For centuries Jews were mistrusted and mistreated. But the Jews believed that they were chosen. They were the descendants of Abraham, Isaac, and Jacob, and after many years of waiting, God led them out of the bondage of slavery under the guidance of Moses and Joshua into a land flowing with milk and honey. For a time, they fought off their enemies and enjoyed a level of peace under their own kings—including David, the warrior king, and his son Solomon, who ruled with wisdom during a brief interlude of affluence.

The Romans were more tolerant and allowed the Jews to keep their temple and conduct their religious practices. But the Jews had no political or military power and were subject to abuse and arrest if they transgressed Roman law.

Jesus Himself was from the house of David. He knew about the captivity, about the persecution of His people, and about the great Exodus story. He grew up following Jewish practices, He quoted the Jewish prophets and the Psalms, and He told people to follow the commandments of Moses. Those followers of Jesus who were Jewish began to separate and become Christians alongside non-Jewish Christians. These new Christians had to work out their own differences, and at the first Council of Jerusalem, Peter and Paul led the debate. Peter believed at first that the followers of Jesus should be circumcised according to Jewish law, but Paul (himself a Jew from Tarsus) argued that the main requirement was a new and lively faith. Some of this is recounted in the New Testament, in the Acts of the Apostles, where you can trace the growth of this new community of Christians.

But the rise of Christianity presented the Jews with a new adversary, and a new, more complicated relationship began. As Paul and his followers were spreading the Christian message, the church began to grow, and the four Gospels were written and also disseminated. It was not safe in many places—particularly in Rome—to be Christian, and Christians learned what it meant to suffer persecution. The fourth Gospel, the Gospel According to John, was written roughly around AD 100, and it's an important part of the story. Remember what I said earlier about the Christian evangelists? They all had the same agenda: that their readers would come to know and follow this Jesus, Who had been killed, but Who had risen from death. The three synoptic Gospels share similar accounts of preaching, healing, suffering, and rising. The fourth Gospel, the Gospel

According to John, was written later, and in it, Jesus speaks at length about His own identity and His relationship with God.

When you read the Gospel According to John, there is a steady and almost chronic reference to the Jews. Over and over, we read "for fear of the Jews," or "because of the Jews"—the Jews, the Jews, the Jews. After a while, to the untrained ear, it begins to take on an *anti* flavor. Did this contribute to anti-Semitism? Did a harsh, dismissive, repetitious reference to "the Jews" in a written work read by Christ's followers and distributed widely throughout the spreading Mediterranean community contribute to a fresh, new wave of anti-Jewish or anti-Semitic thought? Maybe. Jewish wariness and distrust would certainly be understandable.

In all the Passion narratives, the Jews are the ones who have Jesus arrested and tried by the Romans, and that's where the notion of "Christ killers" came from. But that notion was wrong. It was wrong then, and it is wrong now. Bible scholars tell us that when John makes reference to "the Jews," he is referring to everyone who was opposed to Jesus, of all different stripes. Nicodemus and Joseph of Arimathea were Jews and were sympathetic to Jesus. John's Gospel is referring to anyone in Jerusalem during the Passion, death, and resurrection of Jesus who wanted to harm Him and His followers. That's it. It was a collective term—not an accusation. It was misunderstood and misappropriated by some Gospel hearers who did not understand the meaning of the cross and did not accept the Christian imperative to love. But it probably lent itself, or fed into, hatred for the Jews.

The Romans destroyed the Second Jewish Temple in AD 70, and within a couple of hundred years, a Christian—Constantine—became the Emperor of Rome. He wanted those in his kingdom to be baptized, and become Christians. The Jews, who did not accept Jesus as Messiah, were once again at odds with those who had political and military power. The Jews—often viewed as money collectors and the killers of Christ—would be at odds with every culture, and their misery would continue for centuries.

I'm not capable of capturing a full Jewish history here, but their story is consistent. Scholars tell us that in Europe serious problems would continue. The Jews were expelled from England in 1290 and from France in 1306. In the mid-thirteen hundreds, Jews were suspected of spreading the Black Death. In Spain in the late thirteen hundreds, the archdeacon of Seville led an assault on a Jewish ghetto and tore down synagogues. Acts of violence were repeated in Valencia, and from 1412 to 1414 the preaching of Dominican Vincent Ferrer touched off rioting directed at Jews.

Throughout the fourteen hundreds Jews were expelled from places like Vienna and Linz, Cologne, Bavaria, Perugia, and all of Tuscany. The church often tried to help. One pope, Nicholas II, wrote a bull, denouncing exclusion of Jews and Christians from political office based on race, and later, Pope Sixtus IV had the Spanish ambassador to the papal court arrested, insisting that Jews be allowed to have legal counsel in their struggle to maintain their homes and businesses. But the Spanish Inquisition continued, and in 1492, King Ferdinand signed a decree requiring all Jews to convert or leave the country.

Jews were not allowed back in England until 1656, under the rule of Oliver Cromwell. By then Jews were being portrayed in society and on the stage as deceitful and greedy, like the wicked Jewish villain Barabbas in the Christopher Marlowe play, *The Jew of Malta*. And proponents of anti-Semitism used the character Shylock—from Shakespeare's play, the *Merchant of Venice*—to fuel the depiction of Jews as moneyed and lecherous outsiders.

Anti-Semitism spread throughout Europe and made its way to the United States. Even when hardworking Jewish immigrants achieved success in the United States, they were still reviled and mistrusted.

Some were Eastern European Yiddish speaking immigrants with keen minds and great determination, and they found their way into influential positions in newspapers, theatre, and movie-making, swiftly having a great impact on the American culture. People with names like Selznick, Mayer, and Goldwyn produced wonderful images of romance and heroism. Despite entertaining millions, Jews were still called controllers of money, and by the 1930s they would be accused of controlling something else—Hollywood.

The Holocaust marked Jewish history forever and had a direct impact on the relationship between Catholics and Jews. Jewish historians and other scholars can correct me on some of this, but it seems clear that beginning with World War II, the perception of Jews by non-Jews slowly but surely began to change.

During the course of World War II, all Americans were brought together through the war effort. Catholics and Jews fought alongside one another. Everyone was involved, and the country was largely united to defeat the Germans and Japanese and to turn back the evil of Nazism and totalitarianism. When the long, horrible war ended, news of great atrocities were revealed, and we now know that the Nazi regime was responsible for up to ten million executions—more than six million of them Jews. The victorious Americans who had been united in their effort were, generally speaking, united in their horror at the Holocaust. Six million Jews exterminated?

American Catholics, like all Americans, now had a different perspective on the Jewish experience. They could now see and hear from fellow Americans whose families were hated and killed in Germany and Poland. They could begin to glimpse the suffering of innocent people, killed just because they were Jewish. Within eight to ten years after the War, the story of the Jewish Holocaust was being widely expressed and shared. Art, literature, and stories of the destruction and survival were everywhere in the 1950s and '60s.

The Pawnbroker, The Diary of Anne Frank, Judgement at Nuremberg, and many other reflections on the Shoah—in books and on television—increased sensitivity to the Jewish experience of rejection and suffering. In the 1970s a miniseries appeared on national television called *The Holocaust,* and later still, more movies like *Sophie's Choice* and *Schindler's List* were made.

In a sense, Catholics could make a real-life connection to the suffering of the Old Testament Hebrew slaves in their Bible—the descendants of Abraham, Isaac, and Jacob. Jesus came to take on the sins of the world, and the world was filled with evil. Hitler was evil, and Jews were victims.

In addition to real empathy, a sense of affection also began to develop. The music of Al Jolson, Irving Berlin and George Gershwin was popular before the war, but now more Jewish entertainment was coming into American homes through television. American Catholics didn't just watch sermons by Fulton Sheen. They were also entertained by Milton Berle, Sid Caesar, Jack Benny, Mel Brooks, Carl Reiner, Myron Cohen, Neil Simon, Alan King, and Woody Allen—talented artists who made people laugh and think. Jews were smart and funny. Many people had Jewish doctors or dentists, and a more trusting rapport evolved. Although affluent Jews had to start their own country clubs because of discrimination, overt anti-Semitism was less and less in vogue. Since World War II, Catholics and Jews have entertained each other, served in the military together, gone into business together, taught each other, married each other, and cried at each other's funerals.

By the early 1960s, there was still racism and anti-Semitism, and the Civil Rights Movement was well under way. It was in 1963 that Martin Luther King Jr. would make his "I Have a Dream" speech in Washington DC. Many Catholics and Jews joined the movement. What did Vatican Council II do to advance the story?

Here's how I would tell it. After the death of Pius XII in 1958, Angelo Roncalli became Pope John XXIII, and within three months he announced his intention to call for a great council. The purpose of the council would be aggiornamento, an updating or modernizing of the church. Pope John wanted to open the windows of the church and let the fresh air of wisdom flow through, the wisdom of the Holy Spirit. The meetings would take place in the great basilica of St. Peter's Church. Eighty-five cardinals, eight patriarchs, 533 archbishops, 2,131 bishops, twenty-six abbots, and sixty-eight superiors-general of various religious orders were invited to participate. They were to take on the great issues facing the church, a little more than ninety years after the First Vatican Council.

Also invited were over one hundred observers and guests, religious leaders from other churches around the world. These observers had the best seats in the house, nearer to the president's table than even the cardinals. They were intellectuals and theologians from around the world. The Pope and the council fathers wanted input from across the theological spectrum, and some of the best minds of the time were there. One of the guests was a representative of American Jews, Abraham Joshua Heschel. People forget that Jewish periti (experts) attended the council.

Rabbi Heschel was a widely read Jewish theologian, whose works included *God in Search of Man* and *The Prophets*, both of which attracted the attention of Catholic theologians and biblicists. In his own writings, Heschel advanced the idea that religious experience is fundamentally a human impulse, not just a Jewish one. He believed, and stated clearly, that no religious community could claim a monopoly on religious truth.

His main message to the council was something like this, and I'm paraphrasing: "Stop missionizing the Jewish people. Please stop trying to convert Jews. We cannot be friends if the basis of our relationship is a conversion to faith in Jesus Christ. Please respect us, and please refrain from using language in your liturgy that is demeaning to our faith traditions." Through dialogue and debate, he attempted to influence the council to modify references in the Catholic liturgy that demeaned Jews or that referred to an expected conversion to Christianity. One of the bishops at the council was from Poland, and during the council he would be named the Archbishop of Krakow. Archbishop Wojtyla—who was to become Pope John Paul II—was listening.

Pope John Paul II lived through the Holocaust and grew up in the vibrant and prospering Jewish community of Wadowice in Poland. The papal biographer George Weigel wrote of how the young Karol Wojtyla saw and felt the fear and pain of anti-Semitism in war-torn Poland. He had both a real life experience with Jews and a pastoral understanding that reconciliation would require respect and acknowledgment. Bishop Wojtyla and other council fathers worked behind the scenes to make changes in the liturgy that would reflect respect for the Jewish people.

Fifty years later, in 2014, Timothy Cardinal Dolan of New York spoke at the Jewish Theological Seminary in New York and said, "The brave fathers of the council, aided by Jewish experts, could never have envisioned such success five decades ago. The friendship between us, I feel, has never been stronger."[4]

Cardinal Dolan is the Catholic co-chair of the church's dialogue with the National Council of Synagogues and is a strong force in promoting dialogue and goodwill between the church and the Jewish community. Nostra Aetate was a concrete starting point for a long and continuous dialogue between the two great religious traditions. Finally, a process was underway for the healing of one of humanity's deepest wounds.

Angela: *What wounds? What liturgical language was Rabbi Heschel referring to?*

One lingering issue was the prayers used on Good Friday that referred to the Jews. Every Good Friday, in every Catholic Church around the world, there is a celebration of the Passion of Jesus Christ. It includes an important reading from the Bible, solemn intercessions—which are the prayers of the church for the whole world—and veneration or adoration of the cross.

In the Bible the Passion narrative in the Gospel According to John, mentioned earlier, is either read or sung by whole congregations. It is a moment of great reverence and devotion. The focus of attention during this ritual is the act of love expressed in the suffering and dying of Jesus on the cross.

Then, the church prays. It prays for the whole church, for the Pope, for all the bishops and clergy, for those studying for the faith (the catechumens), for the unity of Christians, and then for the Jewish people. Now, before 1962 the language in the prayer asked that *perfidis Judaeis* might be converted to "the truth." The Latin meaning of the word *perfidis* is "unbelieving." So Catholics were praying for Jews who remained unbelieving in the Messiah. But over the centuries, the word *perfidis* (perfidious) acquired the sense of, and was defined as, "treacherous" or "deceitful." That's what Rabbi Heschel referred to as demeaning to Jews. Words matter, and Pope Paul VI approved the changing of these words, which could surely be said to be misguided and hurtful. All language in the Catholic liturgy which could hint at anti-Semitism was reevaluated and has been removed.

Nostra Aetate stated: "Furthermore, in her rejection of every persecution against any man, the church, mindful of the patrimony (inheritance) she shares with the Jews, and moved not by political reasons but by the Gospel's spiritual love, decries hatred, persecutions, displays of anti-Semitism, directed against Jews at any time and by anyone."[5]

Vatican Council II, in all its work, was affirming its belief to all Catholics that to be anti-Semitic was to be anti-Catholic. You cannot be a lover of Jesus and hate Jews.

Fast forward to March 2000. Throughout his papacy, John Paul II had continued his efforts to reconcile the differences between Catholics and Jews. He was the first Pope to visit the Nazi death camps at Auschwitz and the first to attend services at a Roman synagogue. He opened up diplomatic relations between Israel and the Holy See, and in 2000 he met personally with Israeli's political leaders and chief rabbis. On this historic five-day trip, he visited a famous memorial to Holocaust victims and said these words:

> I have come to Yad Vashem to pay homage to the millions of Jewish people who, stripped of everything, especially of their human dignity, were murdered in the Holocaust. Men, women, children cry out to us from the depths of the horror that they knew. How can we fail to heed their cry? No one can forget or ignore what happened. We wish to remember. But we wish to remember for a purpose, namely to ensure that never again will evil prevail as it did for the millions of innocent victims of Nazism.
>
> As bishop of Rome, and successor of the Apostle Peter, I assure the Jewish people that the Catholic Church, motivated by the Gospel law of truth and love and by no political considerations, is deeply saddened by the hatred, acts of persecution and displays of anti-Semitism directed against the Jews by Christians at any time and in any place.[6]

On this pilgrimage he also visited the Western Wall in Jerusalem and offered a prayer. You may remember the images, broadcast around the world, of the now-aging pope quietly placing a note between the stones of the Wall.

"God of our fathers, You chose Abraham and his descendants to bring Your Name to the Nations: we are deeply saddened by the behavior of those who in the course of history have caused these children of Yours to suffer and ask Your forgiveness; we wish to commit ourselves to genuine brotherhood with the people of the covenant."

The wording of the prayer was highly significant, especially to Jewish ears. The Pope referred to the Jews as "the people of the covenant." Had any pope ever uttered these words before? According to Yossi Klein Halevi, an Israeli journalist, no one could recall at any other time in history when a Catholic leader—no less, a pope—had endorsed the notion that two parallel covenants could coexist: one for Christians and one for Jews. If God's covenant with the Jews has never been revoked, then the survival of the Jewish people as an independent entity must be part of His plan.[7] Catholics could plausibly say, "Maybe the role of Jews in history is to be a sign for God's presence in this world!"

Even as the church repudiated anti-Semitism and begged God for forgiveness on Israeli soil, not all Jews were, or are, moved. "Maybe the church is still trying to convert us," they say, "through love now instead of brutality." As Halevi says, "Rather than celebrate one of the great Jewish victories in the post-Holocaust era, many Jews continue to cling to an archaic perception of the church as enemy." And so books still circulate like *A Moral Reckoning: The Role of the Catholic Church in the Holocaust* and *It's Unfulfilled Duty of Repair,* by Daniel Jonah Goldhagen, and *The Popes Against the Jews,* by David Kertzer.

Angela: *Right, don't Jews still blame Pius XII for not helping during World War II?*

Yes, the criticisms of Pope Pius XII have been a nagging issue for years, centered on this question: did Pius do enough to help the Jews during the Holocaust? This story has been around now since the end of World War II, and every time so-called new evidence is uncovered, it gains momentum, and is happily carried by mainstream media.

Pius XII reigned from 1939 to 1958. The story is that, as Cardinal Eugenio Pacelli, he served his predecessor as secretary of state and in 1933, negotiated a treaty with German dictator Adolf Hitler, known as the Reich Concordat. The agreement essentially said Hitler would allow the Vatican to maintain a measure of religious control over the churches in Germany in exchange for German Catholics staying out of politics. The result was that German Catholics (and later Catholics in other occupied countries) who might have protested Hitler's policies remained silent at the Vatican's instructions. Hitler saw the agreement as "particularly significant in the developing struggle against international Jewry."[8]

This is an argument from the past, and I may be leaving something out, but here's what we can say: The Pope's defenders point out that Pius XII was not indifferent to the Jews' plight; he did not speak out because he was convinced it would make matters worse. Quietly, he took measures to save Jews. Father Pierre Blet, a Catholic scholar who spent fifteen years examining documents relating to the period, maintained that "the public silence was the cover for secret activity through Vatican embassies and bishops to try to stop the deportations." Father Blet clearly refutes the suggestion that Pius XII was in any way a Nazi sympathizer. There is a documentary that sets forth an explanation of the Pope's mind-set and activities during this period.

Can we all agree that the Pope was in a ridiculously difficult situation? With no standing army or physical defense, he had to guide the church through the rise of fascism in Italy, the onslaught of the Nazi regime, and the outbreak of a war fought in countries populated by Catholics. How far did his political influence extend, and at what point would it have helped to denounce Hitler publicly? Can we say at least, at times, he did not know what to do or that he did the best he could under the circumstances? Remember at the end of *Schindler's List* when people who were shepherded to safety from deportation came together to thank Oscar Schindler in person? Schindler (whose mother was Catholic) looked at his watch and the car that he owned and realized that if he had sold these items, he would have been able to add more names to his list. He said, "I could have done more. I could have saved more people!" In retrospect, everyone could have done more.

And given all that has happened since 1965, is it healthy or wise to allow feuds over the past to dominate our intercourse or dialogue? Catholics beat themselves up over this issue. Some of the harshest criticism of Christian anti-Semitism has been written by Catholics. James Carroll's *Constantine's Sword* and Edward Flannery's *The Anguish of the Jews* are examples of Christian self-confrontation. These works and others show great remorse for Christian behavior and empathy for Jewish feelings of hurt and doubt.

Bridge building continued. In 2006 Pope Benedict also visited Auschwitz where he recounted the vital historical tie between Christianity and Judaism. And on his famous trip to the United States in 2008, Benedict visited Park East Synagogue on the eve of Passover. Rabbi Arthur Schneier, the leader of Park East, stated that the Pope's visit was a "tangible expression of his [the Pope's] outreach to the largest Jewish community in the world outside of Israel...The very clear message is that Jews and Catholics and Christians, we are in the same boat; we have common concerns for humanity."[9]

WE'RE ALREADY FRIENDS

We have entered a period of friendly relations between Catholics and Jews, with strong potential for more public displays of mutual understanding, respect, and a desire to occupy common ground wherever possible. This movement is not just confined to the clergy. Collaborations abound.

Jews believe in education, and Catholics have a reputation for running good schools. The Harry and Jeanette Weinberg Foundation in Baltimore ranks in the twenty largest foundations in the country, with assets of nearly $2.5 billion and annual giving of almost $100 million. Its mission is to assist the poor by funding direct-service organizations, with an emphasis on supporting the elderly and the Jewish community…and Catholic schools. Donn Weinberg, chairman of this Baltimore-area foundation, said this:

> Now there's a very simple reason why a foundation with a definite Jewish background—you might even call it a Jewish Foundation—gives to Catholic schools. It's that the Catholic schools in Baltimore and across the country take all comers. They're educating poor kids in Baltimore—predominantly from black families. In other American cities, they serve mostly Latino families. Either way, they serve kids from very low-income families.[10]

A powerful Jewish foundation is supporting a Catholic effort to educate some of the poorest children in America. "Another benefit," Weinberg adds, "is part of their mission is to impart American civic norms and values to their students. Of course, they're not the only schools to do this, but they definitely focus on the character, as well as the minds, of their students."[11]

Catholic schools are the largest provider of private education in the in the United States, and the largest amount of non-Catholic support comes from the philanthropic generosity of American Jews. Here's another example of partnership in education. The Partnership for Inner-City Education is a collaboration with the Archdiocese of New York to provide Catholic-school education to low-income children, and help them break the cycle of poverty that continues to exist in parts of Manhattan and the Bronx. As the number of parishes, vocations, and student enrollment have declined, Catholic schools around the country have had to close. Catholic schools have a proven record over several generations of being able to move students out of poverty. The Partnership is dedicated to preserving and strengthening inner-city Catholic schools, so that an excellent Catholic education can still be a reality for low-income students. For more than *twenty years*, the Partnership has been raising money and investing hundreds of millions of dollars to develop programs, resources, scholarships, and capital projects.[12] Most of that effort was shouldered by Catholics who support the Catholic Church, and much of the board of the Partnership is made up of Jewish educators, fund raisers, and philanthropists.

Beyond education, here's another example of collaboration: recently, two venerable nonprofit organizations have merged, with the top officials of both groups raising the possibility of broad affiliations among similar groups around the country. These two groups provide health care and rehabilitation services for blind and visually impaired people. Jewish Guild Healthcare (JGH) and Lighthouse International have merged, and the new entity is now known as Lighthouse Guild International. Dr. Alan Morse, who was president and chief executive of the original JGH and now holds the same titles in the new organization, said, "The Lighthouse is a worldwide household name in terms of vision services, and the Guild has highly developed models within healthcare. This collaboration makes good sense, and both programs will benefit from each other." Mark Ackermann, the president and chief executive of Lighthouse and a practicing Catholic in the Archdiocese of New York, said he and Dr. Morse had been sharing resources seamlessly for many months. As their talks for a formal merger evolved, they said to each other, "Why hadn't we done this before?"[13]

The Hebrew Home at Riverdale in the Bronx, New York, is a huge and well-run nursing home with over eight hundred beds. Naturally, the organization employs a full-time rabbi and offers the full range of religious services for Jews. But they also house and provide for over 250 Catholic residents and their families, and so you will see and hear Catholic services on Fridays and weekends to meet the religious needs of those residents.

Calvary Hospital is a well-known nonprofit institution specializing in hospice and palliative care. For years it was a Catholic hospital, and Dominican nuns assisted in serving the patients there. Now there is a lay administration, but religious people from many different communities and faiths still share in the work of the hospital. There is a Torah on permanent loan to the hospital. Rabbi Rachmiel is a full-time rabbi there, and he explained to me that the Torah is under restoration to make it kosher for use in service and rituals for Jewish patients at Calvary.

Pope Francis has continued deepening the bond. In 2014 the Pope made a three-day pilgrimage to the Holy Land, during which he prayed at the foot of a huge concrete separation barrier that has come to symbolize the divide between Israelis and Palestinians. Soon after that trip, he welcomed Israeli President Shimon Peres and Palestinian President Mahmoud Abbas to the Vatican Gardens, and in a beautiful sunset meeting, Pope Francis invoked Jewish, Christian, and Muslim prayers for peace.

At a day for Catholic-Jewish dialogue, hosted by Cardinal Dolan in 2015, everyone seemed to want to comment on Pope Francis. Rabbi David Saperstein, director of the Religious Action Center of Judaism, made a presentation that touched on the Pope's Holy Land visit:

> There's actually no pope in history who has been as close to the Jewish community and has had as much involvement in the Jewish community as this pope has. I had concerns about the way some of the things he did became politicized. But on the whole this was a very positive visit in his embrace of Israel as a Jewish state in the clearest possible terms. And he has a long record opposing anti-Semitism and Holocaust denial, just recently calling Holocaust denial "madness."[14]

Rabbi Gilbert Rosenthal, executive director of the National Council of Synagogues, characterized the current state of Catholic-Jewish relations as "marvelous—look, before Vatican II, I had no relationship with a priest; I tried, but no dice. Once Vatican II came, the whole atmosphere changed. This," he said, scanning the room where Cardinal Dolan and Catholic priests were enjoying lunch with their Jewish guests, "was impossible sixty years ago."[15] There is no longer a need for a rabbinic ban on stepping inside of a church. That time, thank God, has passed.

For years, Monsignor Tom Hartman and Rabbi Marc Gelman worked together on a television program called the *God Squad*. It featured a Catholic priest and a Jewish rabbi exchanging views on subjects related to religious life, in a respectful and friendly way. They made recurring appearances on *Good Morning America* and on the "Imus in the Morning" radio program, and they were featured as animated characters in an HBO special based on a children's book they wrote together, *How Do You Spell God? Answers to Big Questions from Around the World*, published in 1991. It was obvious that they loved each other, and they raised millions of dollars for medical research, including for AIDS and Parkinson's Disease—the disease that Father Hartman himself battled for sixteen years until his death at the age of sixty-nine in 2016.

The disputes now have only to do with historical, Holocaust-related issues. The 1987 visit to the Vatican by Austrian President Kurt Waldheim, who reportedly had connections to the Third Reich, was one sore point, and the building of crosses at Auschwitz by Polish Catholics in 1998 was another. Cardinal Dolan also recalled the "bickering over Mel Gibson's movie, *The Passion of the Christ*" that included charges of anti-Semitism. "We are family. We argue. That's what a family is all about. We raise our voices when we get scared."[16]

There are conferences and symposia all around the country now, with clergy and theologians discussing subjects like Catholic social teaching, Jewish readings of the New Testament, and a sharing of perspectives on the images of God. In fact a Catholic publication, *America* magazine, has collaborated with St. Joseph's Seminary in New York to sponsor a trialogue, among Catholic, Jewish, and Muslim scholars to discuss and exchange ideas about Pope Francis's Year of Mercy in 2016.

Christina: *Dad, this is all very interesting and, frankly, news to me! But what real impact can it have in the United States or around the world? Do you think people care?*

Well, at this point in history, there is no clear political coalition built up around shared values. The Catholic people are divided about political solutions, as are American Jews. In the 2012 election, more than half of Catholics—and an even higher percentage of Jews—voted for President Obama. So there is no dependable voting bloc that could influence legislation reflective of shared values.

But when we talk about Judeo-Christian values in this country, what do we mean? Doesn't that refer to a shared belief in values that grew out of the Bible: love of God, respect for law and for life, honesty in business, fidelity in marriage, and so forth? First and foremost, Jews and Catholics can stand up for these things and represent God in the world.

What about preserving the sanctity of the Sabbath, by remembering to keep it holy? Can we talk about how to express our faith in a country that glorifies personal choice and tolerance of everything, except religious values?

And how about the shared challenge of passing along the faith from one generation to another? What happens when Catholics and Jews intermarry; is no faith passed on? Can't we discuss ways and offer tools to parents to help them pass along the rich traditions and love of God to the children?

And don't we now have to stand together to defend the Jewish and Christian minorities throughout the world who still face persecution and death at the hands of extremists? There are concrete reasons for Jews and Catholics to continue to coalesce and strengthen their bond.

I realize this is not a topic that many people care or think about. But we all have an obligation to bring peace and joy into the world, and leave a better place than the one we have found. If some people have an opportunity to build up Catholic-Jewish relations and make the world a better place, let's celebrate and encourage it.

But let's return for a minute to Good Friday. Roman Catholics believe that on Good Friday, in particular, we must acknowledge our common fallen nature and acknowledge that Jesus died for all. Catholics have long prayed for many classes of people, both inside and outside the church: for political leaders, for various needs, and for those who do not believe in God.

In a sense, on Good Friday the entire church stands at the foot of the cross and asks for the forgiveness of sins and for the salvation of the whole world, through the saving grace of Jesus Christ. This is part of the revised prayer that every Catholic now prays in church on Good Friday:

> Let us pray also for the Jewish people, to whom the Lord our God spoke first, that He may grant them to advance in love of His name and in faithfulness to His covenant. [Prayer in silence.] Almighty ever-living God, who bestowed Your promises on Abraham and his descendants, hear graciously the prayers of your church, that the people you first made your own may attain the fullness of redemption.

Furthermore, Catholics and Jews can do even more than pray *for* each other; we can pray *together*. The prayers that Catholics and Jews can pray together are the Psalms. The Psalms express the heart of the Catholic Church. The liturgy of the hours is built on the Psalms, and at every Mass a Psalm is read. On Sundays Catholic people sing a Psalm. They express happiness in God's law, and they call out to God for help. They lament the struggles in the world but express trust in God's deliverance.

What if Catholics and Jews could have a meal together and precede it by offering a Psalm of praise to the God of Abraham? Isn't there a value in following the first commandment of God: to put God above all things? How about this Psalm?

> Bless the Lord, my soul!
> Lord, my God, you are great indeed!
> You are clothed with majesty and splendor,
> robed in light as with a cloak.

You spread out the heavens like a tent;
setting the beams of your chambers upon the waters,
You make the clouds your chariot;
traveling on the wings of the wind.
You make the winds your messengers;
flaming fire, your ministers.
I will sing to the Lord all my life;
I will sing praise to my God while I live.
May my meditation be pleasing to him;
I will rejoice in the Lord.
Bless the Lord, my soul! Hallelujah!
(Ps 104:1–5, 33–34, and 35b).

Imagine if we prayed this prayer together in real life. Wouldn't it be a nice way to spend a few minutes on a Saturday or Sunday afternoon? It couldn't hurt!

"Dialogue and friendship with the children of Israel are part of the life of Jesus's disciples."   Pope Francis, Evangelii Gaudium [17]

Endnotes

1. Jewish Virtual Library/American Public Opinion Polls: Attitudes of American Jews, September 2016, https://www.jewishvirtuallibrary.org/jsource/US-Israel/ajcsurvey2016.html.
2. http://www.jewishvirtuallibrary.org/jsource/US-Israel/us-jewpop.html.
3. New York Post Editorial Board/*Europe's Jew-hatred dressed as Anti-Zionism*, July 21, 2014, http://nypost.com/2014/07/21/europes-jew-hatred-dressed-as-anti-zionism/.

4. Claudia McDonnell, *"Cardinal, in Address, Chronicles Revolution of Jewish-Catholic Relations,"* Catholic New York, May 14, 2015.

5. Pope Paul VI, "Nostra Aetate" (In Our Time), October 28, 1965, Section 4 http://www.vatican.va/archive/hist_councils/ii_vatican_council/documents/vat-ii_decl_19651028_nostra-aetate_en.html.

6. http://www.yadvashem.org/yv/en/about/events/pope/john_paul/speech.asp#!prettyPhoto.

7. Yossi Klein Halevi, *Catholicism Is Our Friend*, Jerusalem Post Internet Edition, December 26, 2002.

8. Pierre Blet S. J. (Author), Lawrence J. Johnson (Translator), *Pius XII and the Second World War: According to the Archives of the Vatican* (Mahwah, NJ: Paulist Press 1997).

9. Sewell Chan, *"Pope Makes First Visit to a U.S. Synagogue,"* The New York Times, April 18, 2008, http://cityroom.blogs.nytimes.com/2008/04/18/a-key-moment-in-benedicts-relationship-with-the-jews/.

10. Christopher Levenick, "An Episcopalian, an Atheist, and a Jew Walk into a Catholic School..." *Philanthropy Magazine*, Spring 2010, http://www.philanthropyroundtable.org/topic/k_12_education/an_episcopalian_an_atheist_and_a_jew_walk_into_a_catholic_school.

11. http://www.philanthropyroundtable.org/topic/k_12_education/an_episcopalian_an_atheist_and_a_jew_walk_into_a_catholic_school.

12. Michael Goodwin, "Schools Done Right," *New York Post*, June 20, 2012.

13. James Barron, "Hoping to Raise Awareness, Two Leading Groups for the Blind Plan a Merger," *The New York Times*, September 16, 2013.

14. Ron Lajoie, "Relations Between Catholics and Jews Strong, Dialogue Leaders Say," *Catholic New York*, July 10, 2014.
15. Ibid.
16. Catholic New York News, "Catholics, Jews Find Common Concerns in Dialogue, Cardinal Says," May 28, 2015.
17. Pope Francis, Evangelii Gaudium, 248.

CHAPTER 7

Marriage

§

"I WILL LOVE YOU AND honor you all the days of my life."

I promise.

Marriage is a big commitment—the biggest one in most people's lives. It is an oath to another person for life, in front of a witness or witnesses. Most people have at least a few questions before the ceremony: Am I ready for this? How do I know for sure if this is the right person or the right time? Is marriage for me?

The year 2015 marked a big year for marriage. And it's still a hot topic. The Pope continued a major dialogue about many of the issues related to marriage through his Synod on the Family. The synod has caused Catholic people at all levels around the world to reflect deeply.

In this country the Supreme Court of the Unites States had redefined marriage by making it legal for same-sex couples to marry. I wonder about the impact this has had on how young people think about marriage today.

Angela: *Dad, first of all, I know this is not a revelation to you, but most people I know in their twenties are not in a rush to get married.*

Oh, I realize that. And I've seen well-documented reasons. First, we know that there's been the huge growth in higher education. With an overall higher level of affluence, and with the government subsidizing community colleges and state universities, there has been a dramatic rise in the number of high-school graduates going on to college. And in recent years you, or maybe some of your friends—in pursuit of the American dream—have felt pressured to add years of graduate-school education after bachelor's degrees. So a huge proportion of young people today are not beginning stable careers at eighteen but are extending their formal schooling well into their twenties.

Second, due to the shifting and emerging global economy, we see that graduates are not entering a job market that provides stable, lifelong careers. Young people today are starting their careers with lower security and more frequent job changes. You and your peers know that you need to approach your careers with multiple skills, maximal flexibility, and a readiness to adjust on the fly. As we've discussed, keeping all options open is the best way to navigate. Many young adults are spending five to ten years experimenting with different job and career options before deciding on a long-term career path.

Third, the parents of today's youth are increasingly willing and able to extend financial support to their children well into their twenties and even thirties. More and more college graduates return to live in their parents' home, under their parents' health plan, and drive their parents' cars. These resources help young adults take a good long time before settling into full adulthood.

So sure, more and more young people are waiting to get married.[1] Fifty years ago, many young people were anxious to get out of high school, marry, have children, and start their career. Not anymore. Today's youth take almost ten years after high school to explore life's many options as singles before making the commitment to marry.

Christina: *And even after waiting, the prospects for success are not great. So many of my friends' parents are divorced. It's scary.*

True. Divorce is rampant. Every other week *People* magazine seems to report another Hollywood marriage on the rocks or breaking up. We see marriages crumbling on talk shows before our eyes. We read about wealthy people with multiple marriages, embroiled in bitter divorce disputes over property and custody rights. When a celebrity couple marries, you read and hear people speculating on how long it will last. ("I give it a year, nah, six months, tops.") And we're right. Wasn't Kim Kardashian married for seventy days, and wasn't Brittany Spears married for, like, one day? Not a great model.

Marriages are also popularized as unhappy. We read about conflicts, separations, and abuse. People complain about their spouses, and you hear that sex gets boring or stops completely after marriage. Cheating and unfaithfulness is news, and every affair ultimately seems to come to light. Wives are overbearing, and husbands are emotionally distant. When children come along, different levels of emotional separation creep in. Couples who seek counseling to try and work it out are often told, "You two are really just not compatible." Addictions to shopping, food, drugs, and alcohol all hasten the process of failed marriages.

And divorce is easy, right? There are free divorce e-books, simple, low-cost divorces, and just as you can quickly as you can meet your spouse online, you can now file for divorce online. It's painful, and there are long-range consequences, but it's not difficult to get a divorce. There are fewer taboos, and even Catholic divorces have approached the national average.

Angela: *And what is the national average, 50 percent? Half of all marriages end in divorce, right? I mean we've heard this in the media for years, and everyone quotes that figure. We hear it on television, online, and we've even heard it in church.*

Right, and if 50 percent of all marriages in the United States end in divorce, that is scary. It seems like gambling. How can you make a promise to someone for the rest of your life, if you believe that your marriage has only a fifty-fifty chance to succeed? Anyone would be right to be cautious and wary.

But something about that statistic never seemed right. Don't we see people happily celebrating their twenty-fifty or fiftieth wedding anniversaries every year? I mean Hallmark has cards for those events. When fiftieth wedding anniversaries are celebrated in the diocese, hundreds of couples show up. And in my own parish, I look around and see plenty of couples hanging in there. If your parents and your wife's parents are married, and your sisters and brothers are all married (ok, one's divorced), well, you must be living a life shut off from the outside world. Statistics don't lie! Half of all marriages end in divorce!

But guess what? It turns out that figure is not true! Thank goodness for Shaunti Feldhahn and her husband Jeff. They published a book in 2014, which is now being widely circulated and discussed and is particularly appreciated by marriage counselors, priests, and psychotherapists, called *The Good News about Marriage/Debunking Discouraging Myths about Marriage and Divorce.*

Ms. Feldhahn tells the story of how she was writing one of her newspaper columns in 2006 and was referencing the prevalence of divorce. She wanted to correctly cite the most recent divorce rate but was confused by conflicting sources and articles. She asked her assistant to keep looking, but they found nothing. They called a respected expert on marriage and divorce and asked, "What's the exact divorce rate?" And the answer they got back was "no one knows." What about the Census Bureau? They were told, "The Census Bureau stopped projecting divorce rates in 1996. And even those projections were based on divorce increasing, and it has decreased instead. That won't help you.

The 50 percent divorce rate turned out to be—a myth! In the years since then, Ms. Feldhahn, a Harvard-trained researcher, says she gradually began to discover several other surprising myths about marriage and divorce. And as she says in the book, "That's a really big deal!"

Yes, it is a big deal because we need hope to be successful. Bad news is demotivating. So, here's some highlights of the Feldhahn research:

- The actual divorce rate has never gotten close to 50 percent. According to the Census Bureau, 72 percent of people today are still married to their first spouse. And among the 28 percent who aren't, some of those ended in widowhood, not divorce. So, the current divorce rate is probably closer to 20 to 25 percent.
- Most marriages are happy. In her own surveys, Feldhahn found that 71 percent of couples responded that they were happy with their marriages (34 percent said "very happy"), and in one poll 93 percent said they would marry their spouse all over again.
- The rate of divorce in the church is not the same as the rate among those who don't attend worship services. Every study on this shows that by attending worship services, couples are happier and closer in their marriages, and/or have a significantly lower divorce rate.

So it's not a crap shoot or a fifty-fifty proposition. And most importantly, there are things you can do that will influence your marriage and give it a far greater chance for success than you or anyone else may have imagined! There is hope!

Look, this is a book about faith and about how God speaks to us. There are three virtues that are most important—the theological virtues: faith, hope, and love. They're called theological because they come from God, and their objective is God. They are gifts of grace that come from God, and Catholics believe they are bestowed on us at baptism.

Hope is refraining from despair. It is the capability of not giving up. Hope is the sustained knowledge that God is ever present in our lives. Hope means never giving up on His love for us. It is grace from God, and it is essential in marriage.

If both spouses feel that the marriage is hopeless, what chance does the marriage have? If one spouse truly believes, "Hey, we can get through this," then the marriage has a chance to get back on track and keep moving forward. A therapist or marriage counselor, for all his or her skill and training, cannot place hope in a person's heart. And when marriages get into trouble, a lot of hope is needed.

Christina: *But since marriage is forever, people are cautious and say, "It's too risky. Why don't we just live together?"*

Yes, in fact, priests and ministers tell us that when couples approach the church these days to get married, they already share the same address. It fits in with the overall approach of keeping one's options open. If it doesn't work out, they figure, there's no harm done. But living together before marriage doesn't solve the problem. Yes, you can learn some things about a future spouse when you live together for a few months. You will learn some of the person's habits: whether he squeezes the toothpaste from the bottom or the middle, whether she leaves clipped toenails in the sink, or how badly he snores. You also may see how she is in the morning with a hangover or how his or her moods change on a daily basis.

But there are some things you can't learn by living together. How will he react if he loses his job or gets some other kind of bad news?

What if I get sick? How will we handle a child with needs or, God forbid, an unforeseen tragedy? Does living together really help you hear each other and learn to listen?

Again, back to the theological virtues, love (charity or caritas) is a supernatural virtue that helps us love God and our neighbors more than ourselves. There was a movie once called *Love Story*, and it was pretty good, but its tagline was dumb: "Love means never having to say you're sorry." Wrong. That's not what it means. It means placing someone above yourself, and apologizing when you have hurt or offended that person, even unintentionally.

Think about a song you like that expresses a deep love for another person. The writer seems to capture a phrase that really touches your heart, makes you nod your head in agreement, and say, "Yeah, that's how I feel." The writer talks about endless love, tender love, young love, forever love, baby love, hot love, monsta love. Here are some examples of titles and lyrics: "I Can't Stop Loving You," "If loving you is wrong, I don't want to be right," "Will You Still Love Me Tomorrow?," "Love Me Do," "So Much in Love," "Taking a Chance on Love," "Why Do Fools Fall in Love?," "Can't Buy Me Love," "A World without Love," and, of course, "All You Need Is Love."

Why is it that all this love doesn't stick? Why doesn't love alone, the most powerful force in the world, hold marriages together? Because successful marriages require more than love.

Love isn't something that just happens to us. To love is an act of the will. I promise to love you...in bad times too! When romance fades from a marriage, there remains the commitment. And when a married couple doesn't even like each other anymore—and, let's face it, living with someone can really get on your nerves—there is still a willful commitment.

It was Thomas Aquinas who said it best: "to love is to will the good of another."

We have to make sacrifices for each other. Many people will say, "I'll do anything for my kid!" But would the man who said that do "anything" for the mother of his kid? Would he give up a round of golf on Sunday, or a boy's night on Friday, or something more, just for his wife?

Marriage has been studied and analyzed forever, and very smart people have good suggestions on how to start and build a successful marriage. I am not a marriage counselor, but I've been married to a wonderful woman for over twenty-eight years, and I've learned a lot. Here are my thoughts:

Think, plan, communicate, and discuss. If you meet someone and begin to fall in love, start to work with this person to prepare for your marriage in a careful, thoughtful way. The chances for a successful marriage will greatly increase.

Start by putting the phone down. The greatest threat to marriage in the world today is the cell phone. The cell phone and a spouse are very different animals. The cell phone is a perfect friend. It provides you with only the news you're interested in. It tells the weather, the traffic, and the directions you need. It previews books, movies, and restaurants without pressuring you. It enables you to friend and unfriend people whenever you feel like it. It allows you to announce your opinions to lots of people, check stocks, pay bills, and transfer money. It has pictures of all the beautiful places and people in the world. And it's fully charged and ready to go every morning.

A spouse is different. A spouse sometimes needs things. A spouse gets sick. Sometimes a spouse gets angry with you and sometimes disappointed in you. A spouse may not agree with some of your opinions and sometimes gets tired of hearing them. A spouse is a lot of work. And most spouses don't want to be ignored in favor of a cell phone.

Do people ever say to their phone, "Hey, hold on, I've got to talk to my wife"? No, they say, "Hold on, hon, I'm on the phone," and do not even look up.

Angela: *Funny, Dad.*

Learn to discuss and disagree. It's ok to have an argument, even before you're married. But there are rules. Don't start the argument with "you," as in *"you* always do this or that!" That's an accusation, and you're off to a bad start. State your case by talking about your own feelings. "I feel that when this or that happens, I'm not able to…" And when your partner talks, learn to *listen*! Listening is an art and a craft. You have to use your whole body to listen. Listen to the tone of his or her voice, the expression in his eyes, the posture and tenseness of her body, and listen to the words he or she is saying. Try to restate or repeat back to the person what you have just heard. If you are able to accurately play back the other person's side of the argument, then you've listened. It's not easy.

What does winning the argument look like? If you're mean or smug or sarcastic, can you win? If you put your partner down, you lose. You are hurting the person you love. If you can listen to each other and repeat the other person's point, you can start to negotiate. That's winning. Steer clear of sarcasm, dismissiveness, and contempt. Build up the relationship, and point it in a positive direction.

Work at growing together and not growing apart. Many counselors who treat couples with problems will recommend a date night—time devoted just to each other. That's right; you have to schedule time on your Google calendar to go out, just the two of you. Have dinner and talk. Talk and listen. Don't let the relationship slide. Go for a walk, and hold hands. Keep romance in the relationship. It's too easy for outside forces, or forces from within, to infect the relationship.

Christina: *Dad, you're exhausting us again.*

Hey, this is serious. There are obstacles everywhere; take substance abuse. If one or the other partner has an eating disorder or an addiction to drugs or alcohol, that could set the stage for long-term difficulties in a marriage. Addictions are powerful and destructive. Sometimes one partner will subconsciously adapt to the behavior of the addicted person's behavior and thus, become codependent. And people are often in denial about their personal behaviors.

Dealing with an addiction takes compassion. And honesty. And discipline. Alcoholism is a disease. It affects men and women, young and old. It is not the result of poor moral character. Self-acceptance is the first step toward recovery. Support groups are crucial, and AA meetings are held in church basements all around the country. There is no cure. Total abstinence is the only way to stop the effects of addictive behaviors, and total honesty is needed to identify them.

There are other things to consider. We are in an era where multigenerational homes are more common. If you get married and move back in with your parents, you have to be conscious of preventing resentments or stress. Talk it out, and discuss everyone's expectations. Mutually set up some guidelines and ground rules, and discuss privacy and financial considerations. And set a timeline. If you are moving in, when will you be moving out?

In-law relationships are tricky. You must love and honor both sets of parents, but once you marry, your primary relationship and responsibility is to your spouse. You are building something. St. Paul said, "For this reason a man will leave [his] father and [his] mother and be joined to his wife, and the two will become one flesh" (Eph 5:31). To unite as one, you have to leave home.

And I'm sorry, but you've got to go to church. When you go to Mass, you give glory to God, you confess your sins, and you hear the Gospel proclaimed and preached. You say the Lord's Prayer, and you receive Jesus in communion with others. Going to Mass reinforces a sense of humility and gratitude. That's needed in a marriage. Think of it as life insurance for your marriage. And as they used to say at Mass, "It is profitable toward salvation."

When you make a mistake, can you say, "I'm sorry. No excuses, I messed up. I didn't mean to hurt you; please forgive me"? And if your spouse says that to you, can you forgive lovingly? Blame is a disease that affects so many relationships. Humility, asking for forgiveness, is the medicine for it.

When you wake up in the morning, can you say, "I'm so grateful for you. I thank God you are in my life!" Maybe we do that on Valentine's Day or Mother's Day, but how much better would it be to be grateful every day for the gift of marriage? Grace flows from gratitude.

Marriage must be filled with grace. The story of the wedding at Cana reminds us of this. Jesus is present at the wedding with His mother and His friends. As a result of His presence, there's an abundance of the best wine—overflowing. One of the lessons is that when God is present in the marriage, there's an abundance of grace flowing into the marriage, urging us to forgive, get past the problem, keep the marriage afloat, and keep on loving each other.

And one more thing, in the Catholic tradition, a priest does not "pronounce you man and wife." A justice of the peace or civil magistrate does that. In matrimony two people "take each other" and make a promise to each other before God and before a witness. After they say I do to each other, the witnessing priest says, "You have declared your consent before the church. May the Lord in His goodness strengthen your consent and fill you with his blessings. What God has joined, men must not divide."

You recall that I mentioned Pope Francis called for a Synod on the Family back in 2014. That Synod of Bishops called on priests and laypeople to act as experts and observers, and they talked about a wide range of issues related to the family: the various cultural forms of courtship, marriage preparation, the impact of migration on families, and care for elderly parents. There were public seminars with input from a wide range of delegates. Remember, the Pope is focused on the universal church, not just the problems in America. After the initial meetings, a document was issued summarizing the various points of view that were expressed. That document caused consternation because it was felt by some that the church was opening itself up to a shift in its fundamental values and guiding principles. But it was healthy for the church to let everybody weigh in, and have animated discussions. It's a big church and a big subject; let's hear from everyone.

The Pope reflected for over a year on those discussions, debates, and suggestions, and in 2016 his apostolic exhortation was released: "The Joy of Love experienced by families is also the joy of the Church." Encyclicals by popes are named with the first words of the text, and this one is called "Amoris Laetitia" (The Joy of Love). Clerics, theologians, and members of the media have and will continue to analyze and offer insights into this work. It's 256 pages long, and it takes time, prayer, and discernment to allow for the depth of the teachings to unfold and be understood. I read through it once, and that's not enough. I have to go back and read what I underlined, to reflect on what it means in my marriage and in my life. I need to read it and think about what the Pope is saying to the church and what I can do to reflect its teachings as a deacon—not the headline summaries but the actual text.

Angela: *Dad, those encyclicals are so onerous and difficult to read.* Well, here's what the Pope himself says about the document:

I do not recommend a rushed reading of the text. The greatest benefit for families themselves and for those engaged in

the family apostolate, will come if each part is read patient-
ly and carefully, or if attention is paid to the parts dealing
with their specific needs. It is likely, for example, that married couples will be more concerned with chapters four and
five, and pastoral ministers with chapter six, while everyone
should feel challenged by chapter eight. It is my hope that, in
reading this text, all will feel called to love and cherish family
life, for "families are not a problem; they are first and foremost an opportunity."[2]

For me, the Pope's message is centered and grounded in Christ. He
refers back to the pastoral constitution from Vatican II, Gaudium et
Spes, which aimed "to promote the dignity of marriage and family."
The Pope quotes the following:

Christ the Lord "makes Himself present to the Christian
spouses in the sacrament of marriage" and remains with them.
In the incarnation, He assumes human love, purifies it, and
brings it to fulfilment. By His Spirit, He gives spouses the
capacity to live that love, permeating every part of their lives
of faith, hope, and charity. In this way, the spouses are consecrated and by means of a special grace, build up the Body
of Christ and form a domestic church, so that the church, in
order fully to understand her mystery, looks to the Christian
family, which manifests her in a real way.[3]

A Christian marriage has Jesus at its center, so we can learn to love
and to serve one another. He is living water, a fountain of grace.
Through Him we can put ourselves aside and will the good of our
loved ones. And in so doing, we can complete the joy He came to
bring us—the joy of the Gospel and the joy of love.

There is wonderful instruction and advice for couples all around the world in every culture. The Pope shares insights into the problems that couples face in the real world today and offers encouragement. He wants marriages to be strong and wants families to thrive. They are not all the same, but they do all require work and prayer.

As a good Jesuit, he quotes from the *Spiritual Exercises of St. Ignatius of Loyola*. He proposes a pastoral response to the challenges facing families and invites pastors to adopt a "process of accompaniment and discernment," which would include assisting families in "an examination of conscience."[4]

The church has not changed its rules. There are no new norms or obligations to be put in place. But the document encourages a careful review of everything related to family ministry. The Pope himself acknowledges that people have moved away from God and away from the church. Many feel it's too rigid and unyielding and is not listening. According to the document, much greater attention is now to be placed on the attitude and language used when explaining church teaching. After all, it's good news: the Gospel message!

One of the biggest issues raised during the synod was the question of Holy Communion for Catholics who were divorced and civilly remarried. Pope Francis says that pastors must help each couple look at their actions and circumstances, recognize their share of responsibility for the breakup of their marriage, acknowledge church teaching that marriage is indissoluble, and prayerfully discern what God is calling them to. He's saying "the way of the church is not to condemn anyone forever; it is to pour out the balm of God's mercy on all those who ask for it with a sincere heart." He cautioned though that it would be "grave danger" to give people the impression that "any priest can quickly grant 'exceptions' or that some people can obtain sacramental privileges in exchange for favors."[5]

Angela: *So, the rule is unchanged; a divorced person without an annulment cannot receive communion.*

Generally, without an annulment of their sacramental marriage, a divorced and civilly remarried couple would not be able to receive communion or absolution of their sins unless they promised to live as "brother and sister." But every situation is different, said the Pope, which is why the church does not need new rules but a new commitment on the part of pastors to provide spiritual guidance and assistance with discernment. For example, a spouse who was abandoned—versus being the one who left—is in a different position, and these types of differences make it unwise to issue "a new set of general rules, canonical in nature and applicable to all cases" the Pope said.

He quoted John Paul II: "since the degree of responsibility is not equal in all cases, the consequences or effects of a rule need not necessarily always be the same." Pope Francis says quite frankly in the document that he understood those...

"...who prefer a more rigorous pastoral care, which leaves no room for confusion. But I sincerely believe that Jesus wants a church attentive to the goodness which the Holy Spirit sows in the midst of human weakness, a mother who, while clearly expressing her objective teaching, always does what good she can, even if in the process, her shoes get soiled by the mud of the street."[6]

It's clear to me that Pope Francis is listening. He referred to the responses to questionnaires sent around the world before the synod that "showed that most people in difficult or critical situations do not seek pastoral assistance, since they do not find it sympathetic, realistic, or concerned for individual cases." These responses, he said, are a call to the church "to try and approach marriage crises with greater sensitivity to their burden of hurt and anxiety."[7] "The Joy of Love" was issued during the Pope's Year of Mercy, and the theme of mercy is expressed throughout—for migrant families, for people with special needs, and for all of us.

Christina: *Dad, since the church condemns same-sex marriage, doesn't that mean that the church regards gay people as sinful—that homosexuals are evil?*

Hold on here. First of all, Pope Francis repeated his and the synod's insistence that the church cannot consider same-sex unions to be a marriage but also insisted, "Every person, regardless of sexual orientation, ought to be respected in his or her own dignity." We have to be careful with the word "condemn" There is no condemnation of homosexuals. Catholics are reminded that we are commanded by God to love, and we must respect and be guided by the principle of human dignity for all. That's very helpful to the Catholic people. After all, we all have sons, daughters, nephews, nieces, aunts, and uncles who are gay. You don't see me shunning anyone or being unkind to our gay family members. They are part of our family and part of our church! I am commanded to love them, and I do. We live with them and work with them. We can and must continue to love them and respect them, as should all members of the Catholic Church.

Now, our religion teaches us that marriage is a sacrament: a sign Christ instituted to give grace. The family flows from the marriage. When two people fall in love, they want to be together, to live together, to share their lives together, and to become one. That union can produce others, hopefully conceived in love and brought up in a loving environment. Marriage between a man and a woman is unique because of its capacity for procreation. For Catholics marriage cannot be redefined. We believe it comes from God, and even the Pope does not have the authority or right to change it. A family—even an extended family: a parish, a village, a community—ceases to exist if it does not procreate, and procreation comes from the sexual union of a man and woman, ideally united in God's love.

Listen, we have seen the institution of marriage in the United States damaged in recent decades, and it's not the fault of the gay community. We live in a society in which babies born to unmarried women account for more than 40 percent of births. Huge numbers of children are born out of wedlock, many from what used to be called broken families. Custody battles are waged in court, reducing children to property that can be fought over and divided. So the bond between marriage and procreation has been weakened. Now, by redefining marriage, the Supreme Court has formally and legally eliminated any connection between marriage and procreation. In the eyes of the Court, all marriages are reduced to civil unions. A principle has now been weakened. Little comfort came from Chief Justice Roberts who said in his dissent that "for the good of children and society, sexual relations that can lead to procreation should occur only between a man and a woman committed to a lasting bond."

Angela: *Doesn't that now place Catholics out of the mainstream?*

It sure does, and what happens now? According to an NBC/*Wall Street Journal* poll, only 33 percent of the American public is now opposed to same-sex marriage. If Catholics believe that marriage is a sacrament that binds a man and woman as one, are we now to be marginalized as close-minded and stigmatized as bigots? That was fast.

And is religious liberty still a right? Will the nonprofit tax status of institutions that oppose same-sex marriage be challenged? Will religious charities become ineligible for government grants and contracts? Will religious schools that live out their beliefs be threatened with discrimination lawsuits and risk losing their accreditation? Can a bishop, priest, or minister who refuses to perform a same-sex marriage be arrested, fined, and jailed? Those are legitimate questions, and we'll soon see how far religious freedom is protected under the US Constitution, from judges who are led by the Supreme Court ruling.

I've said this to you all along: being Catholic means going against the grain. If people engage in same-sex civil unions, who am I to judge? I can at once still love my neighbor and maintain my beliefs. The sacrament of marriage is a great act of faith, hope, and love. Young people today need to have courage. Marriage can be successful and it can be fruitful, and it can help you fulfill your destiny. Have hope in marriage. Believe in its beauty. Don't be afraid to love. If God is for us, said St. Paul, who can be against us?

I sincerely hope that you and your generation still aspire to a healthy, caring marriage that's filled with children and goodness and love. I pray every day that you will find suitable partners and that God will guide you into an abundant union that will last forever.

It's a good exercise to renew the promises we make to each other in marriage. Remember when Mom and I renewed our vows in church? We did it after fifteen years and again after twenty-five years of marriage, and with you guys and Joseph present, it was a deeply moving experience. Our thirtieth wedding anniversary is coming up, and here's what I will say to Mom that day:

"Thirty years ago, I pledged my love and commitment to you, but it seems like only yesterday. I promised to love you, honor you, comfort you, and be faithful to you. I pledged to be by your side in sickness and in health, in time of plenty and in time of want, for better or worse, for the rest of our lives. We have had all those things, and you have been by my side as we built our family, our home, and our life together. Today, as your husband, in the presence of God and the church, I renew my vows to you, pledging my love for you, and eagerly awaiting all that life may bring us. In the name of the Father and of the Son and of the Holy Spirit. Amen."

Endnotes

1. Steve Doughty, "People Are Waiting Much Longer to Get Married Now Than They Did Forty Years Ago with Just 14% of Brides Under the Age of 25," *The Daily Mail*, September 25, 2014, http://www.dailymail.co.uk/news/article-2769848/People-waiting-longer-married-did-forty-years-ago-just-14-brides-age-25.html.

2. Pope Francis, *Amoris Laetitia*, Post-Synodal Apostolic Exhortation March 19, 2016. Section 7

3. Pope Paul VI, *Gaudium et Spes*, Pastoral Constitution on the Church in the Modern World, December 7, 1965. Sections 48, 67.

4. *The Spiritual Exercises of St. Ignatius of Loyola*, translated by Elder Mullen, 1914, http://sacred-texts.com/chr/seil/index.htm.

5. Cindy Wooden, "Pope Extends Mercy Through Exhortation on Family," *Catholic New York*, April 14, 2016.

6. Pope Francis, *Amoris Laetitia*, Post-Synodal Apostolic Exhortation March 19, 2016. Section 308.

7. Ibid.

CHAPTER 8

The Mass

§

TRYING TO PERSUADE YOUNG PEOPLE to go to Mass is not easy. Most young adults don't go. The period between leaving their parents' home and finally getting married is a time of exploring, developing future opportunities for success, navigating amorphous relationships, and keeping as many promising options open as possible.

Religion means settling down, which is for later. When you are committed to indefinitely keeping all of your options open, you are far less inclined to commit to the routines and disciplines of religious faith and practice. And when you are the most important person in your world—the center of the universe—the discipline required to worship, honor, and thank someone bigger and more authoritative than yourself just doesn't compute.

Furthermore, when you have been raised to celebrate diversity, embrace multiculturalism, and be inclusive of all differences, it's difficult to join a group of weekly worshipers who seem to be less inclusive, fixed in their beliefs, and judgmental.

Angela: *Dad, I'm not opposed to the idea of going to Mass. It's just that the Mass at a typical parish in our area is just so...boring. The music is ancient, and the sermons are dreary.*

Christina: *When we were in college, we went to Mass every Sunday. What was it that attracted you to the Mass there?*

Christina: *First of all, they were on Sunday evening at 6:00 p.m.—a good time for college students. There was a huge, colorful procession, plenty of Eucharistic ministers, and the choir was inspirational and got everyone to participate and sing.*

Angela: *And the sermons were aimed directly at students, with very relatable messages.*

Ok, that's all good. But the Mass is not a show, something that entertains you. It is a public act of worship. And it is something that you have to enter into. It is most meaningful when you bring *yourself* to celebrate.

There is nothing I can say to you or your friends that will persuade you to suddenly start going to Mass on a weekly basis. As I said earlier, joining a parish is a life-changing, defining moment in a person's life. Ultimately, when you settle down and start having a family, you may revisit the idea of including some religion in your life. After you have your children baptized, what will you teach them about the Mass? Let me share some thoughts.

What Is It?

The Mass is a celebration. But it is not, in and of itself, a visually evangelizing tool. In other words, if you made a video of a Mass—with music and singing and pomp and color—and put it on YouTube, it would not cause people to say, "Hey, that looks neat. I think I'll go to one." It wouldn't have the same effect as a video of a horse race, a Billy Joel concert, a boxing match, or even a spelling bee. Those can be made to look interesting and attractive to outside viewers. But the beauty of the Mass doesn't come from outside; it is experienced from within.

The Catholic Mass is about Jesus. Everything that is said and done at the Mass is there to help us worship and receive Jesus. The more you are personally drawn to Jesus, the more you are personally able to appreciate and participate in the Mass. If you do not have a relationship with Jesus, the Mass doesn't make sense.

To understand the Mass, it helps to think of it as a meal. When you get together with people for a meal, you greet each other, talk a little bit, and then move to the table to eat. You may say a prayer of thanks, pass the food and drink, finish up, and make plans to stay in touch. That's the Mass; you gather, tell stories, share a meal, and affirm your continued friendship.

It's not just any meal; it is a meal in which we celebrate the Eucharist. That word is derived from the Greek, *eukharistia*—which means thanksgiving or gratitude—and it refers to the sacrament in which Christ's Last Supper is commemorated in the consecration of bread and wine. Again, because of transubstantiation, what appears to be bread and wine is no longer bread and wine, but the sacramental sign of the Real Presence of Christ in the Eucharist. A sacrament is a sign instituted by Christ to give grace, and as such, it comes from God and is holy. We celebrate the Holy Eucharist at every Mass.

The bishops at Vatican II described it this way:

At the Last Supper, on the night He was betrayed, our Savior instituted the Eucharistic sacrifice of His body and blood. He did this in order to perpetuate the sacrifice of the cross throughout the centuries until He should come again and in this way entrust to His beloved bride, the church, a memorial of His death and resurrection: a sacrament of love, a sign of unity, a bond of charity, a paschal banquet in which Christ is eaten, the heart is filled with grace, and a pledge of future glory is given to us.[1]

It's all in there: the Last Supper, the sacrifice on the cross, the Resurrection, and future glory. Holy Thursday, Good Friday, and Easter Sunday all contained and expressed in a ritual: the holy sacrifice of the Mass.

It's deep. The body of Christ, in the form of consecrated bread and wine, is offered. We receive the body of Christ at the Mass, and He receives us, and we are in communion with Him and with each other and with God. It is Holy Communion. The priest is the presider who leads the people and acts in the person of Christ on behalf of the people. He says, "Let your Spirit come upon these gifts to make them holy so that they may become for us the body and blood of our Lord, Jesus Christ." The priest is asking God to send the Holy Spirit, to do for us now what Jesus did at the Last Supper. "Then he took the bread, said the blessing, broke it, and gave it to them, saying, 'This is my body, which will be given for you; do this in memory of me'" (Luke 22:19).

It is not just a reminder of the Last Supper. We believe that Jesus gave Himself up for us—sacrificed Himself to save us from our sins. That sacrifice is present to us in this sacrament. By eating the bread, we are not only sharing in His life. He died and rose again, so the Eucharist makes us sharers in the crucified and risen Christ. He is with us, again and again, in the Eucharist. He is present in the bread, and we are nourished through His sustaining power.

He is present at the altar, He is present in the priest, and He is present in the assembly. And we who receive Him are present in this mystery of faith. Through Him, with Him, and in Him, we are "drawn day by day into ever more perfect union with God and with each other, so that finally God may be all in all."[2]

Angela: *A perfect union with God! It seems like you have to be really holy to be worthy or accepted at most churches.*

People don't come to Mass because they are holy. They come because they are in need of holiness. Before we receive Holy Communion, we all say, "Lord, I am not worthy to receive you, but only say the word, and my soul shall be healed." The priest or minister offers us the Body of Christ, and we open our hands and our hearts, and as we receive Him, we respond, "Amen!"

Christina: *Hasn't the Mass changed dramatically? Wasn't the Mass completely changed after Vatican II?*

Well, yes, changes were made, but the Mass did not start with Vatican Council II. And it didn't grow out of the gothic Middle Ages, as a ritual with candles, incense, and blood. It started at the very beginning. Those small communities of believers that formed and spread around the Mediterranean, got together and prayed. They assembled every week because Jesus had told them to "Do this in memory of Me." In John's Gospel, Jesus said, "I am the living bread that came down from heaven; whoever eats this bread will live forever; and the bread that I will give is my flesh for the life of the world" (Jn 6:51). This Gospel began circulating at the beginning of the second century, and Jesus's followers wanted to keep this message very much alive.

We have written evidence of this fact. A man named Justin Martyr lived near Rome and, after seeking truth through the study of Greek philosophy, had become a fervent Christian. Around the year AD 155, the Roman emperor Antoninus Pius, reputed to be a good man but a pagan, asked Justin what these Christ-followers did when they got together. This is what Justin wrote back to the emperor:

On the day we call the day of the Sun, all who dwell in the city or country gather in the same place. The memoirs of the apostles and the writings of the prophets are read, as much as time permits. When the teacher has finished, he who presides over those gathered admonishes and challenges them to imitate these beautiful things.

Then we all rise together and offer prayers for ourselves and for all others wherever they may be, so that we may be found righteous by our life and actions and faithful to the commandments so as to obtain eternal salvation. When the prayers are concluded we exchange the kiss.

Then someone brings bread and a cup of water and wine mixed together to him who presides over the brethren. He takes them and offers praise and glory to the Father of the universe through the name of the Son and of the Holy Spirit and for a considerable time he gives thanks [*eucharistian*] that we have been judged worthy of these gifts. When he has concluded the prayers and thanksgivings, all present give voice to an acclamation by saying: "Amen."

When he who presides has given thanks and the people have responded, those whom we call deacons give to those present the "*echaristed*" bread, wine, and water and take them to those who are absent.

Through all the wars and all the councils, all the sinning and all the sainthood, all the division and all the unity, the one thing that has held the church together for two thousand years is the celebration of the Eucharist at the Mass.

The Eucharist is understood as "the source and summit of the Christian life."[3] That's why Catholics do not worship alone. We all gather together—young and old, rich and poor, with everyone in the world, and with those who have gone before us—to celebrate Jesus's holy sacrifice. That act, that ritual, that practice, has to animate something—make us do something. Pope Benedict wrote, "A

Eucharist which does not pass over into the concrete practice of love is intrinsically fragmented."⁴ When we receive communion, we're challenged—no, commanded—to love. We have to recognize our place in our own parish community and in the greater human family. The Eucharist calls us to charity. Now we bring the light of the Gospel into the world!

Angela: *Dad, I have to admit, when you start to reflect on it, there is a lot of depth and meaning within the Catholic Mass.*

Christina: *But if the Mass is that important and that beautiful, how come people fall asleep, don't pay attention, or just don't go at all?*

Well, after the last-supper meal, when the apostles went out to the garden, what did even they do? They fell asleep. Maybe people need some kind of motivation. People tend to flock to church during times of tragedy. When 9/11 happened, I recall my regular church-going friends commenting about how great it was to be at Mass with the church filled. And for a month, maybe three, lots of people were in church.

There are some things that will surely get people to come to Mass, and I'm familiar with one of them: cancer. You remember I was diagnosed with prostate cancer when I was forty-seven years old and you were just eight and six? It was shocking and mind-numbing news, as everyone who has ever heard it knows. I had been going to Mass, and I was active in the church. I rationalized that I had had a pretty good life and a good marriage, and I could accept leaving early, but when I looked at you two girls and Joseph, I really did not want you to grow up without a father, so I was upset and worried.

During the weeks after surgery, I did a lot of earnest praying. I was begging God to keep me around. I prayed to Jesus, I prayed to Mary, and I prayed to Joseph. I even considered making a deal with God. Don't laugh. One night, I said to God, "If you will spare me and let me get past this problem, I promise to wear a necktie to Mass every Sunday for the rest of my life!"

Angela: *Dad, what? You promised God you'd wear a tie?*

Yes, as time went on, my blood tests kept coming back clean. I remember one Sunday after Mass, a fellow parishioner complimented my tie, and I told him about my little deal with God. Of course, he smiled and thought that was cute and just kind of eased away.

A couple of months later, I saw him again, and when he looked at my suit and how I was dressed, he said, "Oh yeah, yeah, the tie thing." But I think it made an impression on him. He may not have been to Mass for six or eight weeks, and he assumed that I had been coming every week with my tie on. He was bemused but realized I was taking my promise seriously.

The promise I made to God was that I would go to Mass every Sunday, receive Holy Communion, and be thankful for my many blessings. The tie was to remind me of how important that is. It was a cue—like a string on the finger—reminding me that, hey, even if I don't feel like it, this Mass is important today, and I promised.

Once you get out of the habit of going to Mass on a regular basis, it's almost impossible to start attending regularly again. There are just too many other, seemingly better, choices: you have to be someplace else, you were out late the night before, or you're just not feeling it this week.

What Else Is Going On?

Let's walk through the parts of the Mass and see what's actually happening. We'll assume an ideal scenario: we're going to Sunday Mass at 10:30 a.m., and we're not unhappy about it.

As we're getting dressed, we have a lot on our minds. It's been a long week, and we've got a busy day ahead. Even though this is an obligation and something we've imposed on ourselves, we know that we always feel better after we go to Mass. So, a little rushed, we set off.

As we enter the back of the church, a couple of the ushers recognize us, smile, and wave hello. One of them hands us the weekly bulletin. It's nice to be greeted and feel welcomed. We place our fingers in the holy water and make the sign of the cross. That's a reminder of our own baptism, when we were baptized with water and signed with the cross.

When we get to our pew, we genuflect. This practice may have come out of the Middle Ages when people would bow before the king or person of high rank. Since we're here to worship our Lord, it's a sign of reverence to bow or kneel down before sitting.

The music begins, and everyone stands up. We're ready, we are paying attention, and we sing. Now some people don't sing; they don't have a good voice, or it's too early. But, c'mon people, please try; it makes a big difference. "Praise to the Lord, the Almighty, the King of Creation!" It is your active participation in the Mass!

The priest faces the congregation and begins, "in the name of the Father," and we all bless ourselves. The he says, "The Lord be with you." This comes from the Old Testament. In the Book of Ruth, Boaz, returning from Bethlehem, greets the harvesters by saying, "...The LORD be with you..." (Ru 2:4). It's a warm wish. The priest wants God's Spirit to be given to the people.

We respond, "And with your spirit." This is a recent and more accurate translation of the Latin *et cum spiritu tuo*. It doesn't just mean "you too, Father" or "and also with you." At ordination, through the laying on of the hands, the ordained man receives a gift—the power of the Holy Spirit to do things: preside over the Mass, proclaim the Gospel, pray the Eucharistic prayers, and dismiss the assembly. At each of those points in the Mass, the people acknowledge and affirm that the priest's spirit is now aligned with the Spirit of Christ, by saying, "Yes, may the Lord also be with your spirit, Father."

Then we are asked to pause and recall our sins before God. We may all say, "I confess to Almighty God, and to you my brothers and sisters..." That's the Confiteor, a beautiful prayer. Or we may respond to the priest, "Lord have mercy; Christ have mercy." Depending on the season, we may sing the Gloria, also from the Bible: "And suddenly there was a multitude of the heavenly host with the angel, praising God and saying: 'Glory to God in the highest...'" (Lk 2:13). This proclaimed the birth of Jesus.

Ok, we're all gathered together as a worshiping assembly, and the priest will collect all of our intentions into one prayer, to which everyone responds, "Amen"—a Hebrew word meaning "so be it." And then we all sit down.

Most of the words that are used at the Mass are from the Bible. And now, we open up the Bible to begin the Liturgy of the Word. The first reading is often from the Old Testament. Then we sing a Psalm together, from the same Old Testament. And then there is a New Testament reading—either from the letters of Paul or another apostolic reading. The readings are usually done by a lay lector, who has, hopefully, looked at the readings in advance and is prepared to read them so all can hear them clearly. Since Vatican II, the lector is often a woman, standing in the ambo, proclaiming the Word of the Lord without the formerly required veil on her head.

The Catholic who attends Mass on a weekly basis is exposed to almost the entire Bible in a three-year cycle. That surprises some people. The readings are arranged to reflect the seasons of the liturgical calendar, and they highlight the solemnities, memorials, and church celebrations throughout the year.

Then it is time for the Gospel. To hear these words, we all stand in attentive reverence. That's because we believe that Christ "is present in His word, since it is He Himself who speaks when the Holy Scriptures are read in church."[5] The priest again greets us with "the Lord be with you" and then introduces the Gospel reading while marking a small cross on his forehead, lips, and heart with his thumb, and the congregation does the same thing. He makes another cross on the reading itself and begins. If a deacon is present, the deacon is supposed to proclaim the Gospel and then return to his seat. The reading concludes with "the Gospel of the Lord," and we say, "praise to you, Lord Jesus Christ"—once again proclaiming our faith in the presence of Christ in the word. Then we sit to hear the sermon.

HOMILIES

Let's take a minute to focus on this part of the Mass. Catholics call this the homily, and it has a very important place in the Mass. Some people think it is the most important part of the Mass, but it's not. The homily evokes more reaction from the people than just about anything else. Some people claim that they left their parish because the preaching was poor. Even if a homily is wanting, or less than stellar, we've still read from the Bible, and we are going to receive Jesus in the bread. Although some homilies are weak, we're not really losing anything, but admittedly, it can detract from the overall experience at Mass.

Christina: *Don't some people go to Mass just to hear the homily?*

Yes, so that's a reason why it's important. We've just heard the revealed word of God, including the words of Jesus Himself. Now it is up to the preacher to open the minds of the people to the Gospel message. The homily is an act of worship. It must be rooted in the scripture readings that have just been proclaimed. The homily should illuminate the meaning of the celebration and of the scripture and make them relevant to people's lives. It should make people think, and get them to act. It should maintain the flow of the service, from the singing and the hearing to the worshipping and receiving.

There are many books about preaching and homiletics. It's a subject that has been studied, analyzed, and debated. You don't have to be a scholar to have an opinion about the homily. What are the typical things you've heard?

Angela: *Too long—get to the point already!*

Christina: *He starts with a joke, but I can't follow him after that.*

Angela: *Don't retell the story we just heard in the Gospel. It drives me crazy!*

Christina: *Baw-ring! I'm not paying attention!*

Angela: *Short and sweet—that's how I like it.*

Preaching at Sunday Mass is hard. There's a lot happening in a typical parish on a Sunday that can crowd in on the Mass and distract people's attention. One book I read on the subject (called *Preaching Better/Practical Suggestions for Homilists,* by a bishop from Michigan, Ken Untener) addresses many of the challenges and obstacles facing a pastor.

One chapter is called, "Don't Try to Make the Homily Do Everything that Needs to Be Done." He cites a practical reality for a preacher. On any given Sunday, there are a number of things going on that need to be addressed. The example in the book includes the sudden death of a young parishioner because of a drunk driver, a special collection for famine victims that was announced late, a low response to sign ups for religious education, and—last but not least—a challenging passage in the second reading, "wives should be subordinate to their husbands." The author says that many preachers, particularly pastors, would feel the need to deal with each of these things in some way during the course of the homily.

Bishop Untener puts the situation in perspective. He says if we look at the whole event of the Mass, there are opportunities other than the homily to address these concerns. He says that just before Mass, before the entrance procession, would be an excellent time to come out and talk to the people about the child's death—a chance for a good pastor to gather the flock, state the realities, and bring the tragedy and grief into the flow of the liturgy. Then he says that the words of St. Paul about husbands and wives could be dealt with briefly, before the first reading, reminding people as they are just sitting down that these words from Ephesians don't teach us to recreate the primitive social structures of the time, but rather, they call us to understand the timeless truth that Christ's love for us should affect the way we love one another.

As for remarks about the collection, it would be appropriate to mention this issue during the shift from the Liturgy of the Word to the Liturgy of the Gifts. People are normally seated and could stand a very brief and gentle reminder (less than thirty seconds) about the special collection for famine.

And finally, at the end of the Communion Rite, the rubric says that any brief announcements can be made. Here it might seem appropriate to take about two minutes for some well-prepared remarks about the religious education program. All these things can be accomplished in short segments, allowing the homily to really be about the revealed word of God.

Angela: *What about priests that always begin with a joke?*

Somewhere along the line, beginning with a joke or a funny story became popular. The idea is that if people felt more relaxed and comfortable, they might be more receptive to the message. I've seen some priests do this pretty well. But I've also heard strong and serious objections to this approach. The Gospel is good news, but the sermon is not always time for happy talk or laughter.

Some preachers write out their entire sermon, and others use no notes at all. Sometimes a story is appropriate, or a sidebar, and sometimes quotes from other sources are appropriate. Some priests make their sermons very personal, sort of like a heart-to-heart talk, and that can often really draw people in and hold their attention. But Bishop Untener cautions against overpersonalizing, using one's self too much as an example, or adding too much about one's own family or vacations.

The ending is important, and the bishop has a rule: "Don't ever begin a homily unless you know what your last two sentences are going to be." The bell rings in a classroom, and the teacher says, "Ok, that's it; we'll pick up tomorrow where we left off." A homily doesn't end itself. The conclusion is not difficult, but it has to be prepared. Don't use "finally" or "and so," and then talk for a few more minutes. That makes people very uneasy and impatient. And don't just pull the ending out of the air. Prepare it, say what you have to say, and then end the homily with those words.[6]

As for how long, well, that's the issue that everyone comments on. The truth is, if it's a really good sermon, it can be thirty or forty minutes or longer. Think of Billy Graham or Martin Luther King or Fulton Sheen. They were riveting, and they could hold people's attention for lengthy sermons. But the Catholic people have a long-standing, firm, but unspoken expectation: they want their mass to be one hour long. An hour and five minutes? Too long.

There is no set time for a sermon, but we can say this: a homily is too long when people stop listening. The sermon should be in proportion to the whole liturgy. It's usually the longest single part of the Mass. If it exceeds the Eucharistic prayer and the entire communion rite by too great a margin, then it has become disproportionate—the centerpiece of the Mass—which it isn't.

Less is more. This requires discipline, but it's more effective, and the people appreciate it. Mark Twain once wrote a long letter to a friend and apologized for the length, saying it would have been shorter, but he didn't have time. Guest speakers who are invited to Mass to appeal for charity are told, "The longer you speak, the less money you will raise." What's wrong with a short homily? Nothing.

When the homily ends, there are a few moments for silence. We might thank God for His Word and recommit to making the Gospel message part of our lives.

Then we stand up as a community and proclaim our faith. Every week, we say out loud what we believe. We believe in one God, the Father of the Universe, the creator of all things. We believe in Jesus Christ. We believe in the Holy Spirit. We believe in one, holy, catholic (universal), and apostolic church. We believe in the forgiveness of sins. We believe in everlasting life with God. This is our faith. And it was proclaimed for us at our baptism. We proclaimed it ourselves at our confirmation. And we proclaim it at every Mass.

At civic ceremonies, people pledge their allegiance to the flag of the United States and what that represents. The Boy Scouts recite their oath and law: "on my honor, I will do my best…" When people are sworn in and assigned to public office in local communities all across America, they take an oath by raising their right hand. They make a solemn, spoken pledge to God. That's what we do at Mass.

Then, still standing, we say our prayers together as a community: the general intercessions. We pray for the church, for nations and their leaders, for people with special needs, and for the local needs of our parish. The deacon or lector recites these petitions, and we all respond, "Lord, hear our prayer."

At this point, there is a lot of movement in the church. We are celebrating the Liturgy of the Eucharist, and the priest will have to prepare the gifts, recite the Eucharistic Prayer, and perform the communion rite.

The ushers begin the collection, and usually two members of the congregation are selected to bring up the gifts of bread and wine to be used for consecration. The choir begins the offertory hymn. The priest accepts the gifts and takes them to the altar.

Now comes the presentation and preparation of the gifts. The priest takes the paten (the circular gold plate) that holds the bread, slightly raises it, and says, "Blessed are You, Lord God of all creation, for through your goodness we have received the bread we offer you; fruit of the earth and work of human hands, it will become for us the bread of life." The deacon or priest pours the wine and a little water into the chalice and says quietly, "By the mystery of this water and wine may we come to share in the divinity of Christ who humbled Himself to share in our humanity." The priest raises the cup and says, "Blessed are you, Lord God of all creation, for through your goodness we have received the wine we offer you; fruit of the vine and work of human hands, it will become our spiritual drink." And after each prayer—one for the bread and one for the wine—the people respond, "Blessed be God forever."

The priest bows and say, "With humble spirit and contrite heart may we be accepted by you, O Lord, and may our sacrifice in your sight this day be pleasing to you, Lord God." He moves to the side of the altar and rinses his hands and says, "Wash me, O Lord, from my iniquity and cleanse me from my sin."

He returns to the center and faces the people saying, "Pray, brothers and sisters, that my sacrifice and yours may be acceptable to God, the almighty Father," and the people stand and say, "May the Lord accept the sacrifice at your hands for the praise and glory of His name for our good and the good of all his holy church."

Remember, in the olden day before Vatican II, this was all done in Latin, and the priest had his back to the people. In effect, the people were praying through the priest, up through the altar, to God. But it was not done in their native language, and they couldn't see what was going on.

Now, we are all gathered around the table of the Lord together. The priest says the prayer over the offerings, and the people say, "Amen."

The Eucharistic Prayer starts again with "the Lord be with you."

"And with your Spirit."

The priest says, "Lift up your hearts!"

And we say, "We lift them up to the Lord!"

He then says, "Let us give thanks to the Lord our God!" There it is again! Thanks! That's Eucharist!

And we say, "It is right and just."

We pray another prayer called the Preface, and we all sing, "Holy, Holy, Holy…hosanna in the highest!" We all kneel for the Eucharistic prayer.

This is a long prayer but it is the heart of our faith, and it's the heart of the Mass. There are four versions of the Eucharistic prayer, used for different occasions throughout the year. Essentially, the priest says, "God, you are holy, so make these gifts holy. Send the Holy Spirit, so that the gifts may become for us the body and blood of our Lord Jesus Christ. For on the night He was betrayed, and entered willingly into his Passion, He took bread, and giving thanks, broke it and gave it to His disciples, saying, 'Take this, all of you, and eat of it, for this is my body.' Then He took the chalice, and once more giving thanks, He gave it to His disciples saying, 'Take this, all of you, and drink from it, for this is the chalice of My blood. Do this in memory of Me.'"

Whether it's with the Pope on Easter Sunday, or the bishop at Midnight Mass on Christmas Eve, or a young priest in a tiny chapel in the middle of nowhere, the same thing is happening. We are entering into something. We are at table with the Lord, about to receive Him, and we are entering into a sacred mystery. And at this point in the Mass, we all proclaim the mystery of our faith, "When we eat this bread and drink this cup, we proclaim Your death, O

Lord, until You come again." Jesus Himself is now present in the Eucharist, as the sacramental sign of the Real Presence.

The prayer continues, recalling the saving acts of God, and those in heaven, most dear—including Mary, the mother of God, and Joseph her spouse and the apostles and all the martyrs and saints. We pray for the church, the Pope, and the bishop and all the clergy and all the people gathered. We pray for the salvation of all our departed brothers and sisters, that they may all receive the fullness of God's glory. And with the body and blood of Jesus raised up before us, the priest concludes with "through Him, with Him, and in Him, O God Almighty Father, in the unity of the Holy Spirit, all glory and honor is Yours, forever and ever."

Now the communion rite begins by saying the Our Father, the prayer that Jesus Himself taught us. The priest says, "The peace of the Lord be with you always," and again the people say, "And with your spirit." We are asked to offer each other the sign of peace. It's a great part of the Mass, a chance to smile and greet people near us. Justin Martyr said, "When prayers are concluded, we exchange the kiss." We should receive Jesus with gratitude and purity of heart, reconciling ourselves to God, so it's important to offer a gesture of unity and forgiveness to those around us and to offer them a sincere sign of peace.

The priest then places a tiny piece of bread into the cup and says quietly, "May this mingling of the body and blood of our Lord Jesus Christ bring eternal life to us who receive it."

Then, "Lamb of God, You take away the sins of the world; have mercy on us, and grant us peace."

The priest holds up the broken host, and the chalice, and says, "Behold the Lamb of God, behold Him who takes away the sins of the world. Blessed are those who are called to the supper of the Lamb."

And everyone responds, "Lord, I am not worthy that You should enter under my roof, but only say the word, and my soul shall be healed."

It's time to receive. We're prepared now. And we are in communion. Just as God fed our Jewish ancestors in the desert on their pilgrimage, God now gives us food for our spiritual journey together. We process together to the altar, reverently, united in song. And we are united in the body and blood of Christ. The minister offers us the body of Christ, and we receive Him in our hands, and once again we respond, "Amen." During communion we pray silently in our hearts, thanking and praising God, and asking for the grace that this sacrament promises.

Finally, the priest says, "Let us pray," and we stand for the final blessing and dismissal. We bow our heads as the priest blesses us in the name of the Father, Son, and Holy Spirit. The priest or deacon dismisses the assembly: "Go in peace, glorifying the Lord by your life!" We are now propelled back into the world to be witnesses to Christ, ready to share the Gospel of love. It's a good exercise, a pretty good way to spend an hour each week.

Angela: *It's just not easy to do every week.*

Well, if you want to get in shape, or prepare for a race, you have to exercise. You get on the treadmill, run a certain distance, and record your progress. You do the same regimen every day, or three times per week. You track your progress. If you want to lose weight, you weigh yourself; if you want to get faster, you time yourself. You become more conscious of how much you eat, and you start to eliminate some things. You drink more water and get more rest.

And for any endeavor, you need to manage your time. Try to make a record of how you spend your time. How much time each day do you spend exercising, going through e-mails, shopping, talking on the phone, and sleeping? How much face time do you spend with other people? How much time at meals or commuting or watching TV? Then multiply that by seven days or thirty days. Make a chart; I bet it will be pretty shocking.

How much time do you set aside for God? One hour a week? Ten minutes each night? I mean, if you look at your life from the point of view of time management, and you start tracking your activities, there's plenty of time for prayer and worship. You just have to move some things around and adjust your priorities.

If you want or need an enriched spiritual life, you have to devote some time to it. Start exercising. Talk to God before you go to bed. And greet Him when you wake up in the morning. Remember the Proverb, "In all your ways be mindful of Him, and He will make straight your paths" (Prv 3:6). Look at the Bible, and see if you can encounter Jesus. Ask Jesus to come into your life, or at least let yourself be loved by Him. If you start exercising, going to church is not hard work. It's just what you do and who you are. Come celebrate the Mass.

In talking about the church earlier, I mentioned that the Mass is celebrated every day. Actually, that's not true. On Good Friday and the following day, the church does not celebrate the sacraments at all, except for Penance and the Anointing of the Sick. The church celebrates the Lord's Passion, and the altar is left completely bare: no cloths, no candles, and no cross. Holy Communion is distributed only within the Good Friday service, but it can be brought to the sick at any time.

It's a beautiful moment in time. In a real sense, on Holy Saturday the entire church waits at the Lord's tomb. We pray and fast and meditate on the Passion and death of our Lord and on His descent into hell. The whole church waits in silence for His resurrection.

When night falls, it is time for the Easter Vigil Mass. This is the greatest of all solemnities throughout the entire liturgical year. It hearkens back to the Passover ritual, described in the twelfth chapter of the book of Exodus. It is a ritual of remembrance—when the Lord struck the land of Egypt but passed over the houses of the Israelites, who had applied the blood of lambs to the doorposts and lintels where they were eating the meal. "This was a night of vigil for the LORD, when He brought them out of the land of Egypt; so on this night all Israelites must keep a vigil for the LORD throughout their generations" (Ex 12:42).

The entire Easter Vigil Mass takes place at night. On this night, the universal church meditates on the wonders the Lord God has done for His people from the beginning. It is the longest Mass of the year, and essentially contains four parts. It begins at the back of a darkened church with the blessing of the fire and the preparation of the paschal or Easter candle. A small fire is started just outside the church and blessed by the priest. The paschal candle is brought to him, and he cuts into the candle with a stylus. First he cuts a cross and then the Greek letter for alpha, above the cross, and the letter omega below, and then the four numerals of the current year between the arms of the cross.

The paschal candle is lit, and the deacon takes it into the church. The priest and all the people hold unlit candles. The deacon holds the candle up, and three separate times sings, "The light of Christ," and the people respond, "Thanks be to God." The priest and all the people light their candles from the paschal flame, and the darkened church is lit by candles. The paschal candle is placed in its stand, and the lights are lit throughout the church.

Then something beautiful takes place—again, only once each year. The deacon sings a hymn of praise from the ambo (lectern). It is called the "Exsultet," sung a cappella, and it takes about ten minutes. It recounts all the wondrous deeds the Lord has done. It is sung before the paschal candle and ends with these words:

Therefore, O Lord, we pray You that this candle, hallowed to the honor of Your name, may persevere undimmed, to overcome the darkness of this night. Receive it as a pleasing fragrance, and let it mingle with the lights of heaven. May this flame be found still burning with the Morning Star; the one Morning Star who never sets, Christ Your Son, who, coming back from death's domain, has shed His peaceful light on humanity, and lives and reigns forever and ever.[7]

During the next part of the Mass, the Liturgy of the Word, no less than nine readings are provided: seven from the Old Testament, one Epistle, and one Gospel. We read about the time of Creation and of Abraham in Genesis and of Moses in Exodus. We hear from the prophets Isaiah, Baruch, and Ezekiel, and from the letter of Saint Paul to the Romans. And then we read the Gospel—about the first day of the week when they came to the tomb and saw that Jesus was not there. Then it is time for a reflection, the homily.

The next part of the Mass is also unique. It is time for those who have been preparing and studying to be baptized and/or confirmed. These are the catechumens, those who have been receiving instruction in their faith. Beneath the light of the paschal candle, the rite of baptism is carried out, including the parents, godparents, the anointing, the white garment, and the baptismal washing. It's is a moment of joy for the families and of pride for the whole congregation. Now, if adults have been baptized, or if any other people are prepared, the priest is advised to administer the rite of confirmation, with the sponsors present.

After this sacramental celebration is completed, all in the church stand with their lighted candles in their hands. The whole community will renew their promises. The priest says, "Dear brothers and sisters, through the paschal mystery, we have been buried with

Christ in baptism so that we may walk with Him in newness of life. And so, now that our Lenten observance is concluded, let us renew the promises of holy baptism by which we once renounced Satan and his works and promised to serve God in the holy Catholic Church."

"Do you renounce Satan? Do you renounce sin?" I do! The priest then sprinkles the people with holy water, while the people chant an appropriate hymn for baptism. I find it to be bracing and beautiful.

The fourth and final part of the Vigil Mass is carried out—the Liturgy of the Eucharist—and it takes places according to the standard rites, just like at a regular Mass. At the end of this long celebration, the priest's solemn blessing may say, "Now that the days of the Lord's Passion have drawn to a close, may you who celebrate the gladness of the paschal feast come with Christ's help, and exulting in spirit, to those feasts that are celebrated in eternal joy!" Amen!

EASTER

More people attend Mass on Easter Sunday than any other day of the year. I think the Catholic people instinctively know that God is real and that the time to celebrate and worship together is on Easter. The people who went to the church on Ash Wednesday make it back there on Easter Sunday, now dressed in their Sunday best.

The entire church celebrates, rejoices! The Easter Mass in Rome is televised and beamed around the world. Sing joyfully to the Lord, all you lands! Men wear suits and ties, and women wear beautiful spring dresses. People take pictures. In many cultures, people order lamb for dinner that day. *Buona Pasqua*! Happy Easter!

It's a good time to ask, "When is God present in my life?" The first followers of Jesus became aware of Him in a place called Galilee. It was a time in history long ago. They had a personal encounter with Jesus and were called by Him. He taught them and healed them. He loved them and died for them. He loved us and died for us. We believe that He rose from the dead to conquer death, to conquer sin. He said, "Do this in memory of me." Are you ready to receive Him?

The Mass helps us to renew Him in us. We return to the Mass, over and over, to become witnesses to the Resurrection. We return to the Mass to receive Him and to renew our love for Him. If you love Jesus, it's not hard. Celebrate! He is risen!

Endnotes

1. Pope Paul VI, *Constitution on the Sacred Liturgy*, December 4, 1963, Section 47.

2. Pope Paul VI, *Constitution on the Sacred Liturgy*, December 4, 1963, Section 48.

3. *Catechism of the Catholic Church* (Liguori, MO: Liguori Publications, 1994), 1324.

4. Pope Benedict XVI, *Deus Caritas Est* (God is Love) Section 14.

5. Pope Paul VI, *Constitution on the Sacred Liturgy*, December 4, 1963, Section 7.

6. Ken Untener, *Preaching Better—Practical Suggestions for Homilists* (Mahwah: Paulist Press, 1999), 29–110.

7. The Exsultet: The Proclamation of Easter, http://www.us-ccb.org/prayer-and-worship/liturgical-year/easter/easter-proclamation-exsultet.cfm.

CHAPTER 9

The Commandments

§

We've been talking in this book about the ways in which we encounter God. We can't complete this discussion without considering God's law, as expressed in His Ten Commandments.

Angela: *Here's where you may lose us. The Ten Commandments are not exactly a hot topic of discussion.*

Christina: *You never hear them discussed. Are they even relevant today?*

Well, people certainly still care about what's right and wrong, don't they? Aren't the laws today designed to ensure fairness? Don't most people today still want to do the right thing? I've read that over 60 percent of American companies now have detailed codes of conduct. They are designed to translate basic company values into specific modes of behavior: language and dress codes, hiring and firing policies, and so forth. And now almost one-third of American firms have either ethics training programs or full-time ethics officers on staff. Companies now hire accounting firms and law firms to assist them in designing comprehensive ethics programs. And yet, corporate malfeasance at all levels still thrives.

Angela: *But where do the commandments fit it? Most people can't name them all.*

Christina: *I know seven or eight; two of them are the same. I know thou shall not kill, thou shall not steal, thou shall not commit adultery, don't curse, mmm, that's it. Dad, people don't even argue about them or think about them anymore.*

I know; I think the last we heard about them was a few years ago. Remember that exquisite block of granite with the chiseled commandments that stood in a courthouse in Texas? It was defended by the local official there, against a call to have it removed from a public space. Remember what happened? The Ten Commandments were removed. It was not a fight over the meaning of the commandments, it was over whether an expression of religion could be displayed in a building paid for by taxpayers—not a fruitful discussion.

In today's society, people do not like to be told what to do. They do not trust authority and resist absolutes. They don't like dogma, dictums, directives, proscriptions, precepts, or rules, and they certainly do not pay attention to commandments.

But I say they might be relevant if we thought of them differently.

What if we thought of them as a helpful guide offered to us by a generous benefactor?

Let's say we are a group of parents and Boy Scouts going on an overnight camping trip up and over a mountain. We have what we need: tent, backpacks, mess kits, flashlight, bug spray, and so forth. One member of the group has taken the trail before, and he pretty much knows the way. He knows some good stopping points and thinks he remembers the ideal camping spot for the overnight stay. But just before the group is about to set off, the ranger suggests that the group take along the camper guidebook, which has lots of stuff in it that will be helpful and needed for a hike of this kind. So, off they go with their guide.

There are different kinds of directives in the guide, some pointed and very specific. The guidebook says no fires—not because the ranger doesn't want people to enjoy a nice campfire, but for two reasons: one, fires at certain times of the year, tend to attract bears and other unfriendly critters (skunks), and two, this is a leaf and dry-wooded area, and a small untended fire could spread and become a major problem for everyone. Some of the people are disappointed, but they accept and understand the reason for this rule.

Another directive is "at night be sure to place all of your food in a closed bag, and suspend it on a hanging branch, away from your sleeping tents." This is an annoyance, but it makes sense. If a bear really does show up, he won't be pawing at the tents. He'll be a distance away, and the campers would be safe.

The guide also has information about the trail, like where to be careful crossing streams, where to avoid slippery areas, and where to camp if it is particularly windy or rainy that night. The guide points out good locations for star watching if the sky is clear and how to appreciate the nuanced beauty of the variety of trees, shrubs, and birds. Isn't this guidebook a good idea? It helps us along our journey. We have a better chance of avoiding injury, attack, and a number of otherwise unforeseen difficulties. We are more aware of things to avoid and better able to appreciate and enjoy the things we encounter. If we follow the guide carefully, we have a much better chance of getting to our destination safely and satisfactorily.

That's one way we should still think of the Ten Commandments; they are instructions that will help us reach our destination safely.

When God handed these "ordinances, statutes, and decrees" to His people, He also gave the people the reason for them and an explanation that they could give their children. God said this in the Old Testament:

...When your son asks you, "What do these...[things]... mean?"...You shall say to your son, "We were once slaves of

Pharaoh in Egypt, but the LORD brought us...from there, to lead us into the land he promised on oath to our ancestors. The LORD commanded us to observe all these statutes...so that we may always have as good a life as we have today" (Dt 6:20–21, 23–24).

The Ten Commandments are a guide into freedom. Still today, they are a guide out of our weaknesses, shortcomings, and sinfulness into a life of abundance, joy, and peace.

Some people notice that there are two different versions of the Ten Commandments (the decalogue). The commandments are found twice in the Pentateuch (the first five books of Hebrew scripture), one in Exodus 20, and one in Deuteronomy 5.

Jews and Christians all have Ten Commandments, but they are numbered slightly differently. Jews make the Roman Catholic first commandment into two separate ones, and they combine the ninth and tenth commandments into a single one: "you shall not covet."

Among Christians, Roman Catholics and Lutherans usually summarize the texts from Deuteronomy. Anglicans, Orthodox, Presbyterians, and Baptists summarize Exodus. The essential meanings are the same; the biggest difference between the two is the ordering of items not to covet.

As we know them, here are the Ten Commandments:

1. I am the LORD your God; you shall not have strange gods before Me.
2. You shall not take the name of the LORD your God in vain.
3. Remember to keep holy the Lord's Day.
4. Honor your father and your mother.
5. You shall not kill.

6. You shall not commit adultery.
7. You shall not steal.
8. You shall not bear false witness against your neighbor.
9. You shall not covet your neighbor's wife.
10. You shall not covet your neighbor's goods.

The first three commandments have to do with our relationship with God. They challenge our faith and call us into a relationship. The first is "I am the LORD your God; you shall not have strange (other) gods before me." What things in our life do we place before God? What do we hold as more valuable then God? Be honest. Our list might include our home, our money, our possessions, our time, our level of influence, ourselves! We think of ourselves, and just about everything else, before—and more often—than God. The first commandment calls us to attention. If God is the creator of all things, then God must be placed in our life before all things!

Second is "you shall not take the name of the Lord your God in vain." When we are in relationship with God, we would never use His name to curse something or someone or use the name of Jesus in vain. Words matter, and what we say can have a lasting and powerful impact on ourselves and how we act. The words we use can shape our attitudes and opinions. Taking God's name in vain? You shall not!

The third commandment says we must worship God on a regular basis. We'll spend a little more time on this below, but let's face it, many people no longer worship on Sunday. Once you get used to not worshiping, it gets harder to do it. We're lazy, and there are too many good things to do on a Sunday morning. But God's commandment is "keep holy the Lord's day"!

THE FOURTH COMMANDMENT

The remaining seven commandments have to do with our relationship with the world and how we should live. What do these commandments mean to us, and how can we apply them? Let's look at a few a little more deeply, starting with the fourth commandment: "honor thy father and thy mother." This commandment means a lot more than simply being good to your parents.

When you were very young, you were dependent on Mom and me for everything: for your food, clothing, protection, and education. And as teenagers, you needed us for discipline and guidance and financial and moral support. When you become parents, your children are dependent on you. In fact, when many people become parents, they learn and experience true selflessness for the first time in their lives. Parents come to realize that they would do anything for their children, even take food out of their own mouths to feed them. How often have we heard of people working two jobs to feed their children or to get them the best education possible?

When Mom and I get old, we will become dependent on you as well. Most of my peers now, the baby boomers, have to deal with the issue of providing proper care for their parents. In this faster-paced, more complicated world, people are not always able to have their aging and ailing parents live with them. They have to work full time, pay the mortgage, and support all the needs of their own immediate family. They may feel that they cannot provide the proper care and medical attention needed and have to place their parents in some kind of assisted-living or full-time nursing home. Some of these environments are less than ideal, and yet the alternative is worse. My friends and I grapple with guilt about these choices and find the pressure of simultaneously raising our own children and taking responsibility for our parents to be a heavy burden, and one that may last for years.

People are quick to judge or criticize, but none of these decisions are easy. If, God forbid, your mom and I were afflicted with dementia or some serious illness, what is the proper care we should receive? These situations can go on for years and cause long periods of physical separation. End-of-life considerations come into play, and they are complicated. There are cases where years and years of burdensome health-care costs are thrust on the children of aging parents, and resources are not unlimited.

And think about the people who live in nursing homes now and have no one to visit them. How do they feel, and what are they thinking? Have their children moved away or passed away? What does it mean to honor them?

The fourth commandment serves to remind us to do everything we can to ease their way. We have to do everything in our power to help them maintain their sense of dignity. If dementia or Alzheimer's afflict them, we do what we can to make sure that they receive loving, prayerful, pastoral care.

There may be issues with our extended family. How many people do you know who have had disagreements, serious issues, and separations from their in-laws? Perhaps there was an argument one Christmas, some breach of trust over money, or a decision about the grandchildren—something that causes a rift that doesn't get addressed for months and years. Bad feelings harden. People stay apart and don't try anymore. Have you ever heard someone say, "I can't stand my mother-in-law," or "we're not on speaking terms"?

These are not easy rifts to mend, but the fourth commandment forces us to consider something: if I really love my husband or wife, how can I not love his or her parents? It's similar to the question I posed earlier: "if I really love my own children, how can I not love their mother?" Who takes responsibility for these damaged relationships? We do. We have to look for opportunities to bridge the gaps or separations. We have to be strong, try to forgive and forget, and move on. We have to become the source of peace within our own family.

What's wrong with trying to follow the fourth commandment? Absolutely nothing. It encourages a sense of respect, a sense of responsibility, and a sense of gratitude. It engenders an appreciation for the whole family: for your parents, for their parents, and even for their brothers and sisters. It is something to hand on to your own children, thus, keeping a tradition alive. We are all urged to be agents of peace within our entire family and to set an example for everyone. It may encourage your own children to honor you one day; so work toward becoming worthy of that honor. The fourth commandment is the only one that includes words of encouragement; it says in Exodus, "Honor your father and your mother, that you may have a long life in the land, which the Lord your God is giving you" (Ex 20:12).

Many good people in the world today make sacrifices to ensure that their parents are safe, cared for, and loved. And by fulfilling this commandment of God, I believe they receive a special grace, and as the saying goes, their reward will be great in heaven.

The Third Commandment

Let's go back to that third commandment: "remember to keep holy the Sabbath day."

We've talked about weekly worship, and this is a commandment that most people have brushed aside or completely ignored. On any given Sunday morning, just look around. The soccer fields are packed, tee times at golf courses are taken, there are lines for brunches at restaurants, liquor stores are open, and shopping malls across America are bustling. Church anyone?

How about this? If you believe in God, doesn't God have the right to command that a day be set aside to honor Him?

A long time ago, the president of the United States issued a proclamation:

> Now, therefore, I, Abraham Lincoln, president of the United States, do hereby appoint and set apart the last Thursday in November next as a day which I desire to be observed by all my fellow-citizens, wherever they may be then, as a day of thanksgiving and praise to Almighty God, the beneficent Creator and Ruler of the universe. And I do further recommend to my fellow citizens aforesaid, that on that occasion they do reverently humble themselves in the dust, and from thence offer up penitent and fervent prayers and supplications to the great Disposer of events for a return of the inestimable blessings of peace, union, and harmony throughout the land which it has pleased Him to assign as a dwelling place for ourselves and for our posterity throughout all generations" (Abraham Lincoln, sixteenth president of the United States, 1863).[1]

Everyone loves Thanksgiving. It's our favorite holiday, right? No presents, no major preparation, just a parade, a great dinner with family and friends, and some football.

Here's the proclamation from God, the Creator of all things, as found in Deuteronomy:

> Observe the Sabbath day—keep it holy, as the Lord, your God, commanded you. Six days you may labor and do all your work; but the seventh day is a Sabbath of the Lord, your God. You shall not do any work, either you, your son or your

daughter, your male or female slave, your ox or donkey or any work animal, or the resident alien who lives within your gates, so that your male and female slave may rest as you do. Remember that you too were once slaves in the land of Egypt, and the Lord, your God brought you from there with his strong hand and outstretched arm. That is why the Lord, your God, has commanded you to observe the Sabbath day (Dt 5:12–15).

So the commandment as expressed in Deuteronomy emphasizes rest from human activity, so that human activity does not constantly distract us from God. God insists on rest from constant human labor (and Jesus encourages rest too: "come away and rest with me awhile"). In Exodus the commandment says you may labor for six days, but on the seventh day you must rest because the Lord rested on the seventh day from the work of Creation. Thus the Lord blessed the Sabbath and made it holy. God said, "Remember to keep it holy."

Abraham Joshua Heschel wrote *The Sabbath*, first published in 1951, and it is essential reading for all who take interest in the third commandment. In it, he beautifully develops the idea of an "architecture of holiness" that appears not in space but in time. To encounter God in the Bible, one must understand this:

The Bible is more concerned with time than with space. It sees the world in the dimension of time. It pays more attention to generations, to events, than to countries, to things; it is more concerned with history than geography. To understand the teaching of the Bible, one must accept its premise that time has a meaning for life which is at least equal to that of space; that time has a significance and sovereignty of its own.

Judaism is a religion of time aiming at the sanctification of time. The meaning of the Sabbath is to celebrate time rather than space. Six days a week we live under the tyranny of things of space; on the Sabbath we try to become attuned to *holiness in time*. It is a day on which we are called upon to share in what is eternal in time, to turn from the results of creation to the mystery of creation; from the world of creation to the creation of the world.[2]

For Catholics, and all Christians, Sunday replaced the Sabbath. Jesus was an observant Jew and followed all righteousness, but after His Passion and death, He rose from the dead "on the third day." Since Sunday is the day that Jesus rose from the dead, it has become the basis point for every Christian's spirituality. The Resurrection freed us from sin and death and is the dawn of a new creation. The catechism explains, "In Christ's Passover, Sunday fulfills the spiritual truth of the Jewish Sabbath and announces our eternal rest in God."[3]

Since Jesus gave us Himself at the first Eucharist, the best way to celebrate the Lord's Day is by going to Mass and receiving Holy Communion. Millions of people do this and then have dinner with their friends and families.

For those who do not attend Mass, I would say, start the day with a prayer. Acknowledge God, and talk to Him. Take a step closer to God. Alter some daily or weekly behavior; change something in your life that may open you up to a sense of the spiritual. If you are not ready to take a full step, consider a half step: add a simple prayer at night; "Lord Jesus, come into my life." And if you are not ready for that, then just lean in, and let God love you.

After prayer to God, we can celebrate and enjoy all of His creation. Sunday dinner with family is a tradition for many. A walk in the park or along the beach allows us to breathe and take in the world's beauty and God's creation. A round of golf with friends is wonderful, and it should be done with a sense of appreciation and gratitude for all God has provided.

Christina: *What about people who have to work on Sunday?*

Try to offer the day up in sacrifice to God. Try to be mindful of God throughout the day. And make time to remember.

Angela: *But all the soccer and baseball games—it's a big day for kids' sports.*

Ok so the world has changed. The scheduling of children's sporting activities on Sunday morning is really a shame, and many a pastor have expressed great frustration with this stubborn reality. I don't have the answer. People must figure out a way to fulfill their obligation to worship and figure out a way to keep the day holy. The third commandment is not a suggestion or a neat idea. It is a way to bring God back into the center of your life and draw you ever closer to the promise of an eternal peace that passes all understanding.

THE FIFTH COMMANDMENT

The fifth commandment is "thou shall not kill." Since the time that Cain killed his brother Abel, mankind has broken this commandment in every century and in every society. Killing occurs every day. But this commandment goes beyond murder. It touches many aspects of modern life, so let's try to unpack it.

First, why are Catholics pro-life?

In the Bible it says, "God created man in His image; in the divine image He created them; male and female He created them" (Gn 1:27). And "God looked at everything He had made, and found it very good" (Gn 1:31). Since God made everything and found it very good, and since God made mankind in His own image, then man is holy or sacred. The belief that man is holy or sacred—the belief in the sacredness of human life—is the basis and foundation of a moral vision for society.

Since the very beginning, the church has taught or preached a moral vision. And over the centuries—through the councils, proclamations, bulls, and sermons—the church has refined and clarified its social teaching. Earlier, I mentioned *Reram Novarum* (Latin for "Revolutionary Change"), Pope Leo XIII's encyclical that addressed the condition of the working classes during the height of the Industrial Revolution. It supported the rights of labor to form unions, it rejected socialism and unrestricted capitalism, and affirmed the right to private property. It was a foundational text of modern Catholic social teaching. Later encyclicals expounded on this and developed into "Seven Themes of Catholic Social Teaching."[4]

Again, in Centesimus annus, John Paul II said,

> All **Catholic social doctrine is based on the dignity of the human person.** Man derives both his dignity and his social nature from the fact that he is made in the image and likeness of God. God is a community of loving relationships between the three Persons of the Blessed Trinity. Man similarly seeks out loving relationships in his life on earth. As man by his very nature desires to live in loving community with others and with God, Catholic social doctrine seeks to support all that facilitates this endeavor, and seeks to eliminate all that hampers this endeavor.[5]

The belief that human life is sacred is the foundation of all the principles of Catholic social teaching. The first of the seven themes is the "Life and Dignity of the Human Person." This theme of Catholic social teaching addresses all the major issues related to life: war, capital punishment, embryonic stem-cell research, euthanasia, physician-assisted suicide, and abortion.

WAR

Angela: *If the commandment is "thou shall not kill," then how can any war be justified?*

St. Augustine, writing back in the fourth century, was probably the first to grapple with a moral code for mortal combat by coming up with what is known as the just war doctrine. It is often referred to in discussions of major conflicts.

We think of World War II as a legitimate and just war, with the forces of good against the evil of Nazism and Fascism. Your grandfather, like many World War II veterans, often said, "If we hadn't stopped Japan, the war might have continued for years, and many more millions of people would have died." That surely seems true. But as we look back at the bombings of Hiroshima and Nagasaki, what do we see? To end the war, the atomic bomb was used on two cites, and some 140,000 people were incinerated—burned to death—and subsequent generations were scarred. It took years for people to finally see the stark reality of that event from film and documentaries.

From a wider view, it's been written that in the twentieth century alone, over one hundred million human beings were killed by other human beings. For any follower of Jesus, the killing of innocent people is a troubling and painful thought. It is difficult to accept or defend aggressive military action that results in the loss of innocent human life.

The catechism says that for military force to be considered legitimate or just, these conditions must be met:

A. Damage inflicted by the aggressor must be "lasting, grave, and certain."

B. All other means of putting an end to the conflict must have been shown to be impractical or ineffective.

C. There must be serious prospects for success.

D. The use of arms must not produce evils and disorders graver than the evil to be eliminated.[6]

Christina: *But even if these conditions are met, it's still war, and it's still killing.*

Many good Catholic men and women have served heroically for just causes in war, and we are not judging anyone in this discussion. We are trying to understand the meaning and value of the fifth commandment of God. It's one thing if appropriate public authorities meet criteria for a just war; the hope is that the people who make decisions about war draw from and include a sense of morality. I agree, Christina, it's extremely difficult to justify war. It's not just a question of being a hawk or dove. What happens when we kneel before God? As followers of Jesus Christ, could we stand before God and defend any war as just? When we examine our own consciences, can Catholics take pride in or boast of war? "We had no choice, Lord; we had to kill them."

Military action is necessary to defend our way of life—currently to protect ourselves from the onslaught of Islamic jihad or Islamic terrorism (ironically taken up in God's name, as so many wars have been). God will be our judge, and deciding on the legitimacy of war is not an easy or satisfying exercise. We have to approach the justification of all military actions with fear and trembling.

CAPITAL PUNISHMENT

Angela: *Where is the church on the death penalty?*

For years, when I was younger, I thought the death penalty was justified, just on the basis of logic. Society had the right to express its outrage toward a person who had killed a valued human being: a politician (like the president), a prominent leader (a bishop or a general), or any defenseless person (a nun, a doctor, a child, or any unarmed person for that matter). But my reasoning didn't make sense because every human being has value.

In the past, many Catholics supported the death penalty, and church teaching tolerated it. The death penalty was justified if it was the only possible way of effectively defending human lives against an unjust aggressor. But the teaching in the catechism is "if nonlethal means are sufficient to defend and protect people's safety... Authority will limit itself to such means." And once a guilty party's identity and responsibility are fully determined, the state now has the means to incarcerate and render an offender incapable of doing harm. Therefore, "cases in which the execution of the offender is an absolute necessity, 'are very rare, if not practically nonexistent.'"[7] So, it cannot be said that the Catholic Church approves of, or condones, capital punishment.

EUTHANASIA

Christina: *There were a number of articles a year or two ago about the value of assisted suicide. Remember the young woman who had terminal brain cancer and decided to end her life on her own terms?*

Yes, this is a serious area of concern, and it's evolving. I think people had assumed that this issue had quieted down or gone away, but it is still advancing under the radar of daily national news. There is an aggressive effort underway in several states to legalize physician-assisted suicide and euthanasia.

At the end of 2014, a bill was introduced in the New York State Senate called the Death with Dignity Act, and a similar bill was introduced in the New York State Assembly with this rationale: When an individual has a terminal illness, the effects are often debilitating, filled with discomfort and agony. "They should be able to decide for themselves how and when they die. These patients, when mentally competent, should be afforded this right. Patients seek to die with dignity, on their own terms."[8]

So we are talking now about peaceful dying and dying with dignity and expressions like, "facing death on my own terms." The proponents of physician-assisted suicide and euthanasia are trying (with success) to make it more palatable to the public by using this language. Lots of new terms have cropped up to help us understand pro-death. When a sick person chooses to commit suicide on his or her own, phrases like "self-deliverance," "patient-directed dying," and "choice-in-dying" have been employed to soften potential criticism. And when a doctor is brought in to prescribe a lethal overdose, terms like "physician-managed death," "medically assisted dying," and "aid-in-dying" have been used.

Angela: *Relieving suffering does contain an element of compassion.*

Ok, but how did we get here? I mean, doctors helping people to die? May I sketch some history? Even before the birth of Christ, the ancient Greeks and Romans were familiar with and tolerant of some form of mercy killing. In the fourth century BC, Hippocrates resisted this idea and provided guidance. He devised an oath (the Hippocratic Oath) that would prohibit doctors from giving a deadly drug to help someone voluntarily end their life. Down through the centuries, Jews and Christians also resisted this notion and developed strength in their opposition to euthanasia. In many societies laws were developed to restrict the practice of suicide. But advocacy for euthanasia continued, and a milestone in the debate occurred in the nineteenth century, with the more widespread use of morphine—not only to alleviate pain but also to intentionally end a life. Legal battles in Europe and the United States continued.

By the 1970s and '80s the pro-choice movement grew in influence, and people again began to talk about putting an end to the suffering that people experienced in old age. In the name of compassion, people said it was time to help the sick to avoid a horrible, painful death. The movement began to gain traction in Western Europe (particularly propelled by the Dutch and the Swiss) and in England. In California a small association called the Hemlock Society USA[9] was started by a man named Derek Humphrey in 1990. It went on to become the largest and oldest right-to-die organization in America, fighting for voluntary euthanasia and physician-assisted suicide to be made legal for terminally ill adults.

Within a short period of ten to fifteen years, voluntary euthanasia gained traction. The Hemlock Society began to be sourced in medical and legal texts and gained respect as one of the pioneer right-to-die organizations in the world. School textbooks almost always include at least one proactive essay on the subject of euthanasia. Humphrey's book entitled *Final Exit* showed readers exactly how to exercise their ultimate "civil liberty." The name hemlock was a clever choice; the noun "hemlock" refers to a conifer tree or a waterweed. It was the root of the weed that was used in classical Greek and Roman times as a deadly poison when either the state ordered death by suicide or a rational person chose it.[10]

Enter Jack Kevorkian, known as Dr. Death. He pushed the envelope and openly tried to get the American medical profession to change its attitude on euthanasia. He taped dying sessions with potential suicide patients and made bold statements in interviews on television. He was a pathologist, not a general practitioner, and more of a media circus performer than a dedicated campaigner. He alone thought he could alter the attitudes of the huge American medical profession. He underestimated the respect doctors have for the law and for their oath. Without law reform accompanying it, most doctors—even those sympathetic to his cause—would not take the same chances that he would. Kevorkian ended up going to jail, and his failure helped set the movement back for a time.

But the right-to-die movement did not die. In November of 2016 Colorado became the sixth state in the nation with a 'right-to-die' law, joining Washington, Oregon, California, Vermont and Montana. Now New Jersey has joined New York State in the ongoing effort to make assisted suicide legal. Just as with abortion, people take to the courts to try and force change. For now, the general public is going along.

A May 2006 Gallup Poll found that 69 percent of Americans answered yes to the question "when a person has a disease that cannot be cured, do you think doctors should be allowed by law to end the patient's life by some painless means if the patient and his family request it?" In fact most of the current polling, as of 2015, on the subject of physician-assisted suicide reveals that the general public's support is as high as 70 percent!

Catholics are not alone in opposing physician-assisted suicide, though. Evangelical Christians, Latter-day Saints, the Greek Orthodox, and Orthodox Jews also oppose the idea. These groups believe that, with elder abuse on the rise, if old people begin to feel that they have become a burden or hardship for their families, some could be pressured into ending their lives prematurely by their families, their doctors, and by insurance companies.

Are doctors willing to help patients end their lives? Well, the American Medical Association (AMA) had always opposed physician-assisted suicide. Up until 2016 an opinion posted on the AMA website said that the practice was "fundamentally incompatible with the physician's role as a healer." Logically, people reach out to their doctors to help them heal and recover, but if a doctor is seen as a potential agent for ending life, it could be a blow to the reputation and credibility of the entire medical profession. However, as of 2016, the AMA has decided to publicly take "no position" on physician-assisted suicide.

You know of palliative care, right? That's hospital care that alleviates a patient's symptoms, even if there is no hope of a cure by other means. It focuses on the relief of pain, symptoms, and the emotional stress brought on by a serious illness. You do not have to have a terminal illness to qualify for palliative care. In some cases, palliative treatments may be used to relieve, for example, the nausea that comes with chemotherapy, which may then help the patient tolerate more aggressive or longer-term treatment. Effective palliative care involves figuring out what bothers the patient the most (nausea, pain, confusion, delirium, psychosis) and treating that symptom aggressively. At a certain point, when a disease is determined to be terminal—and specific criteria are met to determine this—a patient is eligible for hospice.

Hospice is a type of palliative care and is covered by Medicare. People who have reached the point where hospice has been recommended are those who, surrounded by love and care, can face the end and truly experience dying with dignity.

Angela: *Is the church clear and consistent on this?*

Yes, I believe so, because there are fundamental moral principles at work. Human life is sacred because it is created by God. We are made in the image and likeness of God and are, therefore, holy. We did not choose the hour or the day that we were to be born. And we cannot choose the hour or the day that we are to die. God alone is the Lord of life—from beginning to end...from conception to natural death. It is wrong to say, "It's my life, and I can kill myself if I want to." It is illegal and immoral. We come from God, we belong to God, and God wants us to return to Him. "Thou shall not kill."

According to the catechism, "Whatever its motives and means, direct euthanasia consists in putting an end to the lives of handicapped, sick, or dying persons. It is morally unacceptable."[11]

Even if death is thought to be imminent, the ordinary care owed to a sick person cannot legitimately be interrupted. The use of painkillers to alleviate the sufferings of the dying, even at the risk of shortening their days, can be morally in conformity with human dignity if death is not willed as either an end or a means, but only as foreseen and tolerated as inevitable. Palliative care is a special form of charity. As such, it should be encouraged. [12]

Discontinuing medical procedures that are burdensome, dangerous, extraordinary, or disproportionate to the expected outcome, can be legitimate; it is the refusal of "overzealous" treatment. One does not will to cause death; one's inability to impede it is merely accepted. The decisions should be made by the patient if he is competent and able or, if not, by those legally and legitimately entitled to act for the patient.[13]

CLONING

Angela: *Related to all of this, I guess the issue of embryonic stem-cell research still fall under the fifth commandment. The church is always criticized for seeming to be antiscience.*

True, but that's really no longer valid. Tons of medical research is done at Catholic hospitals and universities around the world, including stem-cell research. But the teaching is consistent. We are taught that we cannot take human life and dispose of it, even for research. The catechism is clear on this: "It is immoral to produce human embryos intended for exploitation as disposable biological material."[14] Therefore, stem-cell research is acceptable but not research with human embryos.

When the Planned Parenthood videos were revealed in 2015, it stirred lots of reaction. Issues like funding for Planned Parenthood and the legality of surreptitiously obtaining and distributing the videos were discussed. But for many people of faith, the Planned Parenthood episodes pulled backed the curtain and exposed a chilling and corrosive element in our progressive society. When people discuss things like "harvesting" human tissue, and when we can casually discuss the ease of obtaining and sharing human body parts for research (over salad and red wine), we have arrived in a new dimension of science and morality. This is really what a culture of death looks like. It's not the *Prince of Darkness*, or some Darth Vader–like creature invading us. It is the tossing away of human life. It is the loss of awareness of the holiness of human life.

Angela: *So, again, Dad, do you believe the church has been consistent in its teaching about life?*

Yes. Peace not war, life in prison—not the death penalty, no suicide (even physician-assisted), and no harvesting of human life for research. There should be consistency if one is trying to develop a world view based on morality.

Abortion

Finally, let's turn to one more topic related to the life and dignity of the human person and the fifth commandment—probably the most deeply divisive of all: abortion. Let's talk about this calmly.

We now hear from the Centers for Disease Control and Prevention that the number of abortions performed in the United States since 1970 is over fifty-four million. It's hard to imagine that many human beings disposed of before birth. It's been a long struggle since Roe v. Wade (now approaching fifty years), a struggle between the proponents of life and the proponents of choice. There has been plenty of misrepresentation and confusion on both sides.

Christina: *Well, I can tell you what a majority of young women think today. We do not want someone telling us what we can or cannot do with our ovaries.*

First, I'd like to ask, what is it like for a woman to have an abortion? I don't mean a back-alley or botched abortion. I mean an abortion that is advertised as safe and legal? What is the experience like, and what is the aftermath? I read a moving op-ed piece in the *New York Times* in 2014 by a woman named Lisa Selin Davis. It was entitled, "I Couldn't Turn My Abortion into Art."[15] It was a straightforward description of her own abortion at the age of twenty-two. She told about how she had an affair in the mid-1990s with a married thirty-six-year-old man at work and got pregnant. She told her boss she intended to get an abortion and had a creative idea: she would take her video camera, record the entire experience, and turn the abortion into an experimental feminist video. She figured it shouldn't be a problem; her expectations about abortion were the same as all her friends—safe, legal, no big deal.

When she got to the clinic, her impressions changed. It was a cold environment with ten other women in the room, all avoiding eye contact. They had to sign a series of forms, including their anesthetic options. Lisa thought she would opt for local so she could be awake and record everything, but she was losing her nerve and was not allowed to use the camera anyway. She got her general anesthesia and nodded off. From there, she picks up the narrative:

The first thing I thought when I awoke from the anesthesia was that I'd never be pregnant again, that I had just squandered my only chance at motherhood. I was sobbing—I had arisen from the depths of the medication this way—as they rolled me into the recovery room where the other women were lying, almost all of them with a friend or partner or relative to brush their hair back or offer them ice chips. I could not stop crying, big heaves and gulps of it. The nurse came over at first to soothe me and then to quiet me. "You're upsetting the other girls," she said. "It hurts," I answered.

She sent the doctor over. "Sometimes we have to massage the womb," he said, inserting his hand inside me and pressing. This did not stop the crying, but eventually it stopped the pain. Or, at least, it stopped the physical pain. The experience was too traumatic for me to make art of. Or maybe it was just that I wasn't a good enough artist to transform that level of trauma into something that others could learn from and use. I had been taught that a woman's right to choose was the most important thing to fight for, but I hadn't known what a brutal choice it was. I wish that someone had alerted me to the harshness of the experience, acknowledged the layers of regret that built and fell away as the months and years passed. I want my daughters to have the option of safe and legal abortion, of course. I just don't want them to have to use it.

I was moved when I read this. The writer refers to the "harshness of the experience" and to "layers of regret." She says she wishes someone has alerted her. Haven't you heard stories like this?

It seems that, more and more, women are alerting each other to the harshness and regret. Did you see the *Rolling Stone* interview with pop-star rapper Nicki Minaj? She revealed that she had had an abortion as a teen. She said, "I thought I was going to die...It was the hardest thing I have ever gone through...It has haunted me all my life."[16]

And then recording star Toni Braxton revealed in her memoir, *Unbreak My Heart*, that her abortion filled her with guilt and remorse. She said she felt like God was punishing her for her abortion when her subsequent son was diagnosed with autism. Other celebrities like Sharon Osborne have had abortions and also describe the experience sorrowfully. Osborne's description is similar to Minaj's. She said, "I would never recommend it to anyone because it comes back to haunt you."[17]

Christina: *But they all seem to remain pro-choice.*

You're right; the writer of the *New York Times* piece said, "I want my daughters to have the option of safe and legal abortion, of course. I just don't want them to have to use it." And Minaj also clings to the label pro-choice, telling *Rolling Stone*, "It'd be contradictory if I said I wasn't pro-choice. I wasn't ready. I didn't have anything to offer a child." But more and more, these real-life testimonies express that even for those who embrace a pro-choice position, the decision to have an abortion is heartbreaking and haunts many women for the rest of their lives.

The pro-abortion movement still wants people to believe that it's not a complicated procedure, it does not have moral implications, and it's really no big deal. You can go online and read accounts of women who have to steel their nerves and emotions against the impact of an abortion. Merritt Tierce confronted abortion in a *New York Times* article ("This Is What an Abortion Looks Like") this way. "We have to stop categorizing abortions as justified or unjustified. The best thing you can do if you support reproductive rights is to force people to realize that abortion is common, and the most common abortion is a five to fifteen minute procedure elected early in the first trimester by someone who doesn't want to be pregnant or have a child. It's our job to say it's ok if that's the end of the story. It's ok if it's boring or not traumatic or even if you don't know what it was."[18]

Planned Parenthood president, Cecile Richards, recently wrote that having an abortion "was the right decision for me and my husband and it wasn't a difficult decision."[19] And a woman named Katha Pollit wrote a book called *"Pro: Reclaiming Abortion Rights"* saying that women have been brainwashed by the pro-life movement, tying themselves up with descriptions of their abortions as "complex" or "difficult," "instead of doing what they should be doing, which is saying out loud that abortion is a positive social good."[20]

Pro-choice people believe that since abortion involves life within one's own womb, the decision to kill is a personal matter—a matter of personal choice. Similar to suicide, a person will say, "It's my body, my life. I am free to make my own choices, and I can choose to kill the baby in my own womb. How dare the state or the church or any person try to interfere with my right to choose to kill." Pro-abortion leaders insist that they are protecting women. But they are surely not protecting little baby girls who are killed in the womb. And so the killing continues.

Here are my questions to you: Is it that difficult to understand or accept that millions of Catholics are motivated by their belief in the sanctity of human life and that they take a pro-life position from a place of love? Can it be understood that people are opposed to abortion because of what it so obviously does to the child and what it does to the mother? Can opposition to abortion not be viewed as condemning people or taking away freedom or imposing one's views on others but instead as a deeply felt opinion or conviction—based on God's law—that all human beings have a fundamental right to life?

Christina: *Yes, but you can't impose your views on others.*

The tide of public opinion has been turning, ever so slowly, in favor of the pro-life position. In a 2012 Gallup Survey, an all-time high of 50 percent identified themselves a pro-life, while a new record-low 41 percent said they were pro-choice, although that 50 percent figure had slipped back to 44 percent by 2015.[21] A recent national poll shows a strong majority of Americans—including a majority of those who consider themselves "pro-choice" on abortion—support substantial abortion limits.[22] Solid majorities now reveal that people want Congress to protect children in the womb who have reached twenty weeks of development.

You guys have grown up with modern technology and ultrasound images that plainly show that it is really a little baby in the mother's womb. We know now that an unborn baby's heart starts beating twenty-two days after conception and that the eyes, nose, mouth, and tongue are formed after six weeks. With surging electrical brain activity, the unborn baby feels pain after eight weeks and starts sucking his or her thumb at nine weeks. Contrast these images with images of disposed fetuses and the determined fight to preserve partial-birth abortion. There is no longer an effort to make abortions safe, legal, and rare—just legal everywhere. No wonder young people are trending more and more away from pro-abortion positions.

Angela: *But even within the church, aren't there pro-choice Catholics?*

For years the media has chronically reported that a majority of Catholics are pro-choice. But who are they polling? Churchgoing Catholics? People who hear the gospel and receive the sacraments? No way. There really is no such thing as a pro-choice Catholic. The position of the church is clear. "Since the first century, the church has affirmed the moral evil of every procured abortion. This teaching has not changed and remains unchangeable. Direct abortion, that is to say, abortion willed as an end or a means, is gravely contrary to the moral law."[23] But we have prominent politicians in Washington, DC, and elsewhere who say that their Catholic faith is deeply important to them, and yet they do everything in their power to block any attempt to limit or discourage abortion. Non-Catholics must wonder.

Angela: *What do you say about activists who threaten doctors or blow up clinics?*

It's wrong. When an act of violence or murder is committed in the name of justice, as when someone shoots an abortion doctor or attempts to blow up a clinic, it is morally wrong and utterly rejected by the pro-life movement. And pro-abortion people have used this issue as fuel to characterize all pro-lifers as fanatics.

Christina: *What is a woman to do then, who is—in effect—forced to have a child without means to support it?*

If a woman is not able to support her child, adoption options exist. Mother Teresa, now Saint Teresa of Kolkata, had this to say, "The biggest disease today is not leprosy or tuberculosis, but rather the feeling of being unwanted, uncared for and deserted by everybody. If you know anyone who does not want the child, who is afraid of the child, then tell them to give that child to me."[24] Listen, it would not be loving or wise to be opposed to abortion and not offer a realistic and caring alternative. The church provides for those who choose not to kill the child in their womb. The Catholic Church in the United States has set up services, missions, and shelters all around the country dedicated to helping young mothers through the latter stages of pregnancy, to the safe delivery of their child.

Here's one example: Father Frank Pavone has led New York based Priests for Life since 1993. Its goal is to restore protection to children in the womb. Priests for Life train the clergy and their churches to provide alternatives to abortion for those who feel they have no choice. They also provide compassionate counseling for young women through something called Rachel's Vineyard, the largest ministry in the world for healing after abortion.

They started a campaign called Silent No More that gives voice to many women and men who regret their abortion experiences and say so publicly. And by the way, Dr. Martin Luther King's niece, Alveda King, is affiliated with them and leads a compassionate outreach to African American women.

In the Archdiocese of New York, Catholic Guardian Services (CGS) addresses the needs of young pregnant mothers. The stated mission of CGS is to protect and nurture disadvantaged children and individuals with disabilities, to increase their prospects for self-sufficiency, and to strengthen the family structures integral to their support. Catholic Guardian Services is a licensed nonprofit adoption agency committed to the sacredness of human life. They help women deliver their babies safely. They provide the means and skills to help young mothers blend back into the community with a chance to make it. No woman or girl should be left with the burden of choosing an abortion as the only way out. The church prays that women, whose own lives may be compromised or threatened with an unwanted pregnancy, will choose life. And the church has the means and desire to help.

And prayer continues. You have heard of the March for Life. It is an annual pro-life rally protesting abortion that is held in Washington, DC, on or around the anniversary of the United States Supreme Court's decision in the case Roe v. Wade, in late January. The overall goal of the march is to overturn the Roe v. Wade decision and reduce access to the abortion procedure. Between 2003 and 2009, the march had an attendance of around 250,000, but this number has since increased. The 2011 and 2012 marches drew an estimated 400,000 each, and the 2013 march drew an estimated 650,000. An estimated 800,000 people attended the 2015 march. Every January, in Catholic churches all around the country, people pray for the well-being of the marchers and the success and protection of the cause. Think of all the love that goes into the protection of animals—dogs and cats that are abused and horses that are mistreated. The hope and prayer is that society will turn its affections and protection toward unborn babies—those most vulnerable humans who are unwanted and unloved.

Christina: *Dad, what would you do if I got pregnant and had an abortion?*

Well, you are an adult now living on your own. What would I do? I would pray—pray for guidance, wisdom, and protection. But what could I do? Would I judge you? Condemn you?

First, I would love you. Then I would protect you and help you. I hope that, after that, I would love you some more and offer more help. Since I was, hypothetically, not able to encourage you to choose life, I would offer to help you where I found you, in your current need. If you felt remorse, I would guide you toward the sacraments—first the sacrament of reconciliation. I would guide you in prayer and support you in whatever penance you were given. And I hope that, enveloped in the healing light of Christ and in God's endless love, you would avoid the haunting guilt that so many women have spoken of. But please remember that I am your father, and I will always love you, no matter what.

For any woman who lives with guilt or remorse over an abortion in her own past, there is a place for her to go. There is healing and forgiveness and reconciliation with God through the sacraments. There is nothing called the sacrament of condemnation. The sacrament of penance is available to us all.

So the fifth commandment stands as God's directive to mankind, passed down through the centuries from the time of Moses to the present. It still stands today. All the commandments are still relevant because they point out evils that we must all try to avoid in our daily life. People don't like the "you shall not" motif; they certainly don't like the word "commandment." Jesus Himself referred directly to the Ten Commandments. He wanted us to follow them, yes, but even more, He wanted us to accept them from within. He wants us to change.

In the Sermon on the Mount, recounted only in Matthew's Gospel, He said, "You have heard that it was said to your ancestors, 'You shall not kill; and whoever kills will be liable to judgment.' But I say to you that everyone who is angry with his brother will be liable to judgment" (Mt 5:21–22). Knowing that anger was a self-destructive force within us, He forbade even the motivation to kill. The Prince of Peace, who laid down His own life out of love, prohibited anger, hatred, and vengeance. He taught His disciples to offer their enemies no resistance but to turn the other cheek. He taught them all to love their enemies.

In fact, through the eight beatitudes, Jesus deepens our commitment to the Ten Commandments by calling us to humility and love. He offers us a way of living on earth that promises eternal life with God in heaven. When preaching about the beatitudes, Pope Francis said that "they are Jesus's practical guide on how to live the Christian life, which often goes against what the world tells us. Because Christianity is a practical religion: it is not just to be imagined, it is to be practiced."[25]

Lamenting the many injustices that are created by what the world tells us, the Pope stated that "blessed are the merciful for they will be shown mercy." The merciful are "those who forgive and understand the mistakes of others," he noted, adding that Jesus does not tell us "blessed are they who seek revenge." And "blessed are they who forgive, who are merciful. Because we are all part of an army of people who have been forgiven! We have all been forgiven. That is why blessed is he who undertakes this path of forgiveness."[26] We all bear the guilt of sin, but we come from—and believe in—a God of mercy.

EXAMINE OUR CONSCIENCE

If we can still think of the Ten Commandments as a guide, then they can help us do a thorough examination of our conscience. The commandments help us measure our own life and behavior in relation to God—not in relation to other people, but by the standards God set.

So when you move on to the sixth commandment, "you shall not commit adultery," you can ask yourself straightforward questions. Have I been faithful to my marriage vows in thought and action? Do I place myself in situations where there is temptation to be unfaithful? Do I inappropriately engage women or men on social media? Am I always respectful to members of the opposite sex, or do I regard them, at times, as objects? Have I kept the promise I made in marriage?

The seventh commandment is "you shall not steal." Many people might say, "Well, no, I don't steal things." But do I pay my debts, my taxes, and my bills promptly? Do I withhold the full value of my services at work by wasting time? Have I taken or kept what is not mine?

The eighth commandment is "you shall not bear false witness." Am I unjustly critical, negative, or uncharitable when speaking about other people? Have I harmed someone's reputation by talking behind their back? Have I lied about something or someone?

Finally, we come to the last two commandments: the ones with the word "covet." Covet means to desire wrongfully or without due regard for the rights of others. It addresses the spiritual warfare that goes on inside all of us. "You shall not covet your neighbor's wife" is the ninth commandment. Do I try to banish thoughts about desiring another woman? Do I overindulge in conversations about women that would be considered impure and disrespectful?

The tenth commandment is "you shall not covet your neighbor's goods." With all the affluence around me, am I jealous of what other people have? Do I envy others' success? Have material possessions become my passion in life?

There's a lot to consider, and when we do a thorough examination of conscience, we not only find ourselves falling short, we sometimes find the Ten Commandments overwhelming or too burdensome. We can't seem to measure up to God's standards. That's why we need Jesus, and that's why He is our Lord and Savior. He gives us His peace in the midst of our trials and tribulations on earth.

One of the scribes asked Jesus this question at one point:

> "Which is the first of all the commandments?" Jesus replied, "The first is this: 'Hear, O Israel! The Lord our God is Lord alone! You shall love the Lord your God with all your heart, with all your soul, with all your mind, and with all your strength.' The second is this: 'You shall love your neighbor as yourself.' There is no other commandment greater than these" (Mk 12:28–31).

Jesus was not replacing the Ten Commandments with these two. He was deepening our commitment to them through the imperative to love.

Remember that the commandments were meant to release people from bondage—to aid us on our journey into freedom. Can we accept them—not as a burden but as a gift? Psalm 119 expresses how we can understand the commandments through a true sense of gratitude:

> Let your mercy come to me Lord, salvation
> in accord with your promise
> I will keep your law always, for all time and forever
> I will walk freely in an open space because I cherish your precepts.

I will speak openly of your testimonies,
without fear even before kings.
I will delight in our commandments, which I dearly love.
I lift up my hands to your commandments;
I study your statutes, which I love.
(Ps 119:41, 44–48).

Jesus said to His disciples, "As the Father loves Me, so I also love you. Remain in My love. If you keep My commandments, you will remain in My love, just as I have kept My Father's commandments and remain in His love. I have told you this so that My joy might be in you and your joy might be complete" (Jn 15:9–11).

Endnotes

1. Abraham Lincoln, *"Proclamation 106, Thanksgiving Day,"* October 3, 1863.
2. Abraham Joshua Heschel, *The Sabbath* (New York: Farrar, Strauss and Giroux, 1979), 6–10.
3. *Catechism of the Catholic Church* (Liguori, MO: Liguori Publications 1994), 2175.
4. Seven Themes of Catholic Social Teaching, http://www.usccb.org/beliefs-and-teachings/what-we-believe/catholic-social-teaching/seven-themes-of-catholic-social-teaching.cfm.
5. John Paul II, Centisimus Annus, May 1, 1991, Centenary of the Encyclical Rerum Novarum.
6. *Catechism of the Catholic Church*, 2309.
7. Ibid., 2267.
8. New York State Assembly, Memorandum in Support of Legislation A10059, http://assembly.state.ny.us/leg/?default_fld=&leg_

video=&bn=A10059&term=2015&Summary=Y&Actions=Y&Fl
oor%26nbspVotes=Y&Memo=Y&Text=Y.

9. History of Final Exit Network, http://www.finalexitnetwork.
org/About-Us.html.

10. Derek Humphrey, *"Assisted Suicide, Farewell to Hemlock: Killed by its Name,"* February 21, 2005, http://www.assistedsuicide.
org/farewell-to-hemlock.html.

11. *Catechism of the Catholic Church*, 2277.

12. Ibid., 2279.

13. Ibid., 2278.

14. Ibid., 2275.

15. Lisa Selin Davis, "I Couldn't Turn My Abortion Into Art," *The New York Times*, July 2, 2014.

16. Julianne Ishler, "Nicki Minaj Reveals Heartbreaking Abortion That She's Haunted By," *Rolling Stone*, December 30, 2014.

17. Steven Ertelt, "Sharon Osbourne: Having an Abortion Was the 'Worst Thing I Ever Did,'" LifeNews.com, June 5, 2014.

18. Merritt Tierce, "This Is What an Abortion Looks Like," *The New York Times*, September 12, 2014.

19. Steven Ertelt, "Cecile Richards: Having an Abortion Wasn't a Difficult Decision," LifeNews.com, October 17, 2014

20. Hanna Rosin, What Women Really Think, *"Abortion Is Great,"* Slate, October 13, 2014.

21. Lydia Saad, Gallup/Social Issues, May 29, 2015.

22. Steven Ertelt, "New Poll Shows Americans Are Pro-Life on Abortion as Roe v. Wade Turns 43," LifeNews.com, January 19, 2016.

23. *Catechism of the Catholic Church* (Liguori, MO: Liguori Publications 1994), 2271.

24. Catholic News Service, "Mother Teresa: 'Do Small Things with Great Love,'" September 4, 2016.

25. Pope Francis, Daily Mass Homily, September 6, 2014.

26. Ibid.

EPILOGUE/WHAT'S OUT THERE

§

FROM MY PERSPECTIVE AS AN Ordained Deacon in the Archdiocese of New York, I've attempted to weave a central theme through this book: The Living God speaks to us in the world today. He spoke first through the Jewish prophets in the Old Testament. He manifests Himself through Jesus Christ. We can encounter this Jesus, through the Bible. We receive Jesus through the sacraments and through His Church. Priests are Christ's Ordained representatives on earth. We are brothers of the Jews, who first received God's covenant. Jesus is present today, in the marriage and in the family. The mass expresses the full meaning of our faith. And the Commandments are our guide to eternal life with God. I believe we should talk to each other about these things. My hope is that this book contributes in some small way to the dialogue.

I'd like to hear from anyone who has read the book. Whether you are Catholic or non-Catholic, cleric or layperson, baby-boomer or millennial, please feel free to share your comments and thoughts with me at: john@jc.training and I will try and respond.

As important as words are, words alone cannot convert or bring people to Christ. Setting an example by living the faith is the best way to communicate the gospel of love, particularly to young people. And I believe that living one's faith has to be accompanied by daily prayer—an ongoing dialogue with God, who speaks to us in so many ways. We are on a journey of faith together, and we need each other to help manifest the Holy Spirit of God in the world today. In this faith community, people experience God in different ways with different levels of intensity. We have to look out for each other, and we have to be willing to allow others—who can instruct us, guide us, and care for us—to love us. We must "be not afraid" to come to Christ and let Him come to us.

I have offered plenty of suggestions on sources of inspiration, starting of course with the *New American Bible* for daily reading. As I said earlier, look for books that help explain the Bible. Try the St. Paul Center for Biblical Theology; they have a huge online library of books that provide instruction at any level. You can even enroll in some online courses, if that is of interest. Also, be sure to subscribe to the *Magnificat* for the readings and reflections on the daily Mass. And for quiet inspiration each morning, get a copy of *God Calling* (Edited by A.J. Russell).

Today the church is blessed with many articulate representatives of Catholic life who aren't limited to prayer and raising money. I want to mention three people in particular who are superb representatives of the Catholic Church.

First, if you don't know of him already let me introduce to you Robert Barron. Bishop Barron is an author, speaker, and theologian and has served for years in the Archdiocese of Chicago. He was ordained in 1986, and since September of 2015, he has served as auxiliary bishop in the Archdiocese of Los Angeles. In 1999 he launched a website called Word On Fire (wordonfire.org), drawing over a million visitors a year from every continent. He is prolific. His video clips, homilies, and sermons, are widely used by hundreds of thousands of visitors every month. He offers commentary on Fox News, NBC, CNN, and EWTN. Bishop Barron has a confident, credible, accessible Midwestern demeanor, and his delivery leaves no doubt about his knowledge or convictions.

He is probably best known now because of the video series that he created and hosted, called *Catholicism*, released in 2010. It is a documentary on the essential truths and beliefs of the Catholic people, and it brilliantly blends beautiful music with pictures of significant Catholic locations around the world. The series has been aired by parishes, universities, and media outlets in many countries and will be an important part of every Catholic library for years to come. It made a great impression on all Catholics; it has been very soothing and reassuring. The reaction to it has been something like "whew, I'm glad everything is still standing just as I remember it." Now there is a sequel, a new series entitled *The Pivotal Players* about six great voices in the church. If you have any questions, search YouTube for Bishop Robert Barron.

Scott Hahn is a powerful proponent and spokesman of the scripture-based rationale for a Catholic life. Dr. Hahn is a scholar in the fields of philosophy, divinity, and biblical theology. He is also widely known by many Catholics through television and print. He has an infectious enthusiasm when discussing and lecturing on the Bible. I think his personal story is intensely interesting. On his website he describes his journey of faith, a journey that took him "from being a fervent Presbyterian minister and professor of theology at a major Protestant seminary, to become a Roman Catholic theologian and internationally known explainer and defender of the Catholic Church."[1] Through study and prayer, Scott Hahn came to realize that the truth of the Catholic Church is firmly rooted in scripture.

I'd like my Protestant friends, and all Catholics, to know about Scott Hahn. He is an intellectual who made his way into the Catholic

Church through the Bible. If you want another perspective on what it means to be a Catholic, check out Dr. Scott Hahn.

The third person I want to mention here is Tom Peterson. Mr. Peterson is the founder and president of Catholics Come Home. He is a very friendly and well-spoken man who appears at Catholic conferences and pro-life events all around the world. He has presented to the United States Conference of Catholic Bishops and also at the Vatican. He has appeared many times on EWTN and Fox News and is heard on Catholic radio stations all around the country.

You've seen commercials around Christmastime that show beautiful images of worship that appeal to the heart of those who may be in need. Tom Peterson is the force behind the production of those commercials and of the strategic buys of TV time that represent the best in modern evangelization. The central message is a call to come home—to return to one's spiritual roots...the church one grew up in. But there's more.

Go to catholicscomehome.org; it is a beautiful website with tons of helpful information for people who are curious but who may not be religious at all. It's also for Protestants or Evangelicals who can find resources that will help them understand what Catholics believe and why. And a section called "How do I talk to my friends and family about coming home?" offers educational and evangelical tools for Catholics who are trying to reach out to people and invite them back to an enriching life in the Church.

There are some outstanding broadcast outlets that feature Catholic news, opinion, and worship services. The biggest and best is EWTN (Eternal World Television Network), an American cable network started by Mother Angelica in Alabama in 1981. This network now covers world events from a global Catholic perspective, and it has become a huge multimedia enterprise, with numerous high-quality programs and personalities. There's also an EWTN app that allows you to follow and read all of Pope Francis's words.

I am also a big fan of Telecare television, carried by a number of cable systems in the New York, New Jersey, and Connecticut tri-state area. Msgr. Tom Hartman started the station in 1969, and its facility is located on the premises of my old high school, Maria Regina, now Kellenberg Memorial High School in Uniondale, New York. It is now run by Msgr. Jim Vlaun and has a twenty-four hour schedule of quality programs, including coverage of all major Vatican and papal events, as well as several local masses and worship services.

You can also find scores of effective Catholic bloggers who promote dialogue and offer a variety of views and insights. I very much like Ed Mechmann, who has a blog entitled "Stepping Out of the Boat." Ed was one of my teachers during my diaconate formation, and he is posted on the site for the Archdiocese of New York. He is an attorney and the director of the Safe Environment Office, overseeing child-protection programs. Ed aims straight and hits hard, providing soothing reading for bruised Catholics.

I'd like to mention some other people who have also moved me. Since ultimately all Christians will one day reconcile, we should listen to each other now and again—to hear all the ways that love for Jesus can be expressed, before defining our differences. Some non-Catholics I like include these:

I included *The Third Jesus* in my bibliography. This book was written by Deepak Chopra, the well-known scholar and author who attended Catholic school in India as a child. Dr. Chopra maintains that the first two representations of Jesus—the Jesus swept away and lost in history and the Jesus presented through the complex theology offered by organized religion—are regrettable misinterpretations.

He wants to present a third version: the possibility that Jesus was indeed a savior and that Jesus intended to save the world by showing others the path to God-consciousness.

I like the book. I very much appreciate the author's thoughtful and scholarly reflections on the words of Jesus. His viewpoint is refreshing because it comes from someone with a different perspective. He has little patience for American right-wing Christian fundamentalists, and I see his point. But I believe there is great insight and true witnessing of Jesus within organized religion and within the Catholic Church. As an American, conservative Catholic, I was relieved not to feel the direct sting of his ire.

Charles Frazier Stanley is the senior pastor of First Baptist Church in northern Atlanta, Georgia. He is the founder and president of *In Touch Ministries*. On television, Dr. Stanley impresses me as a sober, intelligent, experienced preacher of the Gospel. He has a rich, soothing voice and the countenance of a youthful grandfather. I really like the way Dr. Stanley opens up the Bible and preaches.

Joyce Meyer is a charismatic Christian author and speaker. Ms. Meyer has an earthy demeanor and seems like someone who has been transformed by her relationship with Christ. She talks easily about her previous life before knowing the Lord, and she appears to be accessible and empathetic, with strong appeal, and a good example for women. She knows her Bible, and she can preach. I like Joyce Meyer.

Crefalo Dollar is a pastor with the nondenominational *World Changers Church International*. He is another Christian preacher who can be seen on a number of cable systems. I like his intensity and the way he can modulate and vary his delivery. He prowls the stage and preaches the word of God! He seems to go deep into a given Bible passage and helps people to see it and hear it and accept it.

Thomas Dexter "T. D." Jakes, Sr. is the apostle/bishop of the Potter's House Church, a nondenominational American megachurch in Dallas with thirty thousand members.[2] Pastor Jakes can preach! He has a joyous, soulful, intense manner of preaching. He too walks around and works himself and his people into a lather! I like seeing people get excited about the Lord!

And then there is Joel Osteen. He is the well-known American preacher, televangelist, author, and senior pastor of Lakewood Church in Houston, the largest Protestant church in the United States. He is the son of a pastor, and his wife Victoria is part of his ministry.

He was invited to the Vatican in 2015, along with several US officials, and met Pope Francis. Osteen said it was an "amazing" experience and called the pontiff a "warm, kind man, full of joy." He explained, "I went there to express a feeling for unity and to let [the Pope] know that the American pastors support what he's doing. I felt honored to be invited."[3]

Osteen said he is on board with the Pope's message for unity, explaining that he does not have a problem with theological differences among Christians but acknowledging that they need to be handled carefully and respectfully. "There's nothing wrong with denominations, but just don't let it separate us," he said, encouraging people to respect each other regardless of their differences.[4]

From his megachurch in Houston, it is said that he preaches to over forty thousand people a week, and you see his face in bookstores everywhere and hear his voice on the radio. His critics say he teaches a "prosperity gospel," and that he doesn't deal effectively with the issue of Christian suffering, the sense of abandonment, or the effects of carrying the cross, but he says, "There's different approaches. I just know that my gift is encouragement, hopefully to uplift people."[5]

Endnotes

1. Scott Hahn, *"The Scott Hahn Conversion Story,"* Catholic Education Resource Center, http://www.catholiceducation.org/en/religion-and-philosophy/apologetics/the-scott-hahn-conversion-story.html.
2. According to Fact Sheet: Potter's House, https://demoss.com/newsrooms/ph/background/potters-house-fact-sheet.
3. Pastor Hal Mayer, *"Joel Osteen Meets Pope,"* July 22, 2014.
4. Gina Meeks, "Joel Osteen Defends Stance On Hot Button Issues," *Charisma News*, June 13, 2014.
5. Ibid.

THANK YOU

§

I WISH TO THANK MY teachers, particularly my friend Father Peter Bannon. Also Father William Cleary, Father Paul LeBlanc, Father James Villa, Father Innocent Nwachukwu, Msgr. Kenneth Smith, Msgr. Jim Lisante, Msgr. Peter Vaccari, Father Kevin O'Reilly, Msgr. James Turro, Father Stephen Norton, Sister Joan Curtin, Sister Patricia Graham, Deacon Frank Orlando, Deacon James Bello, Deacon John Sadowski, Deacon Joseph Patrona, Deacon Joaquim Pereira, Deacon Steven DeMartino, Dr. Tom Dobbins, Edward Mechmann, Susan George, Marcia Holman, Angela Cox, Susan Deland, Msgr. Robert Ritchie, Msgr. Gregory Mustaciuolo, Msgr. Edward Webber, Father Damian O'Connell, Father Trevor Nicholls, Father Robert DeJulio, and His Eminence, Timothy Cardinal Dolan.

Most especially, I must thank Josephine, who is my love and partner for life, and my beautiful son, Joseph, who inspires me with his kindness and openness to prayer and faith. And of course my two wonderful daughters, Angela and Christina, who challenge me, make me laugh and cry, and teach me to love.

With Angela and Christina

BIBLIOGRAPHY

§

Alter, Robert. *The David Story: A Translation with Commentary of 1 and 2 Samuel*. New York: W. W. Norton & Company, 1999.

Aquinas, Thomas. *Summa Theologiae—Complete American Edition*. Translated by Fathers of the English Dominican Province. Kindle Edition, June 19, 2010.

Blet, Pierre S. J. *Pius XII and the Second World War: According to the Archives of the Vatican*. Translated by Lawrence J. Johnson. New York: Paulist Press, 1999.

Brook, John. *The School of Prayer—An Introduction to the Divine Office for All Christians*. Collegeville, PA: The Liturgical Press, 1992.

Brown, Raymond Edward. *The Death of the Messiah*. New York: Bantam Doubleday Dell Publishing Group, 1995.

—. *An Introduction to the New Testament*. New York: Bantam Doubleday Dell Publishing Group, 1997.

Brueggemann, Walter. *Theology of the Old Testament*. Minneapolis: Fortress Press, 1997.

Bunson, Matthew. *The Pope Encyclopedia*. New York: Random House, 1995.

Catechism of the Catholic Church. New York: Doubleday, 1994.

Catholic Book Publishing Corp, *The Liturgy of the Hours/According to the Roman Rite*. New York: Catholic Book Publishing Corp., 1975.

Chopra, Deepak. *The Third Jesus—The Christ We Cannot Ignore*. New York: Random House/Harmony Books, 2008.

Clayton, Lawrence A. *Bartolome de Las Casas and the Conquest of the Americas*. West Sussex, UK: UK Wiley Blackwell, 2011.

Corbett, David and Richard Hiffins. *Portfolio Life: The New Path to Work, Purpose, and Passion After 50*. San Francisco, CA: John Wiley & Sons, 2007.

Coriden, James A. *An Introduction to Canon Law*. Mahwah, NJ: Mahwah Paulist Press, 2004.

Feldhahn, Shaunti and Tally Whitehead. *The Good News About Marriage*. Colorado Springs, CO: Multnomah Books, 2014.

Foster, Richard. *Celebration of Discipline: The Path to Spiritual Growth*. San Francisco, CA: HarperCollins Publishers Inc., 1998.

Gladwell, Malcolm. *Blink: The Power of Thinking without Thinking*. New York: Little, Brown and Company, 2005.

Heschel, Abraham Joshua. *The Sabbath*. New York: Farrar, Strauss and Giroux, 1979.

Johnson, Kevin Orlin. *Why Do Catholics Do That?—A Guide to the Teachings and Practices of the Catholic Church*. New York: Random House, 1994.

Kohlenberger, John R. III. *The NIV Compact Concordance*. Grand Rapids, MI: Zondervan, 1993.

Martos, Joseph. *The Sacraments, An Interdisciplinary and Interactive Study*. Collegeville, PA: Liturgical Press, 2009

Midgley, John, and Susan Midgley. *A Decision to Love—A Marriage Preparation Program*. New London: Revised edition, 2011. Twenty Third Publications, 2009.

New American Bible, Revised Edition. Charlotte, NC: Saint Benedict Press, 2010.

O'Malley, John W. S. J. *What Happened at Vatican Council II*. Cambridge, MA: The Belknap Press of Harvard University Press, 2008.

Powell, Mark Allen. *Introducing the New Testament—A Historical, Literary, and Theological Survey*. Grand Rapids, MI: Baker Academic, 2009.

Ratzinger, Joseph—Pope Benedict XVI. *Jesus of Nazareth*. New York: Doubleday, 2007.

Ratzinger, Joseph Cardinal. *Pilgrim Fellowship of Faith: The Church as Communion*. San Francisco, CA: Ignatius Press, 2005.

Rocca, Rev. Peter D. CSC. *ORDO—Order of Prayer in the Liturgy of the Hours and Celebration of the Eucharist 2016*. Mahwah, NJ: Paulist Press Ordo, 2015.

Smith, Christian, and Patricia Snell. *Souls in Transition—The Religious and Spiritual Lives of Emerging Adults*. New York: Oxford University Press, 2009.

Tolle, Eckhart. *The Power of Now—A Guide to Spiritual Enlightenment*. Novato, CA: Namaste Publishing and New World Library, 1999.

———. *A New Earth—Awakening to Your Life's Purpose*. New York: Penguin Group, 2005.

Untener, Ken. *Preaching Better—Practical Suggestions for Homilists*. Mahwah, NJ: Paulist Press, 1999.

Vaghi, Peter J. *The Faith We Profess: A Catholic Guide to the Apostles Creed*. Notre Dame: Ave Maria Press, 2008.

———. *The Commandments We Keep: A Catholic Guide to Living a Moral Life*. Notre Dame, IN: Ave Maria Press, 2011.

Vidmar, John OP. *The Catholic Church through the Ages: A History—Second Edition*. Mahwah, NJ: Paulist Press, 2014.

Weigel, George. *Witness to Hope—The Biography of John Paul II*. New York: Harper Collins Publishers, 2009.

Joseph, Christina, Angela, Josephine, and John Catalano
photo by Domenica Comfort

Made in the USA
Middletown, DE
23 June 2017